THE HUNGRY SPIRIT

The Hungry Spirit

*Selected Plays and Prose
by Elsie Park Gowan*

NeWest Press • Edmonton

EDITED WITH INTRODUCTION AND INTERVIEWS BY MOIRA DAY
PRAIRIE PLAY SERIES: 11
SERIES EDITOR, DIANE BESSAI

First Edition
Breeches from Bond Street originally published by Samuel French, Inc., 1952

Rights to perform or produce any of the scripts on stage or in other form are retained by the author. Interested persons are requested to apply for permission and terms to the author.

Canadian Cataloguing in Publication Data

Gowan, Elsie Park.
    The hungry spirit

    (Prairie play series ; 11)
    Includes bibliographical references.
    ISBN 0-920897-19-3

    1. Gowan, Elsie Park – Interviews. I. Day, Moira
Jean, 1953- II. Title. III. Series.
PS8513.0898H8 1992   C812'.54   C92-091145-5
PR9199.3.G69H8 1992

Credits:
Cover design: Connell Design
Cover photograph: Richard G. Proctor
Interior design: Bob Young/ BOOKENDS DESIGNWORKS
Editor for the Press: Diane Bessai
Financial Assistance: NeWest Press gratefully acknowledges the financial assistance of Alberta Culture and Multiculturalism, The Alberta Foundation for the Arts, The Canada Council, and The NeWest Institute for Western Canadian Studies.

Printed and Bound in Canada by Best Gagné Book Manufacturers.

NeWest Publishers Limited
#310, 10359-82 Avenue
Edmonton, Alberta
T6E 1Z9

Every effort has been made to obtain permission for quoted material and photographs. If there is an omission or error the author and publisher would be grateful to be so informed.

Dedicated to the memory of Dr. E.H. Gowan

The editor would like to acknowledge the following people:

Special thanks are due to the staff at the University of Alberta Archives, Diane Bessai, Steve Olson, Anton Wagner and Elsie Park Gowan for their generosity and help in the researching and compiling of this collection.

Special thanks also to my husband, Dr. Norman Gee, for his unfailing support and encouragement on every level and in every way.

The material for this anthology was researched and compiled with the help of a SSHRCC post-doctoral fellowship.

CONTENTS

Executive of Dramatic Society, University of Alberta, 1929-1930.

BIOGRAPHY

Isie Park Gowan (née Young) was born in Helensburgh, Scotland on 9 September 1906 and came to Edmonton, Alberta in 1912. After working as a rural school teacher for four years (1922-1926), she attended the University of Alberta, serving as president of both the Dramatic Society and the Literary Society, and as women's editor of the student paper, *The Gateway*, before graduating in 1930 with a BA in Honors History. During her student years she also came under the influence of the inspirational teacher-director Elizabeth Sterling Haynes who directed her as "Zinida" in Leonid Andreyev's *He Who Gets Slapped* in 1928, "Mrs. Zero" in Elmer Rice's *The Adding Machine* in 1930, and "Mrs. Wrathie" in James Barrie's *Shall We Join the Ladies?*. The latter production also represented Edmonton in the first Alberta Drama League Festival in 1930.

Between 1930 and 1958, Gowan was to prove a dynamic participant in the educational and community theatre of her time. Besides serving frequently as an adjudicator, she also took an active interest in the Edmonton Little Theatre from its founding in 1929, and between 1933 and 1948 served as a board member, editor of the newsletter *The Role Call*, instructor, director and actor. Important roles included "May

1

Daniels" in Hart and Kaufman's *Once in a Lifetime* in 1937, "Christina" in Sidney Howard's *The Silver Cord* in 1938, "Ellen Creed" in Denham and Percy's *Ladies in Retirement* in 1941 and "Ruth" in Noel Coward's *Blithe Spirit* in 1946. She was also a warm supporter of the University of Alberta Department of Drama from its founding in 1946; besides premièring her stage play, *Breeches from Bond Street*, as part of the inaugural bill at the opening of Studio Theatre in 1949, she also played important roles in productions of Jean Giraudoux's *The Madwoman of Chaillot* in 1951, G.B.Shaw's *Great Catherine* in 1953, *Caesar and Cleopatra* in 1955, and Jean Anouilh's *Time Remembered* in 1959.

However, it was as a playwright that Gowan really made her mark. When the second phase of her rural teaching career (1930-1933) ended with her marriage to Dr. Edward Hunter Gowan, a physics professor at the University of Alberta, she turned her considerable talent and energies to writing instead. She first attracted notice when her first three plays – *Homestead* in 1932, *The Giant Killer* in 1933 and *The Royal Touch* in 1934 – won honorable mention, first and second place respectively in the Carnegie Foundation playwriting competitions administered by the University of Alberta for Alberta writers. With the notable exception of *Breeches from Bond Street* and four large-scale historical stage pageants written late in her career – *Who Builds a City* (1954), *The Jasper Story* (1956), *Portrait of Alberta* (1956) and *A Treaty for the Plains* (1977) – most of Gowan's stage plays were written between 1932 and 1942 and premièred by either the Edmonton Little Theatre or other community or educational groups. While her three-act comedy, *The Last Caveman*, was toured over 1946-1947 by the Everyman Theatre, one of Western Canada's first professional theatre companies, limited opportunities for live stage production drew Gowan increasingly towards radio writing.

Commissioned by University station CKUA, Gowan's first

two series of historical plays for radio – *New Lamps for Old*, co-written with Gwen Pharis Ringwood over 1936-1937, and *The Building of Canada* (1937-1938) – helped pioneer radio series writing in the prairie provinces and launched Gowan's radio career when CBC picked up both series for public broadcasting. Between 1939 and 1958, Gowan wrote over 200 scripts for local and national radio, some of them reaching audiences as far away as America, Britain, Australia, the Caribbean and South America. Gowan also taught radio writing to groups within the city, at the Banff School of Fine Arts and at Queen's University Summer School at Kingston.

Gowan's writing career effectively ended with her husband's death in 1958, but she has remained active in the city as an actress, speaker and instructor. Between 1959 and 1971 she taught as an English teacher at Ross Shepherd High School, and has continued teaching writing to senior citizens since her retirement. Honors have included a Canadian Drama award in 1942, a provincial Achievement Award for Excellence in Literature in 1977, and an honorary doctorate from the University of Alberta in 1982 for her many years of service as a teacher, historian and playwright.

Caesar and Cleopatra. Arnold Murray as Pothinus, Elsie Park
Gowan as Ftatateeta, Studio Theatre, University of Alberta
1955.

ELSIE PARK GOWAN:
A HUNGRY SPIRIT

MOIRA DAY

t is a puzzle why some "lost" playwrights are so quickly rediscovered and restored to a position of honour as our spiritual elders, while others, equally well-regarded by the critics of the same generation, remain curiously obscure and more stubbornly resist the restoration process despite their obvious virtues.

Consider the case of Gwen Pharis Ringwood and Elsie Park Gowan, sisters in friendship and fortune if two ever existed. Personally bound by a friendship that lasted some fifty years and only ended with Ringwood's death of cancer in 1984, both women were also very closely linked professionally. While born in other countries – Gowan in Scotland, Ringwood in America – both made their home in Western Canada at an early date and spent some of their most productive years together in the same city – Edmonton, Alberta. Both were also extremely active as teachers, actors, adjudicators, and directors in the community, extension (adult education) and educational theatre that dominated the Canadian theatre scene between 1930 and 1950, and both were significantly hailed as the leading Western Canadian playwrights of their generation.

Yet, while both helped pave the way for the development of the professional theatre during the 1960s and 1970s, neither woman was really to enter the "promised land" that her efforts

5

might have anticipated. Age, awkward domestic situations, distance from major play production centres, regional marginalization and a generally hostile atmosphere for Canadian playwriting conspired to push both women into the background during the post-war decades. By the time the "angry young men" of the seventies had started to build up an indigenous playwriting tradition with a vengeance, Gowan and Ringwood had all but disappeared from the mainstream – the beloved but outmoded ikons of an old-fashioned amateur tradition seen as dominated by school teachers and socialites.

By the late 1970s, this reactionary trend had started to give way to a new interest in reclaiming the past and reinterpreting the present within the context of a long and rich theatrical tradition extending back to the 17th century. Among the first beneficiaries of this explosion of theatre archives and collections projects, the founding of journals and organizations devoted to the study of Canadian drama and theatre history, and the publishing of books and older playscripts was Gwen Pharis Ringwood.

While no one person can claim credit for "rediscovering" Ringwood, there is little doubt that important articles by Anton Wagner, and published interviews and a book-length study by Geraldine Anthony during the late 1970s and early 1980s were major milestones in her revival. So were the collection of her papers at the University of Calgary and a publication of an index to them, the production of a fairly comprehensive collection of her plays by Enid Delgatty Rutland in 1982, and the subsequent appearence of her work in two of the three major Canadian theatre anthologies most used in Canadian Literature and Drama courses. By the early 1990s she has become the subject of several theses and a growing pool of articles in the mainstream and feminist press, as well as a staple in Canadian Literature and Drama courses.

And Elsie Park Gowan? Virtual silence. The odd feature article in a local paper, a seminal article by Anton Wagner and publication of *The Last Caveman* in the *Journal of Canadian Theatre History*, the publication of her one-act play *Breeches from Bond Street* in the 1980 anthology, *Prairie Performance*, now out-of-print, and a chapter on her work in a master's thesis on radio drama in Alberta.

And yet, she was regarded as Ringwood's equal in talent and promise prior to 1960, and if one is to judge a playwright's success by the volume of her work and her ability to get paid for doing it, there is little doubt that Gowan came much closer to earning her living by her pen than did Ringwood. Rutland's bibliography credits Ringwood with 60 dramatic pieces; Gowan wrote over 200. Her work, in many cases produced professionally, was heard by audiences right across the country and internationally in Britain, North and South America, Australia and the Caribbean. Nor is there any question of Gowan simply being a weaker echo of Ringwood. An examination of the 180 odd scripts still extant reveals a highly intelligent and inquiring mind with a very strong and distinct voice of its own.

And yet – silence. Why?

* * *

There is little doubt that accidents of fortune beyond the scope of her work are responsible for some of the difficulties. If Ringwood found her Boswells sooner, it is at least in part because she didn't slip as fully into obscurity as did Gowan, and, in fact, continued to write until her death. While this may reflect differing personal inclinations, it is equally a reflection of differing domestic arrangements. The fact that Gowan had only one child to contend with in an urban environment where family and babysitters were easily had, while Ringwood was raising a family of four mostly in more isolated rural communities may account for the fact that Gowan was able to produce a much larger body of work during the forties and fifties. However, the situation changed during the sixties and seventies. In 1958, Gowan was widowed, and the playwriting career became a casualty not only of the emotional but the financial difficulties of adjusting to single life again after 25 years of an unusually close, secure, and companionable marriage. In discussing her decision to return to work as a schoolteacher to support herself, she explains: "the theory was that I'd do my own writing in the evening. And you can imagine how well *that* worked out."[1] For the next 12 years the educational muse was to supplant completely the creative one in the high school classroom, and after that, in writing classes for seniors. However, just as Gowan's career was going into eclipse, Ringwood's was about to re-emerge. With her family growing up, the energy that had been largely channeled into child-raising over the fifties and sixties began to go back into playwriting over the seventies and eighties, leading to a revival of interest in her as a re-emerging creative artist just at a time when Gowan was fading as one from the public mind.

The real difficulty, however, seems to be that many of the very factors that made Gowan the more successful playwright during her own time, and which distinguish her as a unique dramatic voice separate from Ringwood's, have also conspired to hide her from contemporary notice.

In musing over the reasons why Ringwood's work took such a different direction in tone and subject matter from her own, Gowan suggests that their formative years – or at least their response to certain elements of those years – may have been quite different despite the similarities that bound them. Both were bright, talented young women who spent large portions of their early lives in rural Alberta, found their way into University at a time when few women did, persevered in their writing in the face of obstacles, and possessed a social conscience that surfaced in their community work and writing. At the same time, Ringwood's response to her world was inclined to be more lyrical, poetic and accepting, a celebration

8

of the things of the spirit that gave significance, richness and dignity to the most arid, tragic and commonplace situations around her. Gowan's response, by contrast, was always to be more cerebral, prosaic and critical, a constant inquiry into the pragmatic forces and conditions shaping her world, and an angry, impatient demand that they be changed where they inhibited human growth and progress.

More than Ringwood, Gowan was always to be more consciously aware of the social and personal consequences of having that kind of hungry, demanding, outspoken mind in a female body. In her autobiographical essay, "The Girl Who Is Out of Step," Gowan recalls that she first became painfully conscious of having more brains than was good for her when she entered high school. The school boards who respected her intellectual gifts to such an extent that they accelerated her twice, she comments wryly, should have considered the human consequences of sending a child into high school a full three years younger than the rest of her almost-grown peers:

A tall, rather awkward fourteen year old, I was completely out of step with the seventeen and eighteen year olds who paired off so naturally around me. I came home from parties where I had been a miserable wall flower and stared at myself in the glass. My face *looked* normal . . . what could be the matter with me? . . . I grew more tomboyish, more scornful of the femininity I wanted so much but for some reason didn't seem to have. Since I was a flop socially, I set out to "show them" by leading the class. This made me more of a bookworm than ever, and drove me into the dream world of books as substitute for real living . . . . No help came from a Scots Presbyterian home where it was *right* and *virtuous* not to be interested in boys, and where high marks were next to godliness.[2]

She confesses that her initial interest in drama (under teacher-director E.C.Davis, Victoria High School had one of the most innovative and ambitious drama groups in the city) was an extension of her need for a dream world of escape. But Gowan didn't just play roles in other people's dramatic fantasies; she created her own to combat her sense of adolescent discomfort:

> At least I could dominate the younger fry. . . . Around home in the holidays I was the leader of the neighborhood gang. I organized them in games and in putting on plays in vacant lots . . . plays in which I was always the king or the heavy father who bossed people around.[3]

Normal School followed and at age 16, Gowan began a four year stint in rural Alberta as a school teacher. As with Ringwood, her experience with the land and people outside the larger cities made a lasting impact on the themes and subject matter of her dramatic writing – but her response to the experience of rural life was considerably more ambiguous. Her encounters with the ethnic communities concentrated in the farming districts left her with an abiding sympathy and respect for New Canadians. At a time when such minorities were often treated with condescending humor if they were featured at all, Gowan's sympathetic treatment of Ukrainian, Polish, German and Italian Canadians in many of her radio plays even during the war or early post-war years is noteworthy. Her affection and respect for French Canadians, who also often assume large sympathetic roles especially in her historical dramas, she also credits as a lasting legacy from her teaching days at St. Paul de Métis. On a personal level, she was also to remember her teaching years as an opportunity to gain some much-needed maturity, poise, and social skills.

At the same time, as explored in such early plays as *Homestead* and *The Hungry Spirit*, Gowan again found herself increasingly "the girl who is out of step." However welcome the romantic attentions of the young farmers in confirming the fact that she was developing into an attractive young woman, her critical eye still saw ample proof that marriage entrapped and stultified women as often as it fulfilled them, and that the pastoral life, however engaging to the romantic imagination, offered limited opportunities for intellectual and professional growth to an ambitious young woman. Unlike Ringwood, whose life, work, and drama continued to be closely linked to rural tones and ambiences, Gowan was quickly to become both physically and mentally an urban writer concerned with exploring the larger social, political, and economic forces shaping both the past and present workings of society. In 1926, at age 21, Elsie Young enrolled in Honors History, and her horizons began to expand with gratifying speed.

Looking back across 60 years, Gowan still remembers the excitement of being part of the program and the sparks that flew during the Honors seminars in particular:

> I had such wonderful fellow students. We had the seminar in Professor Burt's office . . . and the other people were George Stanley the man who helped Pearson design the flag and became Lieutenant-Governor of New Brunswick; Ted Manning who became a chief justice; Duncan Innis who became principal of Old Scona, and Wally Sterling who was president of Stanford. And with men like those in this seminar, it was terrific.[4]

However, it was Sterling's older sister who was to influence Gowan most profoundly in her extra-curricular activities, and her reawakening interest in drama in particular. At the time Gowan was a student (1926-30), the most exciting drama work in the city was being done on the University campus, largely under the influence of the inspirational director and teacher, Elizabeth Sterling Haynes. Like her fellow student, Gwen Pharis Ringwood, who enrolled a few years later as an English major, Gowan was to become part of an exciting flowering of amateur drama that exposed students not only to Stanislavskian acting techniques, non-naturalistic writers like

Andreyev and Rice, and expressionistic set design in their drama club productions, but to community-based radio drama via the founding of CKUA and the CKUA Players on campus. Ringwood and Gowan were also to be intimately involved in the rapid expansion of the movement between 1929 and 1936 to include the founding of the Edmonton Little Theatre, The Alberta Drama League, The Dominion Drama Festival, and the Banff School of Fine Arts.

Encouraging local playwrights was certainly one of the mandates of the new amateurism – and Gowan soon responded. *Homestead*, written in 1930 while Gowan was still teaching at Lacombe, not only took an honorable mention in the 1932 Carnegie Playwriting Competition but was performed by the Edmonton Little Theatre in 1933. Her marriage that summer to the play's director, Dr. Ted Gowan, a young physics professor, brought her into the city to stay and with her teaching career now on hold, her playwriting career really began. Ringwood's first play, *The Dragons of Kent*, was performed in 1936 and in the fall of that year, Sheila Marryat of CKUA decided to bring the two promising young talents together to write a series of radio plays on famous figures from history.

Both Gowan and Ringwood remember their work on *New Lamps for Old* – each wrote ten scripts at five dollars each – as valuable training for a future playwriting career, but the series in many ways marked a watershed in their fortunes as playwrights. Where Ringwood largely returned to writing for the live stage after the series was done, Gowan was to increasingly abandon the live stage for radio drama after 1936.

* * *

A large part of the reason for this divergence of paths is that Gowan appears to have been less comfortable than Ringwood with the practical and ideological limitations of writing for the conventional community theatre.

The Madwoman of Chaillot. Elizabeth Sterling Haynes as Madwoman of Chaillot (at the back), Elsie Park Gowan as Mad Woman of Concorde (2nd from the left), Studio Theatre, University of Alberta, 1951.

The Great Catherine. Charles Norman as Patiomkin, Dagney McGregor as Claire, Ben Benson as Edstaston, Elsie Park Gowan as Catherine II, Studio Theatre, University of Alberta, 1953.

13

Gowan, like Ringwood, was always to remain a staunch champion of the artistic integrity and quality of the Little Theatre movement, and to contribute actively to the Edmonton Little Theatre as a director, actor, administrator, teacher, and writer. Nonetheless, she was not blind to the amateur theatre's practical drawbacks: the frustrations of finding suitable theatre spaces and the money to rent or buy the same, the difficulties of finding a large and talented enough pool of volunteer actors, directors and board members to sustain the venture, and the problems of finding a market for mainstage Canadian drama. Gowan was always to treasure the experience of having her full-length comedy, *The Last Caveman* commissioned and performed as part of the Edmonton Little Theatre's mainstage season in 1938, then picked up and toured across the Western provinces in 1946 by the Everyman Theatre company, one of the first Canadian professional theatre groups to emerge after the war. But *Caveman* was an isolated success, all the more frustrating because it was to prove a one-time event.

At the same time, Gowan's strong socialist bent brought her into conflict with some of the social pretensions of the Little Theatre movement. A member of the CCF from its founding, Gowan became increasingly critical during the 1930s of the local drama society's tendency to indulge more in social hoopla and producing the kind of pleasant, escapist plays that enhanced idle socializing than to push strongly for the kind of experimental and socially serious drama that Gowan favored. While the Edmonton Little Theatre premièred such serious works as *The Giant Killer* and *The Last Caveman,* which advocate pacifism, and *The Hungry Spirit,* which upholds a woman's right to a higher education, Gowan as often as not turned to more socialist groups to perform her most experimental or angry work. *You Can't Do That!,* a full-length comedy about national credit (co-written with William Irvine), *Glorious and Free,* about a family facing the Depression, *The Unknown Soldier Speaks,* a Remembrance Day celebration denouncing war, and *The House in Toad Lane*, a play about the birth of the co-operative movement at Rochdale, were all presented by CCYM societies or groups outside the formal amateur theatre movement. Unfortunately, since none of these groups were formal drama societies, their commitment to play production tended to be only on an occasional or project-to-project basis.

Gowan had hopes that the Banff School might prove the cradle for the kind of training and writing still missing from the mainstream Little Theatre movement. In 1937 she wrote about Frederick Koch's playwriting class:

> Something of tremendous importance to the people of Alberta is happening in Banff this month. . . . It has always been a good school. This summer it has become a force of great social significance. *It is creating a people's theatre for Alberta.*
>
> In other sessions, we have worn robes of silk and velvet, played at being kings and queens of long ago. Today our characters wear overalls and sweaters and gingham aprons. They are farmers and miners, grocers and housewives. We are building drama on the humor and tragedy, the triumphs and defeats, the magnificent courage of the people of the Canadian West. . . .
>
> Even timid souls are getting over their fear of "propaganda" plays as they realize that every truly great drama is "propaganda" for something.
>
> When August ends, a hundred and fifty people will return to their own communities with a new understanding. They will know that a powerful social theme can vitalize a play, and a well-produced play can dramatize a social problem . . . There is a force growing here in Banff which can help to change the world.[5]

In the closing years of the decade, however, Gowan was increasingly to come to the conclusion that the real dramatic force for change lay not in Banff, but the airwaves over it. The radio, with its access to professional actors, a nationwide audience, and a continual demand for new materials for which one would be paid, in many ways presented a more promising commercial alternative for an ambitious young writer. But beyond that, the fact that public broadcasting consciously assumed a nationalistic, didactic, and educative mandate towards the Canadian public to combat foreign cultural and commercial imperialism was, from Gowan's perspective, to make the radio a far better instrument than the community theatre for creating a vast socially significant "people's theatre" which could "help to change the world."

* * *

There is something entirely appropriate about the fact that some of the first words of Gowan to go out over the air to CKUA listeners in 1936-37 in the *New Lamps for Old* series were those of Mary Wollstonecraft giving a spirited defense of her *Vindication of the Rights of Women*.

Mary: Will you try for a moment, sir, to forget that I am a wayward and fragile creature. Think of me as a rational human being who has described from the very depths of her heart, the wrongs of half the human race. Will you tell me please why you are so sure we cannot engage in business and the professions.

Walpole: The fundamental inequalities of nature, ma'am.

Mary: What do we know of "fundamental inequalities" in a world which weights the scales against women from the very first? Girls are encouraged to be frail, silly, and shallow, to tremble at the jump of a mouse, or the frown of an old cow. Change all that, give them the same education as their brothers, send them to the same schools. . . .[6]

The play is important insofar as it represents one of Gowan's first attempts to combine her training as a historian and as a teacher – careers which were both sidetracked by the exigencies of Depression economics and her status as a woman married to a successful professional – with her skills as a playwright. However rough the initial results, it was a combination of talents that suited Gowan's taste immensely, and she was to spend most of the next two decades experimenting with and improving on the integration and balancing of the three.

At the same time, the play also sounds the keynote for the kind of strong liberal feminism that implicitly or explicitly dominates much of Gowan's work. In contrast to the gentle, accepting, passive women of many of Ringwood's early plays, Gowan's women – whether they be historical or contemporary in their milieu – tend to be feisty, strongwilled, and articulate individuals who constantly assert their right to be full human beings in the face of social and material inequities which deny them full humanity or visibility. While Gowan's protagonists always demonstrate the importance of the individual will in refusing to be victimized, her larger pacifist and socialist convictions also surface in her insistence that the inequities themselves be explored, challenged and changed to ensure a fairer and more just deal for everyone, including women.

If elements of both preoccupations surface in *New Lamps for Old*, they receive their first mature treatment in Gowan's *Building of Canada* series, which she authored completely by herself and which first drew her to national attention when the series, first done over CKUA in 1937-38, was rebroadcast over CBC in 1938-39.

Gowan was obviously a quick learner. The abrupt and confusing scene transitions which she felt plagued her *Lamps* plays, were more effectively covered by narration and musical bridges. The *Building* plays also show increasingly sophisticated and evocative use of sound effects and music, and more fluid use of time and space as Gowan's mind began moving imaginatively beyond the limitations of the box set and shifting more comfortably between indoor and outdoor, past and present, internal and external expressions of reality.

More importantly, *Building* was to mark Gowan's first mature venture into the kind of epic theatre that was to distinguish her best dramatic work of the 1940s and 1950s. The idea of exposing Canadian listeners to an entertaining but educative pageant of Canada's past was hardly a new one. Merrill Denison had pioneered the historical radio series in 1931 with his *Romance of Canada* series, and by 1936, the CNR-CRBC network had experimented with at least 19 other series on various topics.[7]

However, the *Building* series was seen as unusually good work even by its contemporaries. W. S. Milne wrote in *Letters in Canada, 1937*, that one "had to confess that the Eastern stations have not yet discovered as brilliant a script-writer as has CKUA."[8] Much of its appeal lay in the skill with which Gowan built a cohesive drama of interlinking economic, social and political themes, swiftly unfolding historical action, and ongoing character development over 20 half-hour episodes. Unlike Denison's surviving *Romance* plays which stress only the public manifestations of certain events, and exclude virtually all women, Gowan's series was also innovative in trying to strike a careful balance between the outer world of public affairs where the great speeches, fights and legislation go on – and the parlor and drawingroom where families meet to argue over the impact of these larger affairs on their individual fortunes.

The public realm was undeniably dear to the trained historian's heart, and the listener gets a remarkably evenhanded exposure to the conflicts between French and English Canada, the Western and Eastern experience of settlement, and provincial and federal power sharing as the series pursues the main plotline of Canada's passage from the early days of immigration and colonialization dating back to the 17th century, through to a growing sense of autonomy and self-determination over the 18th and 19th centuries, and finally a sense of rich, multi-ethnic maturity in 1938.

But much of the real genius of the series lies in the private realm and the development not just of individual characters over the years, but whole families over several generations. While Gowan credits Noel Coward's play *Cavalcade* with giving her the idea of focusing the larger historical pageantry around the evolving fortunes of several families, her application of the idea is very much her own.

Undeniably, the main families in the series – the French Morels who arrive in Quebec with Champlain, the English Grants who conquer then intermarry with them, the United Empire Loyalist Steeles who gravitate to Ontario, and the Scottish McLeods who settle in Manitoba – give Gowan ample room for historical and geographical movement.

However, Gowan suggests that the strong emphasis on the family also derives from her pacifist suspicion about the value of military force to resolve problems, and a conviction that the public realm of wars, rebellions and legislation often imposes on the private realm of the home and family in ways that go ignored in the public record:

> For instance, Lord Durham's son-in-law was Lord Elgin, who signed the Rebellion Losses Bill that create a riot in Montreal . . . and I was reading in the Encyclopedia . . . on Lord Elgin, and it said "Victor so-and-so Elgin born so-and-so in the spring of 1849" – and that was the spring when the riots happened. So she was pregnant when this mob was howling in the streets. I mean, here *he* was pursuing a policy which was bringing down upon their house the fury of this mob. And she was pregnant. . . . Public events impinge on private lives. . . . And very often I felt there was a military something-or-another where there wasn't any need for it, really.[9]

The strong family presence also meant that the plays had "plenty of women in them, and . . . usually women who had minds of their own"[10] who made it amply clear to the listener that public "victories" were usually paid for in terms of intense private suffering – romances shattered, families bitterly divided or persecuted, wives widowed and children orphaned. Gowan's own Riel play is unique in that much of the action is centred in the house of an old Scottish homesteader, Jean McLeod, who is inclined to see both Riel and Thomas Scott as immature children who need to grow up before they impose their grand schemes on the world. They mean well, grumbles the old woman, but while they fight, the farming gets neglected, families are disrupted and nuptials delayed, and the network of goodwill created by family helping family is disintegrating. Brushing aside Scott's peevish protest that she just doesn't understand "a man's world," Jean wryly muses as he departs, "Poor laddie. If he had the brains to match his strength and courage . . . he would be a man."[11] Other still, small voices of female reason among the clash of historical forces include Lady Mary Elgin, and 82 year old Louise Morel Grant.

The historical epic was to remain a staple of Gowan's later radio work and to help set the pattern for her successful stage pageants in the mid-fifties. While Gowan credits her interest in the stage form to her discovery of some of Paul Green's outdoor pageant scripts at the Banff School, and her viewing of a 1938 pageant at the San Francisco World Fair, which included "dancing and singing . . . and two trains – the last spike business,"[12] the radio work also helped her deal with the problems of putting the same kind of historical sweep on the live stage. The advent of Alberta's Golden Jubilee in 1955 sparked a province-wide revival of interest in local history, and of the three pageants or "historamas" she wrote as part of the celebrations, *The Jasper Story* (music by Jack McCreath), staged annually between 1956-1960 and 1976-1979 remains a personal favourite of Gowan and one of her most successful later stage plays.

Gowan was always to contend that the same tenets of craftsmanship that applied to good radio writing also applied to the production of stage plays, and she readily applied the same techniques she had learned writing historical drama for the air to writing it for the boards. Confronted with the usual challenge of trying to convert a mountain of oral and documentary historical research into a condensed aesthetic form, she decided that since "the basis of history is economics, the saga had three chapters – Fur, Gold and Steel."[13] Within each of the parts, Gowan again turned to the "good old Gowan" technique of arranging the historical narrative around the fortunes of several representative families (with their own share of strong assertive women, of course), and supplying a narrator/guide as a framing device.

Far more interesting, however, was the way that she adapted to the stage medium the aural evocativeness, large cast size, and freer treatment of time and space associated with her radio writing. *The Jasper Story*, which placed several cars, 12 horses and a cast of 140 local amateur singers, dancers, musicians, actors, and extras on a huge 200 foot stage in an outdoor amphitheatre with the whole of the Palisade mountain range as a backdrop, proved an intriguing foray into what Gowan was to call "'total theatre' using all the theatre's resources of dialogue, song, music, dance, and spectacle."[14] Gowan's visual imagination, stretched by years of radio work, also stood her well in writing scenes particularly suited to the theatre's sprawling natural environment where much of the historical action had actually occurred. As one reviewer noted:

> The sight of the top-hatted and frock-coated Governor Simpson leading a riff raff band of voyageurs into the small clearing which forms the stage has a striking air of reality. The picture of the doomed overlanders singing Luther's hymn, spotlighted against the trees and mountains, brings home with moving impact the courage and isolation of the tiny band. Lewis Swift's story strikes closest to home for it

is acted on almost the exact spot on which the lone homesteader defied the railway to build its line through his property. Behind the stage lies the line the railway finally did build after surrendering to the stubborn man's defense of his home.[15]

To the extent that misscheduled trains roaring through the "set" at inconvenient – and wildly anachronistic – moments in the action was a constant problem, it would appear that the railway had the final word after all. Still the reviewer's good opinion of *The Jasper Story* was confirmed by the fact that by the end of its nine year run, literally thousands of spectators had braved the damp, rain and even snow of the outdoor theatre to watch Gowan's version of "total theatre" in action.

* * *

The Building of Canada not only helped lay the foundations for further dramatic experimentation, it also proved to be the start of a long and fruitful association with CBC that started only two years after the latter's incorporation and was to continue through much of the "Golden Age" of CBC radio drama under Andrew Allan's leadership. Gowan has suggested that marriage to a successful professional man on the prairies left her with neither the time nor mobility to move into the higher bracket of radio writers who could earn up to $15,000 to $20,000 a year from their work.[16] Nonetheless, she felt it was a credit to Allan's determination to make CBC a truly national theatre that he was prepared to cultivate Canadian talent wherever it was to be found, and that a constant stream of assignments continued to find their way to Edmonton over the next two decades.[17]

* * *

Additionally, if radio gave Gowan's historical talents a venue that had previously been denied them, it also gave freer

22

rein to her penchant for social criticism. If she found the social snobbery of the Little Theatre sometimes worked against receptiveness to serious didactic social drama, the CBC's preception of itself as a social and cultural educator worked to her advantage. Working on assignment often meant that Gowan more frequently wrote on topics given to her than freely chosen, but she was allowed a fair amount of artistic license in her treatment of the same, and the projects often pushed her into areas of research she may not have explored on her own.

Her interest in young people continued to manifest itself in dramatizations of history and composition lessons as well as adaptations of short stories and novels for the young. These were sent out not only over CBC but CBS Columbia School of the Air and NBC Inter-American University of the Air. However, it was the education of the older generations that absorbed her interest. In *The Call to Health and Happiness*, she helped alert the public to health difficulties that could be discovered and cured with prompt treatment. With her six episodes each of *Down Our Street Today*, and *Judge for Yourself*, she explored the problems of daycare ("The High Green Gate"), old age pensions, social welfare, mental illness, prison rehabilitation, dysfunctional families, sexual frigidity and promiscuity, wife-beating, and teenage sex and pregnancy, especially in a post-war society still in transition from an agrarian to an urban mode of living. And, as with the historical series, Gowan's training as a researcher stood her in good stead in meeting the challenge of reading umpteen articles, pamphlets and books on her subject, delving into closed files or trial manuscripts, and interviewing and visiting those concerned, while relying on her skills as a playwright to finally condense all the material into a taut, well-crafted 15 or 30 minute episode.

By Gowan's own admission, however, it was her family series, where she got to control the action and development of the characters over the course of several seasons, that display much of her best work and the sharpest critical eye for the social changes that the war and post-war period were bringing to the Canadian public. In many ways, *The Town Grows Up* (1943-44) set the foundation for two of her longest running series, *The People Next Door* (1944-45, 1945-46) and *The Barlows of Beaver Street* (1948-49). With *The Town Grows Up* series, listeners were introduced to the history, social need and functions of such civic services as the library, the police, the public health service, the waterworks and the hospital as they developed in the fictional town of Maplefield. (Typically, Gowan gave high profile to women's groups in promoting the development of certain social services like the library, the hospital, and public and school health, that she felt men, in their pursuit of more economic and political developments, often overlooked or devalued.) In an effort to create some sort of continuity between the episodes, which covered such a wide variety of topics, Gowan invented a kindly old-timer, John Evans, to narrate the series and serve as the binding consciousness which at once knew the town and interacted with its people as they were now, but also had the kind of long, communal memory that could send the action back into the past for the historical sequences of the action.

The fictional town of Maplefield had obviously caught Gowan's imagination, and she was to return to it again for her next important series, *The People Next Door*. Having focused first on the larger public life of her community, Gowan now focused her attention on a block of families within the town, located on Maple Street. (Her research materials include a map of the neighborhood clearly indicating where each family lived and their physical relationship to each other.) John Evans continued to perform as the bridging persona during the 17 episode 1944-45 series, but he was already playing a smaller and smaller part as the voices of the individual families – the Rosaks, the Lyons, the Ferguses, the McKays and the Sinclairs began to take over; by 1945-46, Evans was gone and the individual members of the various families took responsibility for the narration.

Though the series is set against the larger public background of the war and the return of the veterans, Gowan's focus on the public realm's impact on the family again draws the action into the domestic realm of women, and the way the war has changed their fortunes especially with the men overseas. In some cases, the changes are frightening and disruptive. In the first series, she writes about the loneliness and vulnerability of the girls who have left their homes to work in factories and munitions plants ("Transplanting Teresa"); the frustration of young army wives, often with children, struggling to follow their husbands and find accommodation in a tight housing situation ("The Case of the Divided House"); the predicament of English war brides dealing with cultural shock ("Brides from Britain"); and the heartache of a young woman who not only has to cope with the death of her fiancé in action, but the imminent arrival of their out-of-wedlock child ("The Case of the Unofficial Parents").

In the second series, she writes even more jarringly of the conflicts arising out of the men returning home to discover that the homes and families they knew have changed beyond recognition, and the women in particular are marching to the beat of a different drummer. In some cases, the consequences of the hasty war marriage are discovered as people who married as boy and girl are faced with the shock of living with a virtual stranger. While the case of the bored young wife who has already started dating again while her husband is still overseas is explored ("The Case of the Doubtful Bride"), it is the boys who are more frequently seen as returning to their homes as boys while their girls have matured into strong, self-sufficent women, workers and, in some cases, parents ("Marriage is for Adults Only"). In other cases ("Jack Barlow Comes Home," "Mary is a Person, Sergeant"), mature men who have always seen themselves as the heads of their household arrive home to discover that their home is now being run as a co-operative adventure, and the helpless little woman is bristling with all sorts of public poise, and employment and managerial skills he never knew she possessed.

As demonstrated by her lively 1941 comedy, *Back to the Kitchen, Woman!*, Gowan has considerable sympathy for male panic and confusion over women's changing roles. Nonetheless, she suggests in such episodes as "Mary is a Person, Sergeant," that it is the men who ultimately need to grow up and adjust to this new feminine strength:

> Mary: I had to develop muscles in my mind. Do things . . . carry responsibilities. Not because I wanted to. I had to.

> Mac: Uh-huh. But Daddy's home now. . . . Politics are simply not a woman's business! . . . *It's not like you!* Getting up in public . . .

> Mary: I thought "When Mac gets back we'll be better partners in everything." Because if I've changed at all it's to be a bigger person.

> Mac: I liked you the way you were! We were happy.

> Mary: I hoped you'd like me now. That we'd be good friends and have a lot to talk about. And build a home with windows looking out on the world. . . . That takes two.[18]

In another episode,"Janey's Last Chance," which anticipates a number of the themes explored in "The High Green Gate," a young career woman considering the rush of post-war marriages and pressure to join the domestic boom, resists her young man's insistence that there is only one pattern for marriage, the woman home full-time attending to her husband and children's needs:

> Jane: I've seen women that used to be bored,
> discontented . . . buckle into war work that took
> four . . . five hours every day . . . and they loved it.
>
> Ralph: While their children ran the streets, I suppose.
>
> Jane: The small kids went to kindergarten . . . and that's a
> lot happier place for a three year old than shut up with
> one adult female . . .
>
> Ralph: Aw, that's woman's talk. Did you ever meet a full-
> grown man who believed it?[19]

Fortunately for Janey, she meets another young man, who has
more enlightened views about working women, his own
mother having worked full-time as a nurse in the bush while
raising seven children.

All this paved the way for one of Gowan's own favorite
series *The Barlows of Beaver Street*. Conceived as Canada's
answer to such BBC series as *Mrs. Dale's Diaries* and
Coronation Street, which were exposing Canadians to British
life and manners, *The Barlows* was broadcast in 34 chapters
over the CBC International Service to Britain. Returning to the
same community and renaming Maple Street, Beaver Street,
Gowan now focuses in on the fortunes of the Barlows, one of
the families highlighted in *The People Next Door* series: Jim
and Margaret Barlow, the parents; Frank, the eldest boy, a
returned serviceman; Kate, the eldest girl, a feisty young
newspaperwoman with definite opinions on social injustice
and women's place in the professions ("Kate was me," Gowan
frankly admits[20]); Louise, the younger daughter, a department
store worker, and Johnny, the youngest, age 17.

In writing the series, Gowan essentially aimed at creating a
family series that would interest her British listeners on a

human level, while educating them painlessly about Canadian culture and customs. The Barlows were designed to be a large enough family to carry the purely human element of the series: Margaret and Louise were there for people more comfortable with "womanly" women, though even they have something of the distinctive Gowan spark and sense of independence and adventure; Kate was there for the aspiring professional women; Johnny for the adolescents; and Jim and Frank for the mature male listeners. It was through the family's romantic attachments that Gowan tried to supply the educative elements of the program.

Enter Vera, Frank's English war bride, and one of Gowan's best-drawn dramatic characters. Strongly based on Gowan's personal experiences with the airforce couples who lived with her family during the war years, and a close friendship with one British war bride, Vera proved a valuable focus for the series' sympathetic and insightful view of the problems facing young post-war couples trying to start a family, find a home and rebuild careers at a time when families were booming faster than housing and the economy. Equally importantly, the feisty, good-natured Vera served as an important "in" to the Canadian situation for British listeners. She at once slowly discovers and falls in love with the charms and beauties of her adopted country (at least three of the episodes follow Vera's train trip west across Canada to join up with her husband, who is working in Edmonton for the summer), without ever losing the outsider's sharp, dispassionate eye for the contradictions and idiosyncracies of a strange culture especially where they clash with her own British upbringing.

For the larger historical and cultural undertones, Gowan borrowed a page from her *Building of Canada* series, in which many of the larger political and social English-French tensions are explored in the context of the marriage bonds between the Morels and the Grants. Louise's romance with Phil Tremblay, a Western francophone, not only serves as the series' main love interest, but is consciously used as a microcosm of the "two solitudes" struggling to co-exist as Phil and Louise try to wend their way though the pitfalls of differing cultures, customs, languages and religions to achieve a successful union. Gowan further picks up the split between the agrarian and urban realities of the Canadian experience by having Louise struggle with the dilemma of remaining a city girl and marrying her stodgy young Department store boss (whom she has charmed with her outspoken comments about his managerial shortcomings, and suggestion that he give *her* a more responsible position to relieve the problem) or follow Phil out to his new farm in Manitoba. Louise's final decision to marry Phil, with her family and Vera's blessing, thus constitutes not only a vindication of Louise's personal taste in young men, but an affirmation of the agrarian life still found in Western Canada and of the Canadian ability to continue reconciling the differences between the two solitudes with tolerance, good will, hard work and love on both sides.

Gowan was to venture once more into the family series with *The Ferguson Family* in 1954, but it is perhaps a reflection of the more sedate social milieu of the mid-fifties that the six part series moves away from the epic quality of the earlier ones and into the more personal and psychological issues of family life such as sexual repression, adolescent revolt, workaholicism and the proper distribution of roles and responsibilities within the family. Outside of the *Judge for Yourself* series (1955) which again focused on family problems in the context of the family court and social agency case studies, *The Fergusons* was to be the last series that Gowan was to attempt before Dr. Gowan's death in 1958, and the virtual end of Gowan's writing career.

* * *

Musing over her playwriting career in an interview in August, 1991, Elsie Park Gowan, commented wryly, "I often

The program cover from a 1991 production of *Back to the Kitchen, Woman!* by The Central Lions Players.

think it was all written on the air. As Keats said, 'My name is one – whose name was writ in water.' My name was writ on the air and its 'substantial pageant faded.'"[21] Gowan's observation that much of her best work has, in fact, vanished into thin air is not an inappropriate one. Certainly, in deciding to bend her efforts towards radio rather than stage writing at a decisive point in her career, Gowan ensured her professional success as a playwright in her own time at the expense of future posterity.

Until her papers were submitted to the University Archives two years ago, one could only approach Gowan through the few plays of hers that had been published in now out-of-print typescripts and anthologies. That she was published at all at a time when Canadian plays were hardly a marketable commodity argues well for the regard in which she was held by her contemporaries. At the same time, publishers were apt to print only the lighter, more amusing comedies and instructional historical plays that would sell well to the educational and Little Theatre audiences of that time. The indignity of having her name as co-author excluded from the original edition of the political comedy, *You Can't Do That*, (only William Irvine gets credited), is by far surpassed by the indignity of having the whole of this angry, thoughtful writer's canon reduced to four light comedies, three history plays and two fantasies suitable for classroom and Little Theatre use.

Nor has the situation been completely remedied even today. As Howard Fink points out in his index to English Canadian radio drama, there has been a tendency to devalue the importance of radio script writing despite the fact that the radio was in many ways, Canada's national theatre between 1930 and 1950. Of the thousands of scripts written during the Golden Age of Radio Drama, he notes, scarcely more than 100 have ever been printed or anthologized, and only 52 were still in print in 1973.[22] A further complication in trying to anthologize Gowan effectively is that the kind of radio writing

Seniors Writing Class at Strathcona Place in the 1970s. Elsie Park Gowan at table head, Peggy Holmes ("Canada's Oldest broadcaster"), third from instructor's left.

she excelled in was not only the radio play but the radio series. Since the aesthetic of the individual episode – some of them as short as 15 minutes each – values extreme compactness while the aesthetic of the series as a whole stresses size and complexity, publishing individual episodes would be in many ways counter-productive to giving the reader a real sense of Gowan's accomplishment in the form.

One also wonders if Ringwood's stature as the definitive prairie playwright of her generation has not served to push Gowan further into the background than she has deserved. If the same mentality that has led to Ringwood's reputation resting on the strength of her superb folk tragedy, *Still Stands the House,* has not also contributed to Gowan's current reputation resting largely on the witty, little pioneer comedy, *Breeches from Bond Street,* which is in many ways much less representative of Gowan's work – but works in much better with critical theories about Western regional writers being preoccupied with the relationship between man and the land.

Finally, one wonders if Gowan has not been penalized for the fault of being a very different playwright with a very different set of interrelated strengths and deficencies. She may be the more critical and outspoken observer of the times and mores of her society – but that also tends to date her work more quickly since society is nowhere near as universal and unchanging as land. Her fascination with ideas, the sweep of larger historical, social and economic forces, and dedication to social justice especially for minorities and women gives her best work a passion, seriousness and epic quality that still moves the reader, but this breadth – especially in the context of the extremely abbreviated 15 minute episode form – is sometimes acquired at the sacrifice of depth in characterization and treatment of subject matter; as a consequence, where the same issue no longer has the same emotional power it did for the original audience, something of the shrill and didactic can start to creep in. The brisk, witty dialogue charms, but there are none of the deeper poetic overtones and symbolic and archetypal resonances that help keep Ringwood's writing more "universal" in its appeal.

Finally, while Ringwood is associated with a more tragic perspective on the world, Gowan's world view, for all its passion and seriousness is essentially a comic one, and because of that, perhaps easier to trivialize. On an immediate level, the response of many of Gowan's protagonists, when they encounter a gap between the world as it is and how it should be is often a wry, ironic wit that notes the discrepancy. But on a larger scale, Gowan's writing tends to reflect a socialist's faith in being able to eventually bring the real and the ideal into conjunction through the proper employment of clear-minded reasoning, will power, and group and individual action. Her characters tend to be rational, conscious, articulate creations with few hidden demons and subconscious depths precisely, one suspects, because Gowan is inclined to see human frailty, pain and weakness as problems to be analysed and solved, rather than timeless essences to be savored.

Tragedy, in some measure, demands an accepting spirit willing to submit to a glorious defeat at the hands of forces ultimately recognized as greater than oneself. An angry, resistant spirit rejects even that glorious form of victimization, whether it be the work of internal or external forces, simply because to accept it is ultimately to admit limits to how far the human spirit can aspire and succeed. Gowan's is not an accepting spirit.

This introduction has tried to indicate some of the historical, pragmatic and literary factors that can reduce even a writer of talent and insight to invisibility and keep her there even after her contemporaries have been rediscovered and restored with honor. Having done so, it is only fair to acknowledge that the very anthology designed to correct this problem and demarginalize the writer can simultaneously re-marginalize important aspects of her work through editing unavoidably based on practicality, current tastes and personal bias. Nonetheless, we hope that the six plays, one essay and one short story we have chosen to represent Gowan will give a strong enough sense of her skill, variety and vision as a writer that others will take an interest in rediscovering her work, and another significant voice will be restored to the canon of woman's dramatic writing in Western Canada.

University of Saskatchewan
January, 1992

---

1. Elsie Park Gowan, interview with Moira Day, 28 July 1991. (Unless cited otherwise, Gowan's general observations about her life and career in this introduction are drawn from two lengthy interviews made with me on 28 July 1991 and 16 August 1991. The interview excerpts included in the body of the anthology are from the same source. Direct quotations taken from these interviews will continue to be referenced here.)

2. Elsie Park Gowan, "The Girl Who Is Out Of Step," autobiographical script for CBC radio series *Growing Up*, 1948. Elsie Park Gowan Papers, University of Alberta Archives.

3. Ibid.

4. Gowan-Day interview, 16 August 1991.

5. Elsie Park Gowan, "Powerful Social Force at Banff School," Edmonton *People's Weekly*, 14 August 1937.

6. Elsie Park Gowan, "Mary Wollstonecraft," in *New Lamps For Old* series, 1936-37, Elsie Park Gowan Papers, University of Alberta Archives. While Ringwood's scripts from the series have been lost, two of Gowan's, "Mary Wollstonecraft" and "The Coming of Power," are still extant in Gowan's papers.

7. Howard Fink, *Canadian National Theatre On The Air 1925-1961: CBC-CRBC-CNR Radio Drama in English* (Toronto: University of Toronto Press, 1983) 11.

8. W.S. Milne, "Drama" in *Letters in Canada: 1937* (Toronto: University of Toronto Press, 1938) 367.

9. Gowan-Day interview, 16 August 1991.

10. Ibid.

11. Elsie Park Gowan, "Red Star in the West," in *The Building of Canada* series, 1937, Elsie Park Gowan Papers, University of Alberta Archives.

12. Gowan-Day interview, 16 August 1991.

13. Elsie Park Gowan, "History into Theatre," *Canadian Author and Bookman* Vol. 5, No. 1 (Fall, 1975) 8.

14. Ibid.

15. John Dafoe, "Jasper's Colorful Early History Told in Town's Annual Pageant," Edmonton *Journal* (17 July 1958).

16. Elsie Park Gowan, interview with Steve Olson, 21 May 1991.

17. Ibid.

18. Elsie Park Gowan, "Mary is a Person, Sergeant," in *The People Next Door*, Series II 1945-46, Elsie Park Gowan Papers, University of Alberta Archives.

19. Elsie Park Gowan, "Janey's Last Chance," in *The People Next Door*, Series II 1945-46, Elsie Park Gowan Papers, University of Alberta Archives.

20. Gowan-Day interview, 16 August 1991.

21. Ibid.

22. Fink, 3.

Homestead

God Made the Country. Margaret Aldwinckle as Freda, Parker Kent as Hugh, Jack Chalmers as Brandt, University of Alberta Dramatic Society at the Alberta Regional Festival of the DDF, Grand Theatre, Calgary, 1935.

U OF A ARCHIVES (*EVERGREEN AND GOLD*, 1935)

HOMESTEAD: *INTERVIEW*

Day: Let's start talking about *Homestead*. Was this your first play or just the first one that survived?

EPG: That was the first play I had written. You see, I had been at university for four years and I was always involved in something theatrical. And here I was teaching high school in Lacombe and there was no play going on and so I decided to write one. And I had the form of the one-act play in my subconsciousness, I think, from the 16 one-act plays I had seen in the interyear play contests, so that the shape of a play was part of my thinking.

Day: I notice that prior to your marriage you did a lot of teaching in the rural districts particularly after graduation from Normal School, during summers when you were at University and for three years after graduation. Can you talk about your experiences as a rural schoolteacher and what impact they had on the writing of the play? Were Freda, Hugh and Brandt based on real people?.

EPG: Well, *Homestead* was taken almost literally from the place that I stayed at Rocky Mountain House. I was living with a family who were barely on the edge of survival. My hostess was a charming woman . . . I mean, I said to myself, I could have been this person, you know . . . an intelligent, nice girl with three small children and a great big lump of a husband. And I lived with them for six months through the summer. And I saw the struggle they were having, the struggle *she* was having to keep her children fed and have something on the table when I got home from school. And she told me about the forest fire and how she'd seen – I used the line right in the play – seen the little animals running so terrified with the fire, the fire which is a beneficent thing in the stove and a killer in the woods, you know. I was going through at that time, a Hardy fad – reading all of Hardy's books – and the theme of the cruel environment, the pitiless environment that stretches humanity right to the edge was what I was really trying to express.

Well, what we do is a result of what we are, and Freda is the girl who has given into . . . has let her body control her. She's married to this handsome lump who's good with an axe but not much good for anything else. And so, in writing *Homestead*, I had that log cabin in the woods out at Rocky Mountain House very much in my mind.

Day: You said that when you taught in the rural districts, *you* were almost carried off by one of the young farmers as well.

EPG: Well, in those days, everywhere a teacher went, there was always some lonely bachelor who thought she was the answer to his prayers. And a lot of those teachers never came back! However, *I* avoided that.

Day: I notice there are two versions of the play. In one, Freda and Hugh decide to run away but Hugh is killed by a falling tree. In the second, the lovers renounce their love only to recover their hope when the husband is struck down by the tree. Which is the original version and why were the changes made?

EPG: Well, in the original version, of course, Hugh the lover was killed and that bears out the thesis throughout – the cruelty of the environment that cares nothing for human desires or hopes or anything. Of course, some people like a happy ending. I don't know what happened there. Somebody said, "This is so depressing. Couldn't we kill off the other fellow?" So I wrote an ending to please them, but I don't think we should keep that one.

I was nearly killed by a tree myself in that country. I was coming home from Rocky Mountain House one Saturday afternoon, and as we rode along through a part of heavy forest, a wind squall struck the place and the trees started coming down all around me. Crash! Boom! And it was terrific. If I hadn't been riding a little Indian horse, I don't know what would have happened. But the horse instinctively seemed to understand what was going on and it brought me through. So when I had a tree fall on the man, it wasn't out of my imagination. It was based on reality.

Day: I understand that the play was done as part of a bill of one acts at the Masonic Temple in 1933. What do you remember about the first production? I notice that your husband directed it and it had a good Little Theatre cast: Sue Laycock, Max Wershof and Ernest Pelluet.

EPG: Yes, a very distinguished cast. Well, of course, it was a terrific thrill because it was the first time I'd seen one of my plays on the stage and it was, I thought, a very good production. I was living in Lacombe and these Edmonton people got it ready, and it was very exciting to see and hear my dialogue. I always visualize things very clearly, but as the song says: "Did you ever see a dream walking?" Well you write a play and then you see it produced and you see your dream walking. I can still see Mrs. Laycock holding up her lamp.

Day: I understand that a reworked version of the play entitled *God Made The Country* was presented as part of the Dominion Drama Festival in Calgary by the University of Alberta Dramatic Society in 1935. How did the Drama Society end up choosing the play?

EPG: The reason was that Barney Ringwood, who subsequently married Gwen [Pharis Ringwood], was president of the Drama Society, and he was in favor of Canadian plays.

Day: They had done E. J. Thorlakson's *The Derelict* the year before, hadn't they?

EPG: Yes, yes, yes. My sister was in it; she told me that in Ottawa it was quite exciting, that Mackenzie King was sitting in the front row of the audience. And when Thorlakson – you know, the play is about an architect who is going mad because he can't get work in the Depression – came down the stage saying "I must get something to do. I must get something to do," people thought he was going to go right up to Mackenzie King and say "I must get something to do" right at his feet!

Day: That was effective!

EPG: Yes!

Day: The prairie homestead drama appears to have been a very popular genre among playwrights in the twenties and thirties.

EPG: Well, you see, it's my theory that everybody who starts writing plays in Canada writes one play about human nature versus the climate. Gwen wrote *Still Stands the House* which is about a woman going crazy on a baldheaded prairie. I wrote *Homestead*, which is about a woman terribly unhappy in the bush country. Sydney Risk wrote *Fog*, which is about a lighthouse keeper's wife going crazy in the lighthouse – that's the Vancouverite version of the same theme. Robertson Davies did it in *Overlaid;* that's his *Still Stands the House.* And what was that one from Saskatchewan?

Day: That was Minnie Bicknell's *Relief.*

EPG: *Relief,* yes. It was on the same theme. The drought versus people.

Day: It seems everyone did one.

EPG: Because it was an obvious theme, obvious to any thinking person that that was the main problem in Canada. Land.

Day: You seem to have had a love-hate relationship with the genre. When Morley attacked prairie kitchen sink tragedies as morbid and untrue to Canadian life as he experienced it as an adjudicator, you blasted him for thinking that real Canadian drama should look like British witty, drawing-room comedies.[1] You also supported Ringwood's work in the style.

EPG: *Still Stands The House* is the best Canadian one-act play.

Day: At the same time, you said you were increasingly impatient with Frederick Koch's and Robert Gard's emphasis on the folk play [at the Banff School of Fine Arts].

EPG: Well, I thought this log cabin stuff could be carried too far, you know. And not everybody in the class had their feet in the good earth. So that for them to write folk plays was artificial. After you've done one, you move away to different themes. You know, you don't stay in the log cabin forever.

42

Day: Well, *you* certainly moved away from that.

EPG: Yes. But *Homestead* gave me a taste for playwriting. I found I could write a play and somebody would produce it. And that's what got me into radio writing, you see. And into historical writing.

---

1. Malcolm Morley's comments and Gowan's reply are to be found as follows:

Malcolm Morley, "Canada's Kitchen Drama," *Saturday Night*, Vol. 50, No. 40 (10 Aug, 1935) 12; Elsie Park Gowan, "Another Kitchen Stove," *Saturday Night*, Vol. 50, No. 44 (7 September, 1935) 8.

HOMESTEAD: *FIRST PERFORMANCE*

Homestead, under the title of *The Man Who Wouldn't Fight Back*, was first performed by the Edmonton Little Theatre at the Masonic Temple, Edmonton, 31 March, 1933, under the direction of Ted Gowan with the following cast:

Freda Neilson – *Sue Laycock*
Brandt Neilson – *Max Wershof*
Hugh Forbes – *Ernest Pelluet*

A revised version under the title *God Made the Country* was produced by the University of Alberta Dramatic Club at the Alberta Regional of the Dominion Drama Festival, 7 February, 1935, at the Grand Theatre in Calgary under the direction of Norah Young.

H O M E S T E A D

Characters:

Freda Neilson, a young woman, 26
Brandt Neilson, her husband, 27
Hugh Forbes, a bachelor neighbor, 32

Setting:

Time:

7:30, a hot July day, 1930.

Place:

A homestead 20 miles from anywhere.

The scene is Brandt Neilson's log cabin, on his homestead, twenty miles from anywhere. There is a door on the right, a long low window at the back, showing the spruce and jackpine outside. The stove and a crude cupboard are on the left. It is the evening of a hot day in July.

Freda Neilson is putting supper on the table. She is a slight woman of twenty six, with soft brown hair caught on her neck. She wears a cotton dress which is, like herself, too faded and worn to try any more to be pretty.

After a moment Brandt Neilson comes striding in with a high-piled armful of wood. He drops it into the wood box, and puts his axe against the wall. Neilson is a blonde giant of a man, in blue overalls and soft stepping buckskin boots. He pulls out a chair and sits down heavily, saying:

Neilson: There! Maybe that'll keep you quiet a spell. What the hell you do with all the wood I cut is more'n I can figure out.

Freda: I'm sorry, Brandt, I'd have cut it myself to-night, but I been at the garden all day. *She sits down wearily.* Them weeds are awful bad this year. The wind sure had more seeds that I did when I put in the carrots and the beans. They're all over the place, and high, and they choke the garden stuff. I was thinking if we had a cultivator, I could take Barney, and –

Neilson: I need Barney for breaking. *He speaks with his mouth full, in a way that permits no argument.*

Freda: Forbes is breaking on his own place. I could hear the tractor over across the creek this afternoon.

Neilson: Yea! He thinks I'll hire him yet, him and his gas engine. I was breaking land afore he ever saw a homestead, and I'll show him – I'll show him he's not so smart's he thinks he is. Wasn't over here, was he?

Freda: No, but when the wind came from the west, I could hear the tractor, quite plain. *Persuasively.* It had a kind of friendly sound, Brandt, like it was saying, "Here, I'll do this. You rest your back and let me dig this up." I like it.

Neilson: Yeah? Well, I don't like the idea of paying two hundred dollars for breaking, when I got a good team, and there's nothing the matter with my back. *Pause.* How'd he get his team home? Is the road clear?

Freda: Yes, Mrs. Ryan was past this morning, and she told me it took them three hours to come from their place, so many trees was down. Some was two feet across, she said, big strong ones you wouldn't expect to fall for years and years yet.

Neilson: Some wind, I'll tell the world.

Freda: *At the stove.* Now the road's clear, I suppose we'll be going to the picnic at Teepee creek?

Neilson: What for? Who'd ye want to see there?

Freda: Why, nobody . . . everybody I mean. I thought perhaps you'd want to run in the races like you used to.

Neilson: Run in races? An stiff old homesteader like me? I guess not.

Freda: Why we're not – you're not old, Brandt.

Neilson: I'm 28 come next Christmas, and I done all the racing I want chasing that dam' black cow down the pasture. Anyway, I got no time to be driving around the country going to picnics. I got a living to make. Did you fix it up with Mrs. Ryan about coming down here this winter?

Freda: No.

Neilson: Why didn't you? She may be planning on going somewhere else right when you need her.

Freda: I know, but I don't want . . . Brandt, can't I go to the hospital in town?

Neilson: What's the idea? Wha'd you want to make such a fuss about? Nothin' unusual about having a baby, is there? Indian women do right on the trail, or anywhere they happen to be.

Freda: Yes, and die on the trail too, and the rest just move on and leave them behind.

Neilson: Anybody'd think you didn't want it.

Freda: I don't.

Neilson looks at her.

Neilson: Say, what's the matter with you? All women want to have young ones, don't they?

Freda: *A little wildly.* Maybe they do, but I don't want a child in this place, with no decent doctor, or school, or money to send him out, and watch him grow up into a – a timber beast.

Neilson: *Unmoved.* Him? What if it's a girl?

Freda: I hope to God it isn't, but if it is, I'll take good care she never thinks she's in love with a big hulk of a homesteader like . . .

Neilson: *Roused.* Sorry for yourself, ain't you? My God, don't I work hard enough? I work from the time the sun comes up over them trees, 'til it goes down over there. Can I help it if the dam' lumber company don't pay? Can I help it if the hail got that patch of wheat? Can I help it . . .

Freda: *Wearily.* No, Brandt, I guess you can't, not now.

Neilson: Well, what's the use of crabbing about it, then? I'm going hunting.

The tired farmer is lost in the eager woodsman, as he reaches for his gun, which hangs over the door. At this moment Hugh Forbes appears in the doorway, and the men are face to face. Forbes is a dark well-knit man of about 32. He wears breeches, high boots, and a khaki shirt. As Neilson steps back grudgingly, he comes in.

Forbes: G'd evening, Brandt, G'd evening, Mrs. Neilson. Hot day to-day, eh?

Freda: It surely was. *She smoothes back her hair.* But it looks like we might get rain to-night.

48

Forbes: Wouldn't be surprised if we do. How's the breaking going, Brandt?

Neilson stands surly to left of door, still holding his gun.

Neilson: Oh, pretty good.

Freda: Won't you – sit down?

Neilson glares at her.

Forbes: Thanks. Mind if I smoke?

Freda: Why, no. *She becomes positively brazen.* Go right ahead. *She clears the table and takes the dishes to the stove.*

Forbes: *Lighting up and crossing his legs comfortably.* Well, Brandt, how about using twenty horse-power instead of two? I'll be through with the tractor on my place on Wednesday, and can start on your north quarter the day after.

Neilson: No, I guess I can't afford to hire you.

Forbes: But you don't have to pay me 'til next fall, when you take the crop off.

Neilson: Got it all figured out, ain't you? Say, who's running this place, anyway?

Forbes: *Good-humored.* Why you are, man, you and your wife. *He looks at Freda, and decides to tackle the brute again.* I'm going to town to-morrow, and I thought I'd talk over with the fellows that co-operative timber scheme.

Neilson: Yeah?

Forbes: How'd you like to come in on it with us?

Neilson: I figure I get a pretty good deal with the Imperial.

Forbes: Do you know how much the Imperial make on ties?

Neilson: I know how much they pay for ties . . . forty to fifty cents.

Forbes: Forty or fifty cents for ties we've cut an' hewn an' hauled. And they sell them to the mines for around eighty. Now if we formed a company of our own, we could make that profit ourselves. What'd you think of it?

Neilson: Well, I figure these co-operative schemes is all alike. *Spits.* They're alright for a while things going good, but just as soon's money begins to get tight, you'll see 'em all sneaking off to the Imperial again, where they can get credit.

Forbes: We'd have to stick to-gether, that's all.

Neilson: Stick to-gether. I'd like to see the bunch of horse-thieves in these woods stick to-gether. *Spits.*

Forbes: Oh, here, they're not as bad as that. . . . We need someone to take the lead. . . .

Neilson: Yeah, that's another thing. Who's going to run this here company once it's started? Because I'm telling you right now I'm not having Henry Pederson or ol' Pat Ryan butting into my timber deals.

Forbes: Nobody's butting in, man. It's a chance to help ourselves, that's all.

Neilson: Well, nobody's going to help himself with my timber.

Forbes: I'm sorry you see it that way.

Freda: *Emerging from the dishpan, drying her hands.* Why, I think it's a dandy scheme!

50

Neilson: Yeah? Well, you listen to it. I'm going hunting while there's light.

Freda: But, Brandt, it's against the law, and that mounty . . .

Neilson: *Scornfully.* Law? What law? Bunch of white collar guys somewheres think they're goin' to stop me eating wild steak if I want to? That deer's in my woods, and I'll shoot him if I've a mind to. That's the law o' nature, and it's good enough for me.

He goes out.

Freda: I'm sorry, Mr. Forbes. I think maybe you're right about the tractor.

Forbes: Couldn't you persuade him now? *She smiles and shakes her head.* He's got a fine quarter here, if he'd only let me go at it with power.

Freda: Yes, but you know how it is . . . Brandt grew up on a homestead, and he's always been used to horses.

Forbes: Not that he doesn't do a good clean job, but it's slow, far too slow.

Freda: I know. Sometimes I think Brandt doesn't really want his land cleared off. He likes it wild, for hunting.

Forbes: That makes it a bit difficult for you, doesn't it?

Freda: *Quickly.* Oh, he makes good money in the winter. There isn't a better man with a broadaxe in the country, and I'm used to getting along without things.

Forbes: Can I bring you anything from town to-morrow?

Freda: Why, yes, I do want some things. I'll pay you out of my turkey money. Matches . . . *Forbes writes it down,* and salt – a big sack; and baking powder, and coffee; and brown shoe polish . . . and would you get me some soap . . . not laundry soap, but nice smelling soap, like in the advertisements . . . like roses, maybe.

Forbes: I'll get it.

Freda: And when you're in the drug store, would you mind bringing me some magazines, or a book?

Forbes: No trouble at all. What sort of books do you like?

Freda: Well, something about – *She hesitates, then sees her chance.* Did you ever read a book called *Evangeline?*

Forbes: *All his guesses were wrong. Evangeline?* Yes. Yes, I've read it. We learned a bit of it at school when I was a youngster. *He quotes, not unmusically.*

> This is the forest primeval. The murmuring pines, and the hemlocks . . .

Freda: Oh, that's poetry, isn't it? I've never read it, you know, but the last time we were in town, I saw it in the movies. Dolores del Rio was Evangeline, and I thought she was just beautiful. I've cut out a picture of her. *She goes to the shelf and takes the picture from a magazine.* There, isn't she just lovely?

As she looks, her own expression softens and she looks younger. He looks more at her than at the picture.

Forbes: Aye, it's a sweet face.

They are quiet a moment.

Freda: Would you say that bit again, about the forest?

Forbes: *Softly.*

> This is the forest primeval, the murmuring pines and the hemlocks

Bearded with moss and with garments green
Indistinct in the twilight,
Stand like Dryads of old, with voices prophetic of warning . . .

The spell breaks.

I'm afraid that's all I remember. But I've got the book at home
– I'll bring it over.

Freda: Will you? I've got another piece here about a tree, I
cut it out of a magazine, and always think of it when I
look at that big poplar at the door. *She goes over to the*
right wall where the paper is pinned.

Forbes: Read it to me.

Freda: You'll think it's silly.

Forbes: No. I won't – honour bright, I won't.

Freda: It's about a girl, dancing. *She reads with instinctive*
expression.

Slim, young, thing dancing
Firm, brown young thing,
Free!
Dance on your sandalled feet
To a melody
Uprising sweet
From the heart of the tree.
Heart of a tree singing
to the heart of a child
Free!
Beauty is a fragile thing
To touch or to see
It may take wing
With the wind in the tree.

"Wood Girl," by Norreen Masters, Toronto

She turns to him almost fiercely.

Did you ever feel that – that a tree has music and beauty? I used to think so, until I came here and saw nothing but trees, all the time. Now, they're just so much timber. They fall across the roads, they shut me in; they are great heavy things I have to help lift. I . . . I think I'm getting to hate trees.

Forbes: How long have you been in these woods, Freda?

Freda: Eight years. . . .

Forbes: Where did you live before that?

Freda: My folks lived at Scarly, out on the prairie east of here. They moved up from the States when I was a little girl. I hated it on the prairie, it was so dry and bare, and ugly . . . all but the mountains. You could see them all the time, far away and blue. Once when I was nine I ran away and started to walk to them. I walked for miles and miles, I guess. It was dusty and hot but I didn't mind because I kept thinking how lovely it would be when I got there, to the cool trees and the shining mountains. Then I got lost in a coulee, and a cowpuncher took me home. *She smiles a little at the memory.*

Forbes: And how did you come to be on this homestead?

Freda: *Very simply.* They had a sports day and stampede in Scarly, and Brandt came out with a bunch of lumberjacks. I was just seventeen then, and he won all the races. He told me he had a log shack in the woods, and I thought how pretty it would be, like on a calendar.

Forbes: So you came.

Freda: Yes, I came. *Fiercely.* And I got *fooled.* I can't see the mountains. They're just as far away as ever. And the trees aren't beautiful any more.

Forbes: The woods are like a lot of things, I'm thinking. . . . They're good friends and ugly masters. The Saskatchewan's a grand river down there among the hills, but she's a cruel devil in flood time.

Freda: I know, like the fire. It's so friendly in the stove, and so awful when it gets the woods. I remember when the last forest fire came through here, all the poor little animals, the rabbits, and the deer, running, with their eyes all wild and scared, and the wind behind them, driving the fire closer. . . .

Forbes: When I was in France I used to think that if I ever got away to some quiet place like this – back to nature – it would be like heaven. But it's a battle here, too.

Freda: Yes, it's a battle.

Forbes: Do you know, I had a sort of picture in my mind, of nature, like a kind motherly old lady, like old Mrs. Ryan.

Freda: Mrs. Ryan! Kind! Motherly! That's a good joke, that is.

Forbes: *Not seeing it.* Well, ain't she?

Freda: Oh, she's motherly all right. She gets fifteen dollars for every baby born in this settlement, and the more there is, the better she's pleased. She doesn't care if there's no money to bring them up, or what happens to us.

Forbes: What happens to you? You mean . . .

Freda: Yes, that's what I mean.

There is a rumble of thunder. Forbes gets up and goes to the window.

Forbes: I'd best be getting home.

Freda: *Quickly.* No, don't go. I . . . I'm sorry I talked wild like that. Brandt must be home soon now, and if he got the deer, we'll ask him again about the tractor. *She lights the lamp, and the atmosphere becomes less strained.*

Forbes: *Sitting down again and lighting his pipe.* And I suppose if he hasn't got it, you'll want me to bolt through the window there.

Freda: *Flushing.* Why, no, of course not.

They smile at each other.

Forbes: Will we be seeing you at the picnic on Saturday?

Freda: No, I guess we'll be too busy.

Forbes: Now, that's too bad. I was thinking maybe you and I could be having a waltz in the evening, like we had at the school-house last spring.

Freda: *Smoothing her hair.* Oh, I didn't think you'd remember that.

Forbes: Don't I though? You had on a pink dress.

Freda: *Scornful but delighted.* That wasn't pink. That was "rose du bois" in the catalogue. *She calls it "boys."*

Forbes: Well, anyway you looked about eighteen, and the fiddlers played "Annie Rooney," my favorite tune.

Freda: That was lucky, wasn't it?

Forbes: Not altogether – I'd asked them to.

Freda: Oh, I remember that night too . . . how happy I felt. Spring's funny, isn't it? Makes you feel as if things are going to be different. But they never are.

56

Forbes: They can be, if you make them so. A clean chance, that's what spring brings around. A chance to plough in last year's stubble, and raise a new crop on your mistakes.

Freda: *Bitterly, and yet wistful too.* I could raise quite a crop on mine. I used to think when I knew Brandt first, how big and strong he was, and good-looking too, with the sun on his hair. I used to think that he could do anything . . . that he could bend things his way. Women are fools, aren't they?

Forbes: It's no distinction, girl.

Thunder begins

Listen to that now. I wonder was I fool enough to leave my ground wire on? If lightning hits my radio, it's going to be too bad for my shack. *He glances at her.* You're not listening.

Freda: *Tense.* Yes, I'm listening. . . . I'm listening for something else.

Everything is very still.

Oh, why doesn't Brandt come? Why doesn't Brandt come . . . if he's coming?

Forbes: Don't worry, girl, he'll come.

At the touch of his sympathy she begins to cry.

Now – now – don't cry, he'll be here soon. *His control breaks.* Ye do love him, then, Freda, if ye can cry for him.

Freda: I'm not crying for him. He's all right. He's out there in the woods where he belongs. I'm crying because I'm so tired, and I hate this place so, and I'm caught here. . . .

I'm caught here in these awful trees, and I guess I'll stay here 'til I die.

Forbes: Don't say that, Freda, don't . . .

Freda: *Flaring up. You* don't understand. People like you who have a radio, and a tractor, and a car . . . you've been out beyond these damn trees, and you can go out there again. You're free. You don't know how it feels to be chained to a homestead like a dumb beast, with weeds and wind and hail killing everything you'd hoped for –

Forbes: Why shouldn't I understand? Weeds grow on *my* homestead, don't they, and hail bashes down my crop. Those things happen to me, but I'll fight them, I'll fight them every inch of the way. The hail can't hurt me because my crop's insured, and my breaker can tear up the earth. But there's one thing I can't fight.

She looks at him.

Do you think I can be happy when I know that man has you here tormenting you, and working all the sweetness out of you? That's why I'm thinking of selling this place, and going north where I'll never set eyes on you again.

The thunder is becoming ominous, but neither of them pays any heed.

Freda: Oh, no, Hugh, no, don't go.

Forbes: Why shouldn't I go?

Freda: Because if you go . . . away north, there just won't be anything for me.

Forbes: It can't matter to you.

Freda: It does matter.

He looks at her.

Oh, didn't you know that seeing you sometimes, or hearing your tractor across the spruce, or your car go by in the night . . . that that's about all I have, to live for?

Forbes: You mean – you mean that you care – about me?

Freda: Oh, I didn't mean to tell you. I didn't mean you ever to know. But it's true, and I'm glad – I'm glad now I told you. *Half laughing, half crying.* Oh Hugh, did you like the black socks I sent you last winter?

Forbes: *Stupidly.* The black socks . . . with the red heels?

Freda: Yes. Yes, that's them. Don't you remember one day last winter, you came in off the trail, and you took off your shoes to warm your feet, and you had great big holes in the heels? So I knitted those socks and sent them to you in the mail. Did they fit?

Forbes: They were the finest socks I ever wore . . . and to think I never knew you had taken all that trouble for me. . . .

Freda: Oh, it wasn't any trouble, honest it wasn't. I loved doing it. I used to sit over there by the window to get the light, and besides, I could see the smoke coming out of your chimney. Nothing would be any trouble – scrubbing, or baking, or hoeing the weeds even, if I was doing it for you.

Forbes: Don't Freda, don't. You tear the very heart out of me when you talk like that.

Freda: For two years it's been tearing the very heart out of me not to talk like that. Let me talk like that . . . for just this once.

Forbes: I'd like to take you away with me, and show you the world out past yon trees. . . .

Freda: *Coming close to him.* Where would we go, Hugh?

Forbes: *Falling into her mood of make believe.* We'd go back to the Old Land, if you'd like it . . .

Freda: In a ship? I've never seen a ship – only in pictures.

Forbes: Aye, in a ship. And we'd stand in her stern together, like this. *He puts an arm about her.* And we'd watch the green water churning away behind us, and the wind would blow. . . .

Freda: That same wind outside there?

Forbes: That same wind. And I'd hold you tight, and we'd be free. *A pause.* Freda . . .

She looks at him.

We'll go. We won't fight it any longer. We'll go away.

Freda: But we can't.

Forbes: Why can't we? What's there to stop us? Don't you want to come with me?

Freda: Oh yes, I want to, but –

Forbes: Well?

Freda: I'm not free, I'm not free to go with you. I'm tied here.

Forbes: Listen to me, Freda. We've only one life here in this little old world – only one life and it's damn short at that. Let's make the most of it. Come away with me, Freda. You're not afraid are you?

Freda: No, I'm not afraid, only –

Forbes: When we come back, we'll take land in the north, where nobody knows us, and where he'll never find us.

Freda: I wonder if he'd care enough to look very hard. He'd get another stronger woman than me.

Forbes: Will you come then?

Freda: But you're forgetting I'm tied here in other ways. There's going to be his child.

Forbes: Your child, that's how we'll think of him – your child. And we'll have the rearing of him ourselves. I'll be good to him. Freda, I'll be good to you both.

Freda: *Turning to him.* I know you will, Hugh.

Forbes: Then you'll come?

Freda: Yes, I'll come. *She walks deliberately into his arms. Breaking away, breathlessly.* When?

Forbes: Give me a week – I'll need to see about selling the place. They needn't know about it around here. Can you stick it out for another week?

Freda: Oh yes. I can stand it – I can stand anything with the thought of you in my heart.

Forbes: My dear. *He holds her closely for a moment. The storm rises again outside.* I'd best be going now.

Freda: *Her arms about him.* But you've only just come – here.

Forbes: Aye, but I'll be here again, and I'd rather not meet Neilson to-night.

Freda: No, and the storm will drive him home.

Forbes: Goodnight then. Next time I come – you'll go with me.

Freda: Yes – I'll go – away with you. Goodnight. *She kisses him simply and he goes out.*

Freda moves to the window and looks out on the storm. Its fury rises in crescendo and there is a great crash just outside the door. Thunder follows. She runs to the door and opens it. Outside is a tempest of wind and rain.

Freda: *Wildly.* Come back! Hugh, come back!

She falls away from the doorway, her hand across her mouth. It is Neilson who stumbles exhausted across the doorstop, and sinks down on the nearest chair. She shakes his shoulder.

Where is he? Brandt, what happened?

Neilson: *Hoarsely.* It got him, I saw it.

Freda: What got him?

Neilson: *Panting.* The tree, the big poplar. It killed him.

Freda: Killed him . . . !

Neilson: They were coming down – all around me – and in the lightning I saw that one – get him here. *He puts his hand behind his neck.* I had to climb over him. *Pause.* God, it might have been me.

Freda: *In a strangled voice.* Yes, it might have been you.

Neilson: *Getting up and going for his axe.* We'll have to bring him in here, for to-night.

Freda: *Dully.* Yes.

When he has gone, she stands dazed. The poem on the wall catches her eye, and she tears it down. For a moment she leans against the wall. Then she straightens and goes to the couch. She unfolds a rug, spreads it carefully, smoothes the pillow where his head will lie. Standing straight, she looks towards the door and speaks very low.

Freda: Yes, bring him in to me – for to-night.

The End

The Hungry Spirit

The Silver Cord. Frances Garness as Mrs. Phelps, Arthur Clough as Robert, Elsie Park Gowan as Christina, Edmonton Little Theatre, Empire Theatre, 1938. Frances Garness played Mrs. Gale in *The Hungry Spirit.*

THE HUNGRY SPIRIT: *INTERVIEW*

Day: I remember you saying that it was a mixed blessing being from a straight-laced Scots Presbyterian home, where there was a strong emphasis on education and books, but also some rather traditional ideas about woman's role in life.

EPG: Well, there's quite a bit of autobiography in *The Hungry Spirit* because I wrote it as a kind of protest against life in a small Alberta town. What I'm trying to say in *The Hungry Spirit* is that the mind has its hunger. The mind has its needs as well as the body. And in a small town everything is materialistic. Is purely . . . whatever you've got. Freda is a girl who is at the mercy of her bodily urges. Marian isn't.

You see, my father's life was really quite sad. He'd been through University in Edinburgh and he started out very brilliantly. In 1911, there was a great wave of immigration and my father, for some reason, just decided to take a chance on Canada. So he sold his business. He had a beautiful store in Scotland. I remember it to this day. Rows and rows of shining bottles and the lovely smell of the place. He sold it and when he came to Edmonton he had quite a bit of capital. But he lost it all by poor advice and in the real estate boom of 1911-12 and he ended up having this drugstore in this little God-forsaken – as I thought it – town.

Day: Bawlf.

EPG: Bawlf, yes. Where there was nobody – as I would say in a snobbish way – spoke my language. And while my father never had the alcoholic problem that I indicate

66

here, he was wasted, really. He wanted to be his own boss, he had been working for the National Drug Company in their warehouse, and so he bought this business. But there was no future. Just look at my sisters. I had three handsome sisters. They all came and lived with me and got themselves a husband one after another. In Edmonton. If they had stayed in Bawlf, what would have happened?

My mother was a very Victorian-minded person. She admired Queen Victoria, and she was very conventional in her outlook. I never took her as a role model at all. In fact, on the contrary! In those years, I decided never to get married because all I could see was that a married woman was overworked and underpaid. Never had any fun. So there is a strong . . . not strong . . . but there's a reflection of my own family in this play.

My mother read the play . . . and you know, she wanted to play the part!

Day: Really? She wasn't bothered by it?

EPG: No, no. When she was a girl in Scotland, she had been active in the Drama Society and she said she'd like to play that part. *With a Scottish accent.* "I'm an old woman, Marian. I haven't had much happiness in my life. Do this for me now. Do this for me while I'm here." You know?

Day: What does the play say generally about the problems of family life and being a woman in 1935? When I was doing research for my thesis, I kept reading the Dorothy Dix column and that comment on the son in particular could have come right from one of the letters that someone wrote her. Everything was going into the brothers, while the girls worked and brought the money home, and their parents looked right through them.

Letters saying, you know, "for my mother the sun rises and sets on my brothers."

EPG: Ah, that's what Shaw says. That she "would boil Barbara to make soup for Stephen." Yes.

I never ran into any opposition on account of being a girl. I never felt at all put down or held back or anything. You just didn't. It wasn't on the cards. It didn't seem to be happening. Maybe because I didn't have any brothers. "I was all the brothers in my father's house. And all the sisters too." No . . . not all the sisters! One of four. The eldest.

Day: How did your family take to the idea of your going to university?

EPG: I don't remember that my mother ever expressed an opinion about it. I was never terribly close to my mother, you know. We weren't the same kind of cat. My father couldn't understand it. He was really browned off on education. He felt that his hadn't done him any good. He said, "You've got a good job now." I was earning a hundred dollars a month in a country school. He did nothing to help me on. He wasn't able to help me financially. I paid for my education myself.

Day: Did your experience of seeing or hearing the play performed alter your perception of the play?

EPG: No, I don't think so. The first production was in the Empire Theatre and that was a very stupid idea. They had an evening of three one-act plays. And the stage is so enormous! It was hard to put on a play like that in a huge scene. And the casting wasn't perfect either. It isn't the kind of play that a little group is going to pick up, particularly because there's no love interest, no glamour to it.

Andrew Allan did it on the national network in the early 40s. A very successful production. I think Kate Reid played the girl.

Day: I remember that in the radio version you put a narrator in – a doctor.

EPG: Well you see, when Marian discovers the box of her father's books, she gets a new picture of him entirely. And I thought that if there was somebody who remembered him as he was it would strengthen that. So I invented a nice little doctor who had remembered the father as a brilliant man or someone who could have been a brilliant man.

Day: What kind of feedback did you get?

EPG: I got a lot of reaction from that. Mostly male – from young men or moderately young men who themselves taught. From people who had gone through something of the same situation. You know – had had to fight for their education or their freedom or whatever. One of these men I knew was going through a dilemma in his own life. He was very much in love and wanted to get married, and at the same time he wanted to go on and get his doctorate. And in those days you did one thing or the other.

I heard the play at Herriot Bay. I was visiting a colleague of mine called Francis Dickie. I had a contract to write a radio version of one of his novels (*The Altar of the Moon*) and I was staying at the Dickie place while we worked on the general outline, and we listened to *The Hungry Spirit* there. He was very excited about it. He said, "Oh my God, I wish I'd written that!" But then he came from a small town in Manitoba.

Day: Mostly male! Isn't that funny because the person is a woman and she says it's sort of a woman's situation. "You're overlooking me because I'm not a son."

EPG: I've had a lot of arguments about the girl in *The Hungry Spirit*. From people who think she should have given up her hopes of university and given the money to her brother and helped the family, you know. And I think that people complain that she was selfish.

Day: Right.

EPG: But I don't.

Day: What still attracts you about the play?

EPG: Well, nothing really. You see, when I wrote it, I was terribly clueless about history. If I was writing about a small town like Bawlf today I would recognize the fact that it had been pioneered only ten years before and that these Scandinavian people with whom I felt nothing in common were really giants in the earth, you know. They had gone in there – got vacant land – and made it a community of prosperous farms and so on. I would have a different attitude towards them entirely than I had in my snobbish way back then. You see, Marian feels she's imprisoned in this. Uncomfortable, in fact.

   I remember talking to Walter Johns about this play and where he'd seen it, and he said, "If you went back, it wouldn't imprison you now."

Day: It's almost like Gwen Pharis Ringwood. She had to escape, but once she had her windows on the world, it didn't seem so bad for her going back.

EPG: Yes. And it's very thrilling to go to Williams Lake and see the Gwen Pharis Ringwood Theatre there.

Day: I notice that Gwen Ringwood also wrote a mother-daughter conflict play about the same time (*The Days May Be Long*), but in hers the daughter allows herself to be buffaloed into staying. Hester notwithstanding, Ringwood's woman characters of the same era seem to be more gentle, passive and long-suffering than yours.

EPG: I think because my mother had very little influence over me. I never discussed things . . . really discussed my work with her.

Day: Did Gwen discuss her work with her mother? Was she much closer to her own mother?

EPG: Oh yes, very much so. You see, her mother took a degree from the University of Lethbridge when she was 75.

Day: Oh! Quite a character.

EPG: Yes! Gwen was very close to her mother.

Day: She doesn't seem to have had quite the same political agenda in her plays. Her female characters seem much different.

EPG: Well, Gwen used to say, "In Elsie's plays, the women beat the men. In my plays, the men beat the women!" In *The Courtship of Marie Jenvrin*, the hero spanks the gal. And in *Back to the Kitchen, Woman!*, the women chase the guy and pound *him*. But Gwen was a much more "womanly" woman, you know. More loving and giving than I am.

Day: You balanced each other well then, it sounds.

EPG: We did. Gwen and I were very close. We worked together on a lot of things. We were each other's cheering section.

THE HUNGRY SPIRIT: *FIRST PERFORMANCE*

The Hungry Spirit was first performed by Le Cercle Dramatique St-Joachim and The Edmonton Little Theatre at the New Empire Theatre, 6 April, 1935, under the direction of the author, in a setting arranged by Frank Holroyd with the following cast:

Peggy Gale – *Francoise Martin*
Rob Gale – *William Wallace*
Mrs. Gale – *Frances Garness*
Douglas Heath – *John Rule*
Marian – *Dorothy Horrocks (Dahlgren)*

THE HUNGRY SPIRIT

Characters:

Peggy Gale, spoiled but attractive girl, 16
Rob Gale, brother, pleasant, immature boy, 22
Mrs. Emily Gale, mother, small, plump, maternal woman, 50s
Douglas Heath, Marian's "beau," young accountant, mid-20s
Marian Gale, eldest sister, tall, good-looking girl, 24

Setting:

Time:
The Thursday evening before Easter. The 1930s.

Place:
A large town in the Canadian West.

The living room of Mrs. Gale's house on Poplar Street. It has the usual furniture – an old fashioned, shabby chesterfield suite, well worn by the three young Gales. Down stage on the audience's left is a small table with a mirror above it. Two frivolous hats repose on the table at the moment. There is a pot of spring flowers on a table by the chesterfield. The whole effect is of shabby comfort. A desk telephone is the only modern note. The door to the kitchen is on the audience's right. On the left is the hallway, leading outside and up stairs.

When the play begins Peggy is discovered on her knees beside a battered black box which she unsuccessfully tries to jimmy with a variety of tools. The box is old, but of good wood, and placed well down stage, centre.

Peggy is a spoiled but attractive brat of sixteen.

Rob, her brother, is sprawled on the chesterfield, flipping the pages of a movie magazine, and waiting for the phone to ring. He is a likeable boy with nice eyes and a weak mouth. His clothes befit the garage man, cleaned up for his evening off.

Peggy: *Nursing her thumb after the last try.* Rob.

No answer.

Rob!

Rob: Huh?

Peggy: I wish you'd help me get this open.

Rob: I'm tired.

Peggy: Well, I'm tired too, dragging this thing all the way down stairs. It weighs about a ton.

Rob: Hey, why don't you leave the darn old thing where it was?

Peggy: *Doggedly.* I want it down here so I can fix it up.

Rob: It's no good.

Peggy: It is too – for what I want it for.

Silence.

I guess I'll have to undo the screws and take the lid off. Mom says the key's been lost for twenty years.

Rob: What's in it, anyway?

Peggy: I dunno. Some old stuff of Father's.

Rob: Say! If it was his, it's most likely full of bottles. *He rises.* Gimme that screwdriver! *He takes the screwdriver, examines the box, and settles down to have a good time tinkering.*

74

Peggy dances anxiously about behind him.

Peggy: You won't scratch it, will you?

Rob: Gwan, don't bother me.

Peggy: Well, you be careful.

Rob: Say, beat it will you? I'm doing this.

Peggy: All right. *She skips over to the side table and tries on the two frivolous hats. Much preening and primping.* Do you like this one, Rob?

Rob: *Not looking up.* Yeah.

Peggy: The green is more sort of – sophisticated.

Rob: Uh-huh.

Peggy: It's two-ninety-five though. I don't hardly like to stick her up for that much.

Rob: Say, I thought Mom was doing the dishes so you could start your algebra.

Peggy: Well, I will in a minute. I got to have some relaxation, don't I? You don't know how hard that algebra is.

Rob: That's right – rub it in I had to go to work to buy the baby new shoes.

Peggy: *Turning slowly from the mirror.* What baby?

Rob: You, nit-wit. My dear little baby sister.

Peggy: Don't kid yourself, big boy. It isn't your measly thirty a month that buys my shoes. Marian buys them, and everything else that's extra around here.

Rob: Well, gosh, can I help it? I can't give Mom what I haven't got.

Peggy: You'd have more if you didn't hang around the telephone office so darn much.

Rob: You mind your own business! I guess I can do what I like with my own money.

Peggy: Absolutely! And I hope Marian does what she likes with hers.

Rob: *Rising, a weapon in his hand.* What do you mean by that crack?

Peggy: Three guesses . . . and the first two don't count.

Rob: What's the idea . . . picking on me? For two cents I'd bust your darn box of junk wide open –

Peggy: Rob . . . you gimme that hammer . . .

Rob: Yes and I will too!

They struggle furiously, she trying to get the hammer from him, he holding it out of her reach.

Peggy: It's my box – Mom said I could have it . . .

Rob: That's all the thanks I get. . . . Leggo! Leggo my arm.

Peggy bites his wrist.

Owww! Damn little hell-cat!

During the fracas, Mrs. Emily Gale has come in from the kitchen. She is a plump little person who was once pretty in a common place way.

Mrs. Gale: Now Peggy . . . are you quarreling again?

Peggy: He started it.

Rob: *Nursing his wrist.* Yeah, and I'll finish it, too.

Mrs. Gale: *As she begins tidying up the room.* Now get that box out of here.

The box is pushed into a corner, the tools beside it.

Aren't either of you going to meet Marian? It's ten to seven.

Peggy: Sure, I'll go. I'll do my algebra when I get back. Rob can't go, he's waiting for the call to arms.

Rob: *Starting for her again.* Say, you . . . !

Peggy snatches up a jacket and runs giggling into the hall. The front door slams behind her.

Rob: I suppose I ought to go, and carry her grip.

Mrs. Gale: *Complacently.* Douglas will meet the train.

Rob: You'll tell Marian this time, won't you, Mom?

Mrs. Gale: No, Rob, I will not. If you want Marian's help you'll have to ask her yourself. But I don't approve of it.

Rob: Say, isn't Ruby good enough for this familly?

Mrs. Gale: I've nothing against Ruby. She seems a nice quiet little thing and she's very polite on the phone. But you're too young to think of marriage for years yet.

Rob: But I've got to think of it.

Mrs. Gale: What do you mean?

Rob: *Losing his nerve.* Nothing.

Mrs. Gale: You don't mean . . . you don't mean you have to marry her?

Rob: Yes.

Mrs. Gale: Oh, what a thing to happen. . . .

Rob: Now, Mom . . .

Mrs. Gale: Oh, the bad wicked girl . . . !

Rob: Never mind all that! Don't you say a word against Ruby! She's . . . she's . . . gosh I'm crazy about her. I'd want to marry her anyway, and now I'm going to, that's all. You see that, don't you? And if I just had a little money to start. . . . How much has Marian got, anyway?

Mrs. Gale: I've no idea. I know she has been saving all she could for years.

Rob: Gosh, that's swell.

Mrs. Gale: Have you thought how you're going to live?

Rob: Have I thought? Say, I gave a guy too much gas yesterday, just from thinking. Now you wouldn't want us living here . . .

Mrs. Gale: I most certainly would not.

Rob: So I thought we'd rent a little house, or maybe a couple of rooms over a store. And if I could borrow enough to get started, maybe I'll get a raise at the garage, and everything would be swell.

Mrs. Gale: And what about Peggy and me?

Rob: Oh well, Marian won't let you starve.

Mrs. Gale: She's going to resign this June.

Rob: She's *what*?

Mrs. Gale: Why don't you listen to things around here? She's going to university in the fall.

78

Rob: She's crazy. She hasn't resigned yet, has she?

Mrs. Gale: No.

Rob: Well, she just can't that's all. This is important. This is people's lives. Come on, Mom. You'll back me up won't you? You're going to be a grandma, just think of that.

Mrs. Gale: *Shaken.* You ought to be ashamed of yourself.

Rob: Well, I'm not, see? I'm ashamed because I can't give her a home without asking my sister for money, but if I got to, I will!

The phone rings. He flies to it.

Yeah . . . can you get off? That's the good news. I'll be right down! *He hangs up, crosses to his mother and puts an arm around her.* Cheer up, Mom. Everything is going to be swell. I'll just put this up to Marian as a business proposition, and she'll listen to reason.

There is a commotion in the hall.

A Voice Offstage: Thanks Douglas, put it down.

Rob's courage wilts rapidly.

Rob: Heck! Here they are! Tell her I'll be in later.

He retreats through the kitchen just as Marian runs in. She is a rather tall, good-looking girl in travelling clothes. She envelops her mother in a bear-like hug.

Marian: Hi there, old dear! You look wonderful! Who waved your hair?

Mrs. Gale: Peggy did.

Peggy and Douglas come in and cross to the chesterfield where she perches beside him on the arm. He is the accountant in the bank, and the town's most eligible young man. Peggy is not sure if she likes him better than Clark Gable.

Peggy: Sure, I'm the best little fixer-upper around here! You'll let me wave your hair, won't you, Douglas? *She tries it.*

Douglas: Hey, cut that out!

Marian: Oh, it's so grand to be home! Where's Robbie?

Mrs. Gale: He said he'd be in later. Would you like something to eat?

Marian: No thanks, Mums, I had a huge supper. *She moves about the room, savoring the sight and smell of home.* Flowers for Easter! Mmmmmmmmm . . . they're lovely. *Catching sight of the black box.* Hello . . . what's that doing here?

Peggy: *Hastily.* I brought it down.

Marian: It's the dirty old box used to be in the attic.

Peggy: I know. I'm going to fix it up and use it . . . use it to put things in.

Marian: Whose new hat?

Peggy: Hey, that's mine!

Marian: *Teasing.* Oh?

Peggy: I mean, it's only sent up on approval, but I thought . . .

Marian: Well, I approve of it, don't you, Doug?

Douglas: It's the most god-awful thing I ever saw in my life.

Marian: Must be a good hat.

Peggy: Don't you think it a little . . . young for you?

Marian: Nonsense, I like it. It conceals my intelligence.

Peggy: Aw, Marian . . .

Marian: However, I may let you have it. Have you been a good child?

Peggy: *Squirming.* Good as I could.

Marian: Have you done your algebra?

Peggy: Well . . . I was going to, right after supper . . . but of course I had to meet the train . . . and I got all next week . . .

Marian: Too bad there isn't a show in town to-night.

Peggy: *Transfigured.* Oh, there is! Gloria Garbutt, in "Enchanted Ground."

Marian: An educational picture?

Peggy: Oh, awfully educational.

Douglas: I'll bet it is.

Marian: *Handing Peggy money.* Here, scram.

Peggy: *Hugging her.* Oh gee, you're swell! I'll do my algebra to-morrow for sure. Good-night, Doug. Good-night, Mom. I'll call for Gladys. Good-night. *She goes out a-flying.*

Mrs. Gale: You spoil that child, Marian.

Marian: Well, who set me a bad example?

Mrs. Gale: I'm sure I don't spoil Peggy.

Marian: *Teasing.* No, but what about Rob? You're like the mother George Bernard Shaw wrote about, who would "boil Barbara to make soup for Stephen."

Mrs. Gale: That's just the disgusting sort of thing that crazy old fool would say. What do you want to read things like that for, anyway?

Douglas: Because she's a high-brow, Mrs. Gale, and wouldn't be caught dead reading Ethel M. Dell.

Marian: Well, if nobody loves me here, I guess I'll go and wash. You two can discuss Kathleen Norris while I clean up.

Mrs. Gale: Indeed, and it wouldn't be the first time, young lady. Douglas often comes to see me when you're not here.

Marian: *In the doorway.* And I know why . . . banana pie! *She goes up stairs.*

Mrs. Gale: You wouldn't really like a piece of pie, would you Douglas? There's one setting right in the pantry now, and the cream won't keep till morning.

Douglas: Well . . . just to keep it from spoiling . . .

Mrs. Gale: *Very pleased.* I'll get it! *She pops into the kitchen and returns with the pie, a noble specimen.*

Douglas: Say, that's a masterpiece. *He attacks it.*

Mrs. Gale: I'm sure you boys that bache never get half enough to eat.

Douglas: Sure we do.

Mrs. Gale: Well, I notice you never refuse good food when it's offered you. *A pause. She watches him.* Douglas, there's something I want you to do for me.

Douglas: *His mouth full.* Mmmmmmph?

Mrs. Gale: You know Marian thinks of going to university?

Douglas: *Affirmatively.* Mmmmph.

Mrs. Gale: I want you to persuade her not to go.

Douglas: Me?

Mrs. Gale: Yes, I want you to talk her out of it.

Douglas: But what can I say?

Mrs. Gale: You tell her how foolish it is.

Douglas: *Alarmed.* Well, but . . . it's none of my business. I don't want to butt in . . .

Mrs. Gale: It's not butting in, it's for her own good; money thrown away, that's all it will be. She'll get married and forget all about it.

Douglas: But Marian isn't that type. She's . . .

Mrs. Gale: Oh yes she is. She talks big, but at heart she's a fine, home-loving girl. And clever too. She makes nearly all her own clothes. Did you know that, Douglas?

Douglas: Yes, I think that I . . .

Mrs. Gale: Now you help her to be sensible about this, and she'll be grateful to you all her life.

Douglas: But what can I say?

Mrs. Gale: You just advise her in a business-like way. You're a man. You're in touch with . . . oh, financial conditions. I know Marian has a great respect for your opinions, Douglas.

Douglas: *Floundering.* Yes, but look here, I hope you don't think that I . . . I mean, I hope you don't think that Marian . . . well, I mean . . .

Mrs. Gale: I think you have more influence with Marian than any one else, and I'm sure you want her to be happy, don't you?

Douglas: Oh sure, but I . . .

Mrs. Gale: Then you'll talk to her about it, won't you? Oh thank you, Douglas, I knew I could depend on you. This has taken a great load off my mind. . . .

As she picks up the empty pie plate, Marian comes in. She crosses directly to Douglas and kneels on the couch beside him.

Marian: Douglas Heath, you've got pie on your face! *She takes his handkerchief from his breast pocket and wipes his face.*

Douglas: Pretty fresh, aren't you?

Marian: Shucks, I wipe little boys' faces a dozen times a day. Blow their noses, too.

Douglas: Is that all?

Mrs. Gale: *Hurriedly.* If you'll excuse me, I think I'll run over and see Mrs. Parsons about the chicken supper.

Marian: Oh gosh, are we having another one of those?

Mrs. Gale: Yes, on Tuesday. I told the ladies you'd help wait on tables. All the young girls are going to.

Marian: Well, tell them I broke a leg.

Mrs. Gale: *Postponing the debate.* You'll be rested by

Tuesday. Good-night, Douglas.

Douglas: *Half getting up.* Good-night.

She goes out through the kitchen, taking the plate.

Marian: Poor Mother! It's a great sorrow to her I won't be a sweet nice girl and do the things sweet nice girls do. She's always clucking at me from the bank.

Douglas: Howja mean, clucking?

Marian: You know. Hen hatches duck. Duck swims. Hen stands on the bank and tries to cluck me out of the water.

Douglas: Cigarette, ugly duckling?

Marian: Thanks.

He lights up for her. They both lean back on the chesterfield and relax. A pause.

Do you realize this is an historic occasion?

Douglas: How?

Marian: My last holidays from Somerville. Next time I leave that town, it's for good.

Douglas: Or evil.

Marian: For richer or poorer, for better or worse . . .

Douglas: Say, what is this, leap year?

Marian: No, why?

Douglas: Well, first you tell me you're quitting your job, and then we start reciting the shorter catechism . . .

Marian: You're crazy! I'm crazy, too, of course. But not about you.

Douglas: Are you sure?

Marian: Quite sure. *She gets up and moves across the room.* I'm going away from here. I'm going to university next September.

Douglas: What for?

Marian: Because it has just always been for me . . . the green pastures. I'm so hungry for it, Doug! I'm going to take it all in big bites, and the harder it is, the better I'll like it.

Douglas: Now I know you're crazy.

Marian: I am not. That's what I want. Something hard. Something I have to reach up for. I'm so tired of reaching down to children, to a world of nursery rhymes and fairy tales.

Douglas: What's the matter with fairy tales?

Marian: I hate them! "Once upon a time there was king who had three daughters. The two eldest were ugly as sin, but the youngest was a dream of beauty and had a sweet disposition." It's not right! Why does the poor eldest always have to be ugly and bad-tempered? I think they're very un-fairy tales.

Douglas: A pun is the lowest . . .

Marian: I don't care! They are unfair! I'm not ugly and bad tempered – yet. But I will be, if I stay here, year after year. Sometimes I wonder, can I really start my great adventure now – now that I'm nearly 25.

Douglas: You'll never start it younger.

Marian: No, and I'll never start it older, will I? If I'm really going to break away, I've got to do it now. And I don't want to go when I'm too old to look like a sweet girl graduate. Perhaps a strong-minded woman shouldn't care about that, but I do. *Examining herself critically in the mirror.* How about it, Doug . . . do you think I can still get by?

Douglas: I could tell better if you came back over here.

Marian: Not any more. Pale hands you loved have signed the pledge.

Douglas: I don't believe it.

Marian: Why not?

Douglas: You're too darn good-looking.

Marian: That's really all you've cared about, isn't it?

Douglas: What?

Marian: My looks. I've got pretty hair and good legs.

Douglas: What more do you want?

Marian: I'd like to be loved for the things about myself that matter to me.

Douglas: Did I ever say I loved you?

Marian: Do you?

Douglas: I'm damned if I know. But I'll tell you why I've been camping on the doorstep . . .

Marian: Banana pie!

Douglas: Shut up. It's because you're the only girl in town that doesn't pack a pair of handcuffs in her sleeve. You're the only woman that doesn't start inveigling a man into matrimony the first time she gets him in the back seat of a car –

Marian goes off in fits of laughter.

Now what's so funny about that?

Marian: Only that I spent the first year inveigling for all I was worth.

Douglas: You can't tell me . . .

Marian: Oh, but I did it so subtly you never suspected. Defense was the best attack. *Teasing him.* Of course, I was very young in those days and full of illusions. I thought a man who wore such well tailored clothes must be intelligent.

Douglas: *Getting mad.* Say, what is this? I *am* intelligent . . .

Marian: Not terribly, Douglas . . . not enough to hurt.

Douglas: Just because my old man never had the money to send me to college . . .

Marian: Now honestly . . . did you ever want to go? You're not *curious* enough. You're quite content to be a small cog in a big machine, and get all your opinions from the general manager. My dear old thing, you can't even think straight about economics because you imagine you're a banker.

Douglas: I *am* a banker!

Marian: You're an adding machine.

Douglas: What does an ignorant little snipe like you know about it?

Marian: *Roused.* Sure I'm ignorant, but I'm going to do something about it. I'd rather be that way than smug and self-satisfied and – and stodgy. . . .

Douglas: *Furious.* So that's what you think of me, is it?

Marian: Yes, if you must know, it is!

Douglas: Then why in hell do you go out with me?

Marian: I don't know. I guess it got to be a habit!

Douglas: *Grabbing her by the shoulders.* You darned little gold-digger . . .

Marian: I am not!

Douglas: That's what you are, Miss High and Mighty! You'd take a man's money . . .

Marian: You got value for it, didn't you?

Douglas: *Shaking her.* You conceited little fool! You stuck-up conceited little fool. Go to your blasted university . . .

Marian: Thanks, I will!

Douglas: But you're not making a gigolo out of me a minute longer! *He starts for the door, halts in his tracks, and comes back to grab her again.* Mary Ann. *Sternly.* Can you look me in the eye and tell me that's all I've been?

Marian: I haven't said that's all you were, Douglas.

Douglas: If you meant that stuff about stodgy and self-satisfied – do you mean that through all the good times we've had you were just – putting up with me?

Marian: No. It's been more than that.

Douglas: What about that hike to the canyon? You can't tell me you didn't enjoy that moon as much as I did?

Marian: *Smiling.* No. It was a lovely moon.

Douglas: That was real, that night, wasn't it?

Marian: Yes, that was real.

Douglas: Well, so is this! *He kisses her suddenly but thoroughly.* You enjoyed that didn't you?

Marian: *A bit breathless.* Yes. So what?

Douglas: So you're not so darn high-brow as you think you are.

Marian: So I'm a healthy girl that likes your shaving soap.

Douglas: *Pulling her back to the chesterfield where they sit down with a bounce.* Say, listen, let's not fight. Here I haven't seen you for a month, and I shave after supper and run to the train, and all I get is a song and dance about my intelligence.

Marian: I'm sorry, Doug. I didn't mean to fight either. It's just that I'm all lit up, to-night . . .

Douglas: Say, you're not off the wagon at last?

Marian: I mean I'm so excited. The big adventure suddenly seems very close . . .

Douglas: Well, I'm not going to be here all my life either and when I get a move, and a raise . . .

Marian: Don't say it, Doug. You know it would never work. We haven't the same ideas about anything. And I don't want to marry anyone I couldn't give . . . all myself.

Douglas: Well –

Marian: I mean – while I was kissing you just now –

Douglas: You admit you *were* kissing me?

Marian: Why of course! But while I was doing it, there was a little spirit at the back of my mind disapproving of the whole affair. Don't you see? Douglas, I haven't really hurt you, have I? I've been pretty sure we were both just – having fun.

Douglas: Until to-night that's all I was doing, but now . . .

Marian: Now your pride is hurt and making you say things you don't mean. No. I've got to let that hungry little spirit have its innings. Perhaps I'll find that it's all a mistake – *Lightly* – that I haven't any brains or any great contribution to make to mankind. But at least I'm going to find out. My mind is made up, my money's in the bank, and I won't be stopped by fire, flood, or act of God!

The front door bangs. Rob comes in with a look of almost comic resolution.

Marian: Hello, Robbie!

Rob: Hello, kid. Hello, Doug.

Douglas: How's business?

Rob: Rotten, thanks. Not a tack on the highway for miles.

Marian: I've got some poker hands for you. *She gets them from her purse.*

Rob: Thanks. That helps a lot.

Douglas: Saving up for silk stockings, Rob?

Rob: No, curling tongs.

Douglas: Well, I'll be getting along.

Marian: Must you go?

Douglas: I think I'd better run along and do a little adding.

Don't bother to let me out . . . again.

Marian: You can't tell me you're not glad to escape.

Douglas: Don't mention it. Good-night, Rob.

Rob: G'night.

Douglas: Good-night, my learned friend. I hope you choke.

Marian: Good-night, Doug.

He goes. There is silence. Marian wanders to the table and twirls one of Peggy's hats. Rob sits down and lights a cigarette.

Rob: Where's Mom?

Marian: Robbing a roost for the chicken dinner.

Rob: Peg out?

Marian: Gone to the show.

A pause.

Rob: Thanks for the cards, Ann.

Marian: 's all right.

Another pause.

Rob: Say, I didn't butt into anything just now, did I?

Marian: What makes you think so?

Rob: Oh, he looked kind of funny, that's all. Like he was caught short on his cash.

Marian: Bright boy, brother! I was just breaking it gently to Douglas that all is over between us.

Rob: Say, that's fine! I mean, I'm glad to hear it.

92

Marian: Why? Don't you think he is good enough for me?

Rob: It's not that. He just gets my goat, that's all, acting so darn patronizing, just because he's got a white collar job and knows to a nickel just how much we all got in the bank. Marian . . .

Marian: Mmmm?

Rob: I want to get married.

Marian: *What?*

Rob: You heard me. I said I want to get married.

Marian: Why, Rob, you're crazy. You're too young.

Rob: I'm 22.

Marian: I suppose it's Ruby. She's – 18.

Rob: Yes, it's Ruby.

Marian: But anyway, you can't. Mother depends on you.

Rob: She'll have to get along.

Marian: *Really beginning to take him seriously.* But Rob, how can she? You'll have to help her next year.

Rob: I can't do it.

Marian: You'll have to. I've carried the family so far – it's your turn now. That's only fair.

Rob: I can't do it, I tell you.

Marian: Oh, talk sense. Where are you going to live?

Rob: Well, I could get the Larson house cheap.

Marian: And what would you use for money?

Rob: I thought I'd borrow it. *A pause.*

She sees the force of this.

Aw Marian, be a sport. Lend me enough to get started on.

Marian: I will not.

Rob: I'll pay you back.

Marian: Yes, on your salary, with a wife to keep. That's my money. There's just enough to get me through, if I'm careful.

Rob: Heck, what d'you want to go to university for? You got a good job now.

Marian: It's not that. It's just that I want a chance to know, and understand. Oh Robbie, I've been planning this for years. I've saved every nickel I didn't give Mother. Don't spoil everything for me. Wait a few years. Then Peg will be grown up . . .

Rob: I won't wait. Gosh, I never thought you'd be selfish like this.

Marian: Selfish! I like that. Say, I'm through supporting this family for a while. You can take on the job now.

Rob: But I can't.

Marian: Why can't you?

Rob: Well, if you must know, I got another family to support.

Marian: You've got what?

Rob: I've got a family – mine and Ruby's.

A pause.

Marian: *Quietly.* Congratulations.

Rob: You're not mad, are you?

Marian: Why should I be? It's none of my business.

Rob: But that makes all the difference doesn't it? I'm bound to marry Ruby right away –

Marian: That's very generous of you, but it doesn't change my plans in the slightest. If you wanted Ruby as much as that you can face the music now.

Rob: I'm going to. But you'll have to look after Mother and Peg.

Marian: I will not. You can bring Ruby here for a while.

Rob: Yeah, and have Mom bossing us every minute. I'm going to have a home of my own, see? I got a right to.

Marian: What about me? Haven't I a right to live as I like and where I like?

Rob: Aw, what's the matter with where you live right now?

Marian: You wouldn't understand if I did tell you.

Rob: You think you're so darn much better than anybody else –

Marian: I know I'm different, that's all.

Rob: So darn different you don't seem to understand how normal people feel.

Marian: *Roused.* Normal people! Well, if you're normal, I'm glad I'm not. You're just a silly little pup that hasn't enough sense to stay in his own back yard!

Rob: *Shouting.* And you're a darn stuck-up old maid!

Marian: Thanks. I guess there are very few of us left.

Mrs. Gale has come in, in time to hear these last two remarks.

Mrs. Gale: Rob! Is that any way to act? Now you just apologize to Marian right away.

Marian: Not at all. He flatters me.

Rob: *Shouting.* I will not apologize! And what's more, she can keep her old money. I wouldn't touch it with a ten foot pole! *He goes out, slamming the door.*

The women look at one another.

Mrs. Gale: I suppose he told you.

Marian: Yes.

Mrs. Gale: You'll have to help him.

Marian: I will not.

Mrs. Gale: He has no where else to turn.

Marian: I knew you'd take his part.

Mrs. Gale: I'm not taking his part. I'm sorry and ashamed. But you've got to face the fact.

Marian: You'd sacrifice me for him. You've done it all our lives. Because he's a boy, your only son. If I were a man there isn't anything on heaven or earth you wouldn't do to push me on. But because I'm a girl, you'd sacrifice me, all my plans, all my lovely dreams, so that Rob can go up the alley and get away with it.

Mrs. Gale: Marian!

Marian: Do you think I've worked and studied and saved all these years to hand my money over to Ruby Hall?

Mrs. Gale: No, but now this has happened –

Marian: Mother, won't you try to see my side of it? You know I can't be happy here all my life. Deep inside me, I'm so lonely. Nobody speaks my language. All the people in this town care about is what they eat and what they wear, and who they sleep with –

Mrs. Gale: You don't have to be vulgar about it.

Marian: But it's true, isn't it? They're alive only from the neck down. But there's something in me that won't be satisfied with that. I want to be completely alive . . . alive in my mind as well as my body. Let me get away for a while and look for my own kind of life . . . a life of the mind and the spirit. I don't think I'm too old to go yet. The girl who discovered radium was older that I am now when she got to Paris. And I think if I work very hard, I could give the world back something – to make it the better – for having me in it.

Mrs. Gale: That's all very well, but it isn't helping your brother any.

Marian: He can't ask me to go on being the man in this house. It's not fair.

Mrs. Gale: You're the strong one here. We depend on you.

Marian: Then it's time Rob learned not to depend on me. It's time he learned to fight his own battles. If I give in to him now, I'll have to go on doing it till doomsday. It's not good for him.

Mrs. Gale: Marian, you know what Rob is. He's so easily downed. He's too much like his father. *Distressed.* I don't know if you remember . . .

Marian: *Bitterly . . . her memories are not pleasant.* I remember all right.

Mrs. Gale: I'm afraid Rob would – would be the same. But let them have a little home of their own, where he can feel he's his own master. He wouldn't be harrassed by debt if he owed the money to you.

Marian: You mean he wouldn't pay me back at all. I won't be home much this winter. They can have my room.

Mrs. Gale: I'd rather not have Ruby in the house. It would look as if – as if it had to be.

Marian: You mean it would look like a shot-gun wedding.

Mrs. Gale: That's just what people would say.

Marian: And what people would say is more important than ruining my life and making a sponger out of Rob?

Mrs. Gale: Marian, I'm not asking you to do this for Rob, I'm asking you to do it for me. This house has been my home ever since your father carried me in through that door, the first night I got here from the east. You never knew him as he was in those days – tall, and laughing, and good-looking. He set me down on a big packing case, and he made a bow, and said "Here's the Queen of the Castle! *Fiercely.* I've been that for twenty-six years, and I won't have another woman mistress here until I'm gone.

Marian: *Gently.* She wouldn't be that, Mother.

Mrs. Gale: Yes, she would. This would be her house. If I didn't make her feel that it was, she would hate me. She and Rob would both hate me. I'm an old woman, Marian, and I haven't had much happiness in my life. Do this for me – do this for me while I'm here.

There is silence. Marian has turned away. The habit of giving is almost too strong for her. But something her Mother has just said opens a window in her mind darkened and obscure before.

Marian: *Quietly, with wonder.* Mother . . . tell me about my father when he was young.

Mrs. Gale: *In a lifeless voice, tinged with bitterness.* He was very lively and clever, when I knew him first. He was going to college then, and he came down to Belleville in the summer. He was always getting up picnics, and writing funny verses, and making us laugh. . . . . Then we were engaged, and he wanted to come west, because everybody was going west in those days. So he never went back to college . . .

Marian: He never went back – to college –

Mrs. Gale: No. We came out here, and you were born, and for a while we were very happy . . . until your father changed. I've never understood why it was, for God knows I tried to be a good wife to him. But he changed. He wouldn't be friendly any more. He wouldn't go out with me. Before Rob was born he walked to the canyon every Sunday, and left me here, alone. At night he sat here reading his books . . . I've heard him, hours after I went to bed, sitting here talking and arguing with himself, like a crazy man.

Marian: *Eagerly.* Talking – to himself? What did he read? Mother what did he read, here at night?

Mrs. Gale: *Listlessly.* I don't know – I never read them. After a while he wouldn't even look at his books. He threw them into that box, and locked it, and never looked at it again.

99

Marian: Into that box? *She rushes over and tries to lift the end of it.* You mean – you mean his books are still here?

Mrs. Gale: Yes.

Marian drags the box into the middle of the floor.

They've lain in the attic there for 19 years. Marian – ! What are you doing?

Marian: I've got to know! I've got to know what he was. Why didn't you tell me? Why did you hide his books away?

Mrs. Gale: I didn't hide them. I had other things to think about –

Marian: *Fumbling with the lock.* Where's the key to this?

Mrs. Gale: I don't know. I've never seen the key.

Marian: *Taking up the hammer.* Then I'm going to break it open. *On her knees beside the box she thrusts the hammer claw under the lid.*

Mrs. Gale: Be careful – don't smash it! Peggy wants the box for a hope chest.

Marian: *Half laughing, half crying, as she strains at the lid.* A hope chest! . . . Yes, it's a hope chest now . . .

Mrs. Gale: Are you crazy? What's that got to do with . . .

Marian: Don't you understand? The answer to everything is in here!

She gives a final thrust, there is a screaming of nails, a splintering of wood, and the lid comes off. The room is very quiet. Marian is almost afraid to look inside. Slowly, she takes out a book. She hesitates a long moment, then takes courage and opens it. She reads slowly.

The Republic of Plato. Her voice shakes a little. Stephen Gale, 1905. *Holding Plato, she takes out two more books and opens them quickly. Man and Superman – The Origin of Species*, all scored and underlined – he read these! *Still clutching the three books she rises quickly.* He read these! *She looks at her mother strangely, and then beyond her as though at someone else.*

Mrs. Gale: Don't look at me like that . . . what is it?

Marian: *Quietly.* I feel as though my father – my young, *laughing*, father – has just come in and told me what to do. I've never known him before – I thought I did, but I only knew what he was at the end. *With increasing passion.* I can understand why he changed. Oh, how he must have hated it here – hated this place just as I hate it – while his dreams died, and his mind rusted away, till he tried to forget his dreams – in the only way he could. Life did that to him. It broke my father, but by God, it's not going to break me!

Mrs. Gale: You don't mean you're . . .

Marian: I mean I'm going away.

Mrs. Gale: You can't go. I need you.

Marian: You needed my father, too.

Mrs. Gale: I suppose you think it was my fault. You're putting all the blame on me –

Marian: No, I'm not blaming you. I know you tried. You both tried. You were just different kinds of people. But don't you see – now that I know – I can't do anything else – but go?

Mrs. Gale: No. I don't see that. And I never will.

Marian: *Slowly.* No. You can understand a hungry body –
but you don't understand – a hungry spirit, do you,
Mother? So there's no use talking about it – any more.

A silence; neither moves.

Good-night, Mother.

Mrs. Gale: Good-night then.

*She goes. Marian falls on knees beside the books as the
curtain comes slowly down.*

The End

Back to the Kitchen, Woman!

Back to the Kitchen, Woman! Public reading, Banff School of Fine Arts, 1941.

BACK TO THE KITCHEN, WOMAN!: *INTERVIEW*

Day: You said the original inspiration for the play was an article on a woman's strike in Eastern Europe.

EPG: Yes, which I found in a bureau drawer in Yellowstone National Park on a night when I couldn't sleep. We'd driven far too far. And I couldn't sleep. I kept seeing the road coming to me. And there was nothing to read. And I looked in the bureau drawer and here was this newspaper lining the drawer.

Day: Yes. It's a lovely story.

EPG: You're quite right about this Dr. Ludovici (See "Woman in the Twentieth Century"). There was a whole series in England. They put out a series of little handbooks: the future of this and that. The future of marriage, the future of democracy, the future of whatever. And this doctor did one on the future of women in which he deliberately reversed all the current thinking – the current thinking all towards the liberal out-of-the-kitchen philosophy. And he said we must go back to this sheltered existence. If they'd ever had it! He didn't know much history!

Day: In some ways it seems ironic that a play about women being urged to return to the kitchen should be written just at a time when women were leaving their homes in record numbers to be part of the war effort. Did *Kitchen* consciously play off an audience's awareness of this fact and their comfort or discomfort with the idea?

EPG: I just wrote it because I was interested in the situation of the strike. I read in the paper the other day that 500 women somewhere down in the Balkans had marched to protest their sons going to war.

Day: The group action was interesting?

EPG: Yes.

Day: I'd wondered if you'd thought of *Lysistrata* when you wrote the play as well, because you have this war between the sexes.

EPG: Of course! Anyone would think of *Lysistrata*. I once played Lysistrata in workshop in Pasadena at the Playhouse. Ted was working in the big Institute of Technology and I took a summer course at the Pasadena Playhouse, in '39. The war broke out while we were on our way home.

I think the play's brought to some sort of sensible conclusion by the broadminded and intelligent attitude of Mary. Don't you think so?

Day: Oh yes. You seem to be having some fun with the names of the main characters. Mary Godwin . . .

EPG: Well, of course, that's straight out of Wollstonecraft.

Day: Leon Hunter?

EPG: You know – Hunter – primitive. He's looking for a "womanly" woman. I was awfully lucky in the girl we had playing that part here in the first production – Vernis Christie – Vernis McQuaig she is now. Very, very smart. One hundred percent star quality gal. She certainly looked like an opera star.

Day: In comparison to your earlier stage plays, the dramaturgy of this one is much more radio-like with its emphasis on a large cast and frequent changes between indoor and outdoor sets. How big an influence did your radio writing have on the structure of this play? Did you have other models for the fairly fluid structure?

EPG: Well, it was just how that play had to go. You couldn't put it all on in the office and you couldn't put it all on the street. Of course, the mistake I made was having a different office. I had one scene in the publisher's office. Well, that's silly. Because it means moving furniture and going on. If I were producing it now, I'd have one office and one street.

But I have seen it done quite well. In Grande Prairie, for instance, they had a curtain and a couple of yards of forestage on which they had the street scene.

Day: Right.

EPG: And they were very much upset because some of the characters said "damn!"

Day: Oh!

EPG: But the play has been quite popular because people think it's funny. When somebody gets chased down the street and gets a black eye, that's funny. When Leon turns around in the third scene and they realize he has a black eye, the audience just howled.

We did it once for the army. This was a terrible experience. The entire . . . somebody got the idea that Little Theatre plays could be put on to entertain the troops.

Day: Right.

EPG: So the troops were *marched* down there. And a friend of mine had done a picture of Andromache. This was a poster, you see, to publicize Leon's book in the play.

A nude. And this caused so much embarrassment

that the play almost stopped. The men took one look at this and began to giggle and laugh and nudge each other. It almost caused a panic!

Day: A case of things not working the way they were supposed to. And of course, that's still happening today.

EPG: Yes! The *Journal's* going to get some feedback on Michelangelo's "David." Did you notice that in the paper this morning? [Reference to protests over an extremely graphic art exhibit.]

Day: Oh, about the . . .

EPG: "David" was out a fig leaf.

Day: Oh yes!

EPG: *Laughing.* The *Journal's* going to hear about that!

Day: You know, young people coming at the play today with today's emphasis on affirmative action are puzzled that there are not more professional women in the mob and that the main spokespeople are domestics, shopgirls and office help – the people the least likely to view their work as a career anyway.

EPG: Well, you see these are the people, the workers, that would be working . . . that *won't* be working for this man. There are professional women: the doctor's a professional woman, the suffragette's a professional woman, the opera singer's a professional woman. I don't think they're left out. But then it's the people who do the ordinary things that keep life moving – the laundry and the typing and the cleaning and so on. And they're not doing it as a career; they're doing it because they need the money. As Mrs. Brodie says, "mouths to feed and boots to buy."

BACK TO THE KITCHEN, WOMAN!:

FIRST PERFORMANCE

Back to the Kitchen, Woman! was first performed as a public reading at the Banff School of Fine Arts, 25 August, 1941. It was also presented 15 January, 1942 by the Edmonton Little Theatre in a production directed by the author at the Masonic Temple.

This play is designed to be on a stage with an apron. When the curtain is down, the fore-stage represents the street. The action is continuous.

BACK TO THE KITCHEN, WOMAN!

Characters:

Kay Rogers, a stenographer, about 20
Judy Pearson, a shop girl
Mary Godwin, M.D.
J. Leon Hunter, a writer, about 28
Mrs. Brodie, a charwoman, Glasgow Scotch
Brunhilda (Nee Hilda Brown), a singer, about 26
Florence Peters, an ex-suffragette
Arlene Martin, French-Canadian, 20
Mrs. Jenkins, middle-aged Cockney
Annie Sidorsky, another salesgirl
Mr. Philips, an elderly publisher

Setting:

Time:
1941.

Place:
A Canadian city.

The street, morning. People are hurrying by on their way to work. Store windows are understood to be at the edge of the stage, between the actors and the audience. There is a hat shop on the left, a book store centre.

Kay and Judy come in from the left. Kay is quiet, rather serious; Judy is tough and self-reliant. Both are nicely dressed for "business." Judy's eye is caught by the hat shop window.

A crowd of women, people passing on the street. Mr.

Brown and Mr. Black may appear at the director's discretion.

Judy: That's a cute hat. They always got something snappy in this window.

Kay: Which – the blue?

Judy: No, the red one – with the feather.

Kay: Kind of – flashy, don't you think?

Judy: Well, why not? If you wore black all day, like I do, you'd want to break out in something scarlet.

Kay: *Glancing at the next window.* Say, Judy, look! His book is published!

Judy: *Not very interested.* Whose book?

Kay: Mr. Hunter's – the man I'm going to work for. They got the whole window full of it.

Judy: Well . . . Quite a lay out. That's a hot picture on the cover. What's the name of it?

Kay: *Andromache, or Woman Restored!*

Judy: Don't mean a thing to me. . . .

Kay: It's kind of a symbolic title, I guess. Andromache was a Trojan princess, or something – the perfect type of woman.

Judy: Yeah? She'd bust the seams out of a size 36. What kind of a book is it – a ro-mance?

Kay: I don't know. But they must think it's pretty important. . . .

Judy: Well, come on. We don't want to be late for work.

Mary Godwin has come in from the right. Turning from the window, Kay runs into her.

Kay: Excuse me! Oh – good morning, Dr. Godwin!

Mary: Why it's Kay – Kay Rogers. How are you?

Kay: Oh I'm fine thanks. And Dad's wonderful. He says you're the best doctor in town. He says you made a new man of him.

Mary: Good!

Kay: He played 18 holes on Sunday and wasn't even tired.

Judy: *Impatient.* Listen kid – I got to punch a clock . . .

Kay: Good-bye now. I'm on my way to a new job.

Mary: Good-bye, Kay. *Warmly.* Good luck!

Kay and Judy hurry out. The book window takes Mary's eye. As she looks into it, Leon comes in from the left. He stops before the window, trying to look modest, but pride sticks out all over him.

Mary: *Shaking her head a little.* Tt-tt-tt-tt-tt-tt! What a book!

Leon: Did you say something?

Mary: Sorry. I must have been thinking out loud.

Leon: Well?

Mary: I mean – isn't it awful? The books that get published!

Leon: How do you know? Have you read it?

Mary: Well, no – but you can see the sort of stuff this is. History with the dirt left in.

Leon: *With some warmth. Andromache* isn't history. It's a book that can change the world. . . .

Mary: Oh?

Leon: The – the writer – thinks very deeply – of the unhappiness he sees around him.

Mary: Oh, I see. *Amused – realizing this is probably the author.* The unhappiness of – women?

Leon: Yes. Women exploited, little girls like yourself. Serving false gods. Struggling for what can only be dust and ashes in their mouths – success – authority – ambition.

Mary: "And ambition is no substitute for the love of a good man."

Leon: You *have* read *Andromache!*

Mary: *With weary good nature.* No. But I've heard that line before. "Back to the kitchen" – I'll bet that comes in somewhere.

Leon: It does.

Mary: The poor boob!

Leon: What?

Mary: I mean this writer. This – *looking at the books* – "J. Leon Hunter." Some woman must have slapped his face awfully hard.

Leon: Is that so!

Mary: Of course. He's trying to get back at somebody. His type always are.

Leon: That's just like a woman. Let me tell you, Leon

Hunter is a *philosopher*. He's . . .

Mary: Oh, you know him, do you?

Leon: *Drawing back.* Yes. I – I know him – slightly.

Mary: Tell him from me he'll go back to the woodshed, before we go back to the kitchen.

Mary walks away left. Leon, nettled, goes off to the right. He stops and turns as if he had thought of a crushing reply. Mary has stopped before the hat shop. She looks back at him. They exchange glances, hers amused, his annoyed, then both go out quickly.

The curtain rises at once on Leon's office. It is very plainly furnished, with a large writing table for Leon a small desk for his secretary. There is an old-fashioned leather couch with a plain cushion at one end and an old car rug, neatly folded, at the other. Telephone and typewriter are on the small desk. The door is on the left.

Mrs. Brodie, a stout middle-aged charwoman, is dusting with a red flannel duster as Kay opens the door.

Kay: *Hesitating.* Oh – good morning.

Mrs. Brodie: Come in, my dear, come. You'll be the new girl.

Kay: *Dignified.* I'm Kay Rogers. Mr. Hunter's secretary.

Mrs. Brodie: And I'm Mrs. Brodie, cleaning, polishing, disinfecting a specialty. Yon's the place for your hat.

Kay: Thank you.

Mrs. Brodie: As a rule I've the room done by this time, but I'm late today. My Alec – that's my youngest boy – had me up half the night poulticing his bad chest.

Kay: Oh. I hope he's better!

Mrs. Brodie: Aye, he's a bit brighter. Have ye had any experience with writing gentlemen?

Kay: Well, no. This is – this is my first job.

Mrs. Brodie: That's what I thought. Well, he's a quiet lad and no the Bohemian type. Ye'll have no trouble in a *moral* way.

Kay: No, of course not. I –

Mrs. Brodie: He does no live here, you understand. He comes here to do his work.

Kay: *Taking up a large framed photograph on the table.* Is this Mr. Hunter's wife?

Mrs. Brodie: He's no married to her – yet. That's Brunhilda, the opera singer.

Kay: Why, yes! She looks different in fishing clothes. I heard her sing "Isolde" once. She's wonderful!

Mrs. Brodie: I heard her sing on the street corners when she was ten years old. Hilda Brown.

Kay: Hilda Brown? Was that her name?

Mrs. Brodie: That's it. A wee redheaded thing with enough gumption for a half a dozen.

Kay: *Picking up a copy of Andromache.* Mr. Hunter's quite famous, now his new book is out.

Mrs. Brodie: Is that it? I had nae noticed. *She takes the book from Kay.* I like a good book myself. O'Douglas, or Annie S. Swan.

Kay: *Importantly.* The store windows this morning were full of it.

Mrs. Brodie: Mmph. *Andromeche.* Is this her on the cover?

Kay: *Andromache.* She was the Queen of Troy.

Mrs. Brodie: She might have more clothes on the bosom. *She begins to read.*

Kay is at her own desk, settling in. Mrs. Brodie gets more and more indignant.

Blethers!

Kay: What?

Mrs. Brodie: I said blethers! Will you listen to this – "Woman take up your birthright. Return to the splendid destiny nature planned for you – your heritage to minister to the needs of man!"

Kay: Is that in the book?

Mrs. Brodie: On the first page. "Not for you the turmoil of industry, the heat and dust of the race for wealth and fame. Return to your cooking, your sewing, your gardens. Recapture the peace and serenity of a dependent existence." Did you ever hear the like of it?

Kay: *Doubtfully.* You don't suppose it's meant to be funny?

Mrs. Brodie: Well, you can see for yourself –

Kay: *Taking the book.* "Vanity has lead you into professions, into law, journalism, the hurly-burly of politics, where your nerves are shattered by strain and excitement. You waste in factory and workshop the womanly strength designed for service on the hearth, at the spinning wheel." Spinning wheel – gosh!

Mrs. Brodie: So that's what he's been writing. And to think I've been giving his desk an extra polish because he was such a nice young man!

Kay: His other books aren't like that.

Mrs. Brodie: Are you letting him dictate more of this to you?

Kay: Well – I don't know. I suppose it's none of my business what he writes.

Mrs. Brodie: Is it not? Let me tell you, us working women will have to stand together. I'd warm his ear for him – *Leon comes in* – if I had him here.

Leon: Good-morning, Mrs. Brodie. Good-morning, Miss –

Kay: Rogers. Kay Rogers.

Leon: Oh yes. You're the girl the agency sent over. They tell me you're a whirlwind on the keys.

Kay: Thank you!

Leon: You're late this morning, Mrs. Brodie. Dusting not finished yet?

The red duster lies on the desk. Arms folded, she stands dourly, making no move to pick it up.

Well, we've got a lot to do – fan mail and one thing and another, so if you'll –

Mrs. Brodie: You can clean your own office, Mr. Leon Hunter!

Leon: Why – you're not leaving?

Mrs. Brodie: Aye – I'm leaving.

Leon: Well – take the duster along.

Mrs. Brodie: I'll not touch that duster! It may be my heritage to minister to the needs of man, but I'm doing no more of it in this office. I've been reading your precious book, and a worse pack of lying nonsense I've seldom seen.

Leon: Look, Mrs. Brodie, you're hired as a charwoman, not as literary critic –

Mrs. Brodie: Aye, I'm a charwoman. That's my profession, as writing's yours. Did you ever try a dependent existence, Mr. Hunter? Living on a working man's wages, when there's four mouths to feed and boots to buy and doctor's bills to pay?

Leon: That's got nothing to do with it . . .

Mrs. Brodie: *Going right on.* Back to the kitchen indeed! When you've more understanding of life you'll know why women leave their kitchens. It's no for pleasure and it's no for our health, but grim necessity and to hold up our heads in the world. . . .

Leon: Well, go hold it up somewhere else! I'm busy.

Mrs. Brodie: Don't worry lad, I'm going! And I'm not setting foot in this office again. There's always jobs for the likes of me, and I've more pride than work for a traitor to the female sex. Good-bye, Mr. Hunter! *She marches out, slamming the door.*

Leon: Well, I'll be damned! As if it was any of her business. Now let's get started Miss Rogers. If you'll – eh – *He gestures at the duster.*

Kay: Oh – of course. *She drops the duster in the waste paper basket.*

Leon: We'll go through the letters first.

Kay: Yes, Mr. Hunter.

The phone rings. Kay takes it up.

Mr. Leon Hunter's office – yes. Yes, I know – One moment please, I'll ask Mr. Hunter. *To him.* It's the *Tribune.* Dr. Godwin's been made head of the Children's Hospital. They want to know if you'd care to comment.

Leon: Godwin? Who's he?

Kay: Dr. *Mary* Godwin.

Leon: Oh, I see, a woman. Tell them I'll send something over.

Kay: The paper goes to press in an hour.

Leon: All right. We'll call them back.

Kay: *To phone.* I'll have a statement for you in ten minutes – thank you. *She hangs up.*

Leon: We'll clean that off before we start the letters. Take this please.

Kay: *Getting a pad and pencil.* Yes.

Leon: In appointing a woman to the important executive position the directors do a grave injustice to the public, to the hospital, and above all, to the woman herself. Unfitted by nature, for the burden of responsibility, Miss – what's her name?

Kay: *Unhappy.* Dr. Mary Godwin.

Leon: Miss Godwin takes on a job she cannot fill with credit to herself or safety to her patients. Herself highly emotional . . .

Kay: But Mr. Hunter – wait a minute –

Leon: E-m-o-t-i-o-n-a-l.

Kay: I can spell it. But Mary Godwin's not a bit like that.

She's a wonderful doctor. She practically saved my
father's life when he had pneumonia. Dad didn't want to
have her at first, but he –

Leon: I'm not interested in your family history, Miss Rogers.

Kay: I'm sorry. I just happen to know –

Leon: Medicine is no profession for a woman. I dealt with
that in *Andromache*, Chapter V. Now where was I?

Kay: *Flat.* "Takes on a job she cannot discharge with credit
to herself or safety to her patients. Herself highly
emotional. . . . "

Leon: Impartial judgment and scientific detachment are not
to be expected of her.

Kay: But Mr. Hunter, if you say this about Mary and the
Tribune prints it you're going to make things hard for her.

Leon: Can I help that? They asked me for my opinion . . .

Kay: But it's not true and it's not fair! She's had enough
opposition to face without this.

Leon: Miss Rogers, are you taking my dictation?

Kay: It's not impartial or scientific to say things about people
you don't know. You've never even seen her . . .

Leon: I know she's a woman, don't I?

Kay: *Hotly.* I know she's a grand person and a good doctor –

Leon: *Thundering.* Are you taking my dictation?

Kay: Well, no I'm not.

Leon: Oh, for . . .

Kay: I'm sorry, Mr. Hunter. This is my first job and I'd like to make good. But if I went home and told my father I'd helped you write that silly stuff – he wouldn't speak to me. Why it's – it's like stabbing Mary Godwin in the back!

Leon: Now don't be absurd. You women take everything so personally.

Kay: It's not absurd to be loyal to your friends.

Leon: Well, hang the *Tribune*! Sit down and let's get on with these letters.

Kay: I won't sit down. I'm going back to the agency to tell Miss Peters why I resigned here. *At the door she turns.* And if you're going to write another book, Mr. Hunter, I advise you to learn to type! *She goes, defiant.*

Leon: Well! So I can't get along without them, eh? *He gets the telephone directory. Tribune* – R – S – T – Taylor – Towers – *Tribune* –

Kay shoots back into the room, flicks the duster out of the wastebasket, drops it on the desk and marches out without a word. Leon goaded, drops the directory, grabs the duster and starts after her.

Leon: You come back here! You little smart alec – you can't get away with that –

Hilda: *Appearing in the door.* What can't I get away with, Lee?

She is a handsome prima donna of 26, well built, with an air of great physical well-being.

Leon: Hilda!

Hilda: *Coming in and going to the couch.* What goes on here? Playing drop the handkerchief?

Leon: *Casting the duster from him.* That girl – that insufferable little idiot! Blast the little fool! I just fired her.

Hilda: Do you always chase them out of the building?

Leon: Oh, forget her! Hilda – you look magnificent.

Hilda: Why not? That's part of my job. I'm lunching with Bardini our guest conductor.

Leon: That little weasel! Have dinner with me to-night?

Hilda: To-night I'm singing with the Philharmonic. Sit down, Lee. I think it's time we had a little serious talk.

Leon: *Sitting beside her.* Have you – read *Andromache*?

Hilda: Yes. I read it last night.

Leon: *Eagerly.* Well?

Hilda: Well – it rather took my breath away. And why it should be dedicated to me –

Leon: I thought you understood. "To Brunhilda in gratitude." You've been my inspiration.

Hilda: Have I?

Leon: "A perfect woman, nobly planned . . . "

Hilda: *With slight irony.* Thank you.

Leon: Hilda, it's the biggest thing I've done. Old Philips tells me it's selling like hot cakes.

Hilda: People are *buying* this?

Leon: All over the country. Fourteen thousand in three days. Darling. . . . Now I can take you away.

Hilda: Take me away?

Leon: No more – *with distaste* – exhibiting yourself. No more dirty theatres, cheap publicity, weasel-faced Bardinis. We'll have a house in the country – a little house, where we live quietly and simply and naturally.

Hilda: Where I do the cooking and make jams and jellies, while you write books in the attic.

Leon: No, no, not the attic. I'll build a writing room in the garden – away from the telephone and delivery boys . . .

Hilda: Will this little house be on the power and water mains? Or do we haul water overhand in a bucket?

Leon: Hilda – don't make fun of our dreams.

Hilda: *Sincerely.* I'm sorry! I wouldn't make fun of anybody's dreams. I have a few of my own.

Leon: My dear . . .

Hilda: I said – *of my own.* How long have we known each other Leon?

Leon: Almost a year. The second of September – the day you caught the salmon at Blackwater. You remember – we were fishing opposite banks of the river – glaring at each other. . . .

Hilda: *Smiling.* Till I fell in and you waded to the rescue. Parsifal in a checked shirt and waders – ! We've caught a lot of fish since then, and built a lot of camp fires.

Leon: Wonderful days – with the only woman who knows the beauty of silence.

Hilda: *Noticing what she's sitting on.* This is the old rug from the car . . .

Leon: Sure. Smells salmony – when I get lonesome for you I come over and take a good sniff.

Hilda: Oh Lee – I'm sorry . . .

Leon: Sorry? What is there to be sorry about?

Hilda: *Trying for a new opening.* We – haven't talked much about our work on those trips—have we?

Leon: Gosh, no. I go fishing to get away from work.

Hilda: So do I. Just to be lazy, and soak up sunshine. It was playtime for both of us. Maybe that's why – in some ways – we don't know each other very well.

Leon: *Astonished.* Don't know each other?

Hilda: Well, do we? Your book, for instance . . .

Leon: I told you I was writing *Andromache.*

Hilda: I thought it was a love story about the Trojan War. Oh, I knew you had some funny ideas about women. But I never dreamed you'd publish them and put my name on the first page.

Leon: Hilda! The book is my tribute to you.

Hilda: *Getting up.* And what sort of *hausfrau* you saw in me, heaven only knows. If you think I'm ready to give up music and devote myself to frying fish . . .

Leon: But you like cooking – you told me so . . .

Hilda: Sure I like cooking – once in a while. It's a nice change. But give up my singing – do you realize how much music means to me?

123

Leon: Of course I do. It's been your work.

Hilda: It's been my job, and I grouse about it now and then like everybody else. But deeper than that, Lee – music is my life. It isn't just something I do to pass the time. I've slaved at it because I loved it. When I was a kid I went without overshoes to pay for lessons. I waited on tables the year I studied in Italy . . .

Leon: But I don't ask you to stop singing – entirely.

Hilda: You'd expect me to stop working at it. *There is a pause. Wouldn't you?*

Leon: Yes. I would.

Hilda: I know – it's on page one. "Not for you the heat and dust of the race for wealth and fame . . . "

Leon: I'd expect our home – our life together – to mean more to you than – the applause and the spotlights – Hilda! That would be enough –

Hilda: No, Lee. That's why I'm sorry. It wouldn't be enough. . . .

Leon: I know I can't offer you an opera singer's salary . .

Hilda: It isn't the money! Don't you understand? My voice is – *With a deprecating gesture.* If you like, it's something the gods have given me, I have to use it, or die.

Leon: What it amounts to, is that you don't love me.

Hilda: Did you ever ask me – if I loved you?

Leon: No, I . . .

Hilda: No – you took it for granted, along with everything else. Don't you see? None of it has been quite real.

You've been writing a part for me, but I can't play it.

Leon: If you were the girl I thought you were . . .

Hilda: That's what I'm trying to tell you, Lee. You made her up. The woman you thought I was never existed – except in your own imagination.

Leon: Well, so you've been amusing yourself with me. Deliberately letting me think . . .

Hilda: Not deliberately! If you'd asked me – but you didn't. We've had fun together, and it didn't seem to matter –

Leon: You're cold – hard – selfish. Your own ambition means more to you than the most sacred responsibilities of a woman's life.

Hilda: *Losing patience.* Well, it's my life, and I'll do what I like with it! *She makes for the door.* I hope I marry – when I find a man big enough to want me as I am. But I'm going to sing till I'm as old as Schuman-Heink, and make my entrance in a wheel-chair. Good-bye, Lee . . .

Leon: Hilda –

Hilda: *She tosses the book at him.* Good fishing! *She goes.*

The book, awkwardly caught, falls open. He reads, with irony.

Leon: "To Brunhilda, in gratitude."

The phone rings. He picks it up. Irritably.

Hello? – Who? – Oh the *Tribune.* What? Certainly I'll make a statement. No woman has the emotional stability to run a hot dog stand, much less a hospital – Yes, I said a hot dog stand. . . . Yes, you can quote me on that!

He hangs up. Lugging the typewriter from Kay's desk to his own, he sits down, obviously in a very bad temper, and begins pounding out something, using two fingers. There is a firm knock on the door.

Yes? Who is it?

A quiet-looking, middle-aged woman steps in.

Miss Peters: Mr. Hunter?

Leon: Yes.

Miss Peters: I am Florence Peters.

This means nothing to him.

From the employment agency.

Leon: *Getting up.* Well! That's fine. You can start right away.

Miss Peters: I didn't come here to work, Mr. Hunter. Last night I read your book. This morning Kay Rogers reported to me why she had left your office. I have a few things to say to you.

Leon: Now look – Miss Peters – I'm rather busy right now . . .

Miss Peters: Do you know what your book amounts to, young man? Fascism, reaction. The denial of democracy.

Leon: But listen – my dear lady . . .

Miss Peters: You listen to me. . . . Over twenty years ago, Mr. Hunter, I marched in processions for women's suffrage. I went to prison for three months. I fought and worked and suffered, to earn women the right to call their souls their own. . . .

Leon: *Taking the offensive.* Oh. You went to jail. I suppose you're proud of it.

Miss Peters: I am.

Leon: They should have kept you there. Your kind are dangerous. Do you think women are any happier because a lot of old hens went shrieking up and down the country cackling about your precious rights?

Miss Peters: Twenty-five years ago, Mr. Hunter, I wasn't an old hen. I was a good-looking girl, engaged to marry a fine man. That man died in France. He believed he died for freedom. Well, I've lived for freedom. I've fought injustice wherever I saw it. And I'm going to fight you, Mr. Hunter. I'll make you wish you'd never heard of *Andromache or Woman Restored.*

Leon: *Andromache* is the truth. That's why you can't take it.

Miss Peters: It's not the truth. You say women are unhappy. You don't know what our lives were before we marched and cackled for our rights. It's been a long hard fight. We're not out of the woods yet. And we won't be set back by a reactionary young fool like you.

Leon: Look – I don't need a suffragette song and dance. I need a stenographer.

Miss Peters: I'm glad of that. But you won't get one.

Leon: Oh won't I? You don't run the only agency in town.

Miss Peters: I see you don't believe women can be loyal to each other; that's part of your contempt for us. Your education is about to begin . . .

The door has opened abruptly, and Arlene Martin, a pretty girl carrying a large dress box shoots into the room, colliding with Miss Peters.

Arlene: Pardon me, Madame! 'Ere is your laundry, Mistair Huntair.

Leon: Laundry?

Arlene: That is what I say.

Leon: You don't bring that here. Deliver it to my apartment, 18 Riverside . . .

Arlene: I will deliver it – anywhere I like! *Defiantly she yanks open the dress box and throws soiled clothes on the floor.* Voila! 'Ere are the shirts, the towels, the underwear –

Leon: Are you crazy? Get that out of here!!! That hasn't been washed –

Arlene: No – it 'as not been washed. My Mothair and me, we will not wash it. We are not stupids. We 'ave 'eard what you say – that women are good only to do the dirty work. Eh, bien, this is some dirty work that you will do yourself!

Miss Peters: How is that for loyalty, Mr. Hunter? As I was saying, your education is about to begin. Come along my dear. We have a lot to do. *She takes Arlene by the arm and they go out.*

Leon is throwing the laundry back into the box as the curtain falls.
The street. Evening. People passing. Several women stop before the book store window. Mrs. Brodie and her friend Mrs. Jenkins come in from the left.

Mrs. Brodie: Aye, there's the window full of it. I'm telling you, Mrs. Jenkins, the book's an insult to us all.

Mrs. Jenkins: *With cockney accent.* Wot did 'e want to write it for? We ain't done nothing to 'im.

Judy and her friend Annie elbow in before the window.

Judy: That's the book, Annie. "Back to the Kitchen" and all that baloney.

Annie: Have you read it?

Judy: Yeah – I got it out of the store library at lunch time. Gee, did it burn me up!

Annie: Who does the guy think he is?

Mrs. Jenkins: 'e thinks 'e's Mussolini, that's what!

Laughter. There is now a crowd of women around the window.

Judy: He can't tell us what to do!

Agreement from the crowd.

Mrs. Jenkins: I got a mind to 'eave a brick through that window, just to let 'im know wot I thinks of 'im.

Annie: Sure – go on! Bust the window!

Confusion. Miss Peters hurries in with Arlene who carries a soap box. She puts it down. Miss Peters mounts it and harangues the crowd.

Miss Peters: No! There is a better way! Women of a free country – I call on you to stand together! Prove that Leon Hunter cannot force us back into slavery. Lincoln said "A nation cannot exist half slave and half free." The enslavement of women is always the first step in the enslavement of mankind!

Mrs. Jenkins: She's right! Ain't that wot 'itler did?

Applause.

Miss Peters: This man cannot take away our right as human beings, decide what we will do with our lives. If we choose to work within the four walls of a home, we do it gladly, because we love our homes – not because this young dictator thinks we are fit for nothing but drudgery.

Applause.

But if we can serve the world in some other way, Leon Hunter shall not hold us back. Remember Florence Nightingale. Remember Madame Curie. Remember Amelia Earhart! Teach this man that we can stand together. Call on the women of the nation to boycott J. Leon Hunter!

Judy: Boycott Hunter!

Mrs. Jenkins: Boycott Hunter? Wot does she mean?

Judy: She means we won't do nothing for him.

Kay: No dictation! No stenographer!

Mrs. Brodie: I'll no clean his office!

Mrs. Jenkins: Neither will I!

Arlene: I will not wash 'is dirtay shirts!

Annie: Boycott Hunter!

Confusion.

Judy: *Mounting the soap box.* Listen! We got to get organized. I work in the biggest department store in town. By to-morrow no girl in that store is going to sell him anything!

Annie: No girl is going to sell him anything!

Voice: I got a copy of his book. When I get home I'm going to burn it up.

Judy: Burn it now sister! Burn it now!

Mrs. Jenkins: Burn 'is blinkin' book!

Arlene: Let us burn it in the streets!

Miss Peters: Boycott Hunter!

With defiant shouts of "Burn the book," "No dictation," "I won't wait on him" – and "They can't make me!" etc., the crowd begins to move off both ways.
Mr. Brown and Mr. Black, two small inoffensive citizens come in from the left and stand before the bookstore window.

Mr. Brown: Y'know – there may be something in this fellow's ideas.

Mr. Black: Shhh! It's as much as a man's life is worth to say so. *He looks back apprehensively.* Let's get out of here!

They hurry out to the right.

Red light begins to flicker from the right. Down the street, a procession of women come in from the left. They carry banners – "Boycott Hunter," "Back to the Kitchen, Hunter."
Kay and Judy carry a basket full of copies of Andromache.
They all sing as they march –

> Hi ho – hi ho! Into the fire they go!
> We'll keep them burning all night long, hi ho! hi ho! hi ho!
> Leo – Leo! We want to let you know
> We're going to cook your cock-eyed book, Leo – Leo!

Down the street to the right, confusion and noise increase. The song gets louder. The fire light flickers. After mounting to an angry climax, the shouting and singing dies away.

The curtain rises on the office of Philips and Co.
Publishers. Mr. Philips' desk is on the left. There is a shelf
of books with gaudy new wrappers, several sample posters
advertising books.

Leon is standing with his back to us, studying one of the
advertisements. Philips, an elderly man with a slightly
pompous manner, is sitting at his desk. He holds a paper
from which he reads with great satisfaction.

Mr. Philips: Two hundred copies burned at Northton on
Monday. Roughly three hundred in a bonfire outside my
office on Wednesday, and a good blaze at the mass
meeting at the town hall. Splendid, Mr. Hunter, splendid
publicity!

Leon makes an impatient movement. Philips takes up a
handful of newspaper clippings.

We've made the front page of every paper in the country.
"Women declare national boycott of Hunter." "Question
raised in parliament 'Is Hunter's book first step to
Fascism'" – marvellous. There's been nothing like it since
Gone With the Wind. I ordered a fourth edition this
morning.

Leon: That's all very well – but what about me? *Turning, he*
reveals a magnificent black eye.

Mr. Philips: I'd say you're a very lucky young man.

Leon: Lucky, sure, I'm lucky. I *like* being mobbed on the
street. I *enjoy* being chased into a police station . . .

Mr. Philips: Of course, of course – that was very unfortunate.
Very. Although our sales picked up thirty per cent the
next morning.

Leon: Sales – profits – publicity! I bet you're sorry they didn't kill me, just to put over the fourth edition.

Mr. Philips: Now, Mr. Hunter . . .

Leon: *Earnestly.* Did it ever occur to you, Mr. Philips, that I wrote *Andromache* with a purpose?

Mr. Philips: Certainly. I've been a publisher for thirty years. I've never met a writer yet who hadn't a consuming purpose – to write a best seller. Well, you've done it.

Leon: I wanted the world to *read* that book.

Mr. Philips: They are reading it. The more they read it, the madder they get. The more they burn, the more we sell. And now is the time to start thinking about your next book.

Leon: My next book?

Mr. Philips: Exactly. Strike while the iron is hot. In fact – I've had a little idea about that.

Leon: *Gloomily.* You can keep it. I'm tired of seeing my best work go up in smoke.

Mr. Philips: Mr. Hunter – I think you ought to marry.

Leon: *I* ought to marry!

Mr. Philips: Nothing would arouse greater interest in your principles than their application in your own life. Not that I wish to appear dictatorial, but . . .

Leon: And who in hell am I to marry? The Statue of Liberty? No, I wouldn't trust her either. She'd slug me with the chandelier.

Mr. Philips: Now – now – I can't believe there isn't a sweet nice girl who . . .

Leon: There isn't a sweet nice girl in this country who wouldn't love to murder me. *He points to his shiner.*

133

See that? Five foot two, eyes of blue, and she socked me with the heel of her shoe. Have you any idea what I've been through in the past month? Waitresses, shop girls, stenographers – damnit, they won't even speak to me. I haven't had a decent meal or a well-ironed shirt for weeks.

Mr. Philips: Surely you could find a good man-servant –

Leon: *With irony.* Jeeves to the rescue, eh? I hire a man to cook and clean for me – after telling the world that's a woman's business. Bad publicity, Philips.

Mr. Philips: *Hastily.* Yes – yes, I see your point.

Leon: I think I'll retire to a nunnery; I mean a monastery.

Mr. Philips: My dear boy . . .

Leon: If there was any living soul – *man or woman* – who understood what I tried to do –

Mr. Philips: You've had plenty of fan mail.

Leon: Yes. From what kind of man? Snivelling little twerps without the guts of a louse. Women got their jobs away from them. Their wives browbeat them and I'll bet it serves them right. They think I'm on their side.

Mr. Philips: *Interested.* And you're not on their side?

Leon: God, no! No real woman could stand them for five minutes.

Mr. Philips: *Thumping his desk.* There's the idea for your new book!

Leon: Where?

Mr. Philips: Men must be worthy of the new woman.

Leon: I dealt with that in Chapter X.

Mr. Philips: Never mind – play it up! "The Masculine Renaissance." Marvellous. Strength, power, virility – could we sell that! *Excited.* I'll get Bronski to do the cover – a young Greek god. Now the title – this Andromache – did she have a husband?

Leon: Sure. She was a good girl, she was.

Mr. Philips: *Impatient.* Well – what was his name?

Leon: Hector.

Mr. Philips: Hector, that's excellent. Short – easy to say. There's your title – *Hector: The Re-Creation of Man.*

Leon: Look, Philips – I've been hectored enough lately. You'd better give me my cheque and let me go home.

Mr. Philips: *Getting the cheque on his desk.* Here you are, my boy, here you are. And remember – there's plenty more where that came from – if you're smart enough to go after it.

Leon: Thank you.

Mr. Philips: *Going with him to the door.* You'll think about the Hector idea, won't you? We might give the press a few hints – stimulate curiosity –

Leon: I'm not catering to the public appetite for vulgar sensation.

Mr. Philips: Sensation – nonsense! Men have been men and women have been women for thousand of years – but there's still fortune to be made calling attention to the fact. Good morning!

Leon: *Glad to escape.* Good morning. *He goes out.*

Mr. Philips: *Coming back to his desk, vastly pleased with his idea.* Hector: The Re-Creation of Man. *He strikes a classic pose.*

The curtain comes down quickly.
The street – the same day. Mrs. Brodie and Mrs. Jenkins come in from the right, talking as they come.

Mrs. Brodie: And I said to her "If you don't join the movement, Agnes McSkimming, you can think black burning shame to yourself. What's more you'll have no friend on this street."

Mrs. Jenkins: Quite right too. *Looking into window on the right.* Look 'ere, Mrs. Brodie, wot kind of fish would you say that was?

Mrs. Brodie: *Looking.* It's a trout, and artificial at that.

Mrs. Jenkins: Oh, I knew it was artificial, to show off the fishing rods. It ain't got that nice smelly look, a real fish 'as.

They move away.

Go on – wot did she say to that?

Mrs. Brodie: Oh, Agnes said I'm joining the movement. I've brought my girls up to be teachers and they're going into no kitchens but their own.

Mrs. Jenkins: Good for 'er. That's the proper spirit.

Judy, Kay, and Annie come in from the left.

Judy: Hello!

Mrs. Jenkins: 'ello, girls!

Judy: Are you coming to the meeting tonight?

136

Mrs. Brodie: Where's the meeting?

Annie: In the market square. We've made a scarecrow. We're going to burn him in emphasis.

Kay: *Laughing.* Burn him in *effigy!*

Leon has come in right, and is looking at the fishing rods.

Mrs. Jenkins: Oh, you mean you've made a guy of 'unter?

Kay: That's it – like Guy Fawkes.

Mrs. Jenkins: Coo! Won't that be a lark! Wot's 'e made of?

Annie: It's a beautiful guy. It's got a turnip for a head . . .

Judy: Hollowed out and stuffed with his own book . . .

Kay: We're making him eat his own words! *Laughter, suddenly pointing.* Look . . . there he is!

Silence. Leon glances at them, meets five pairs of hostile eyes then quickly turns back to the window.

Mrs. Brodie: You're right – that's him.

Annie: That's the black eye they gave him outside the police station. Gee . . . I wisht I'd been there!

Judy: I'd like to give him a piece of my mind.

Mrs. Jenkins: I'd like to give 'im the back of my 'and. *She advances on Leon.* 'ere you!

Leon: Were you speaking to me?

Mrs. Jenkins: Who do you think you are, Mr. Leon 'unter? Ordering the likes of us abaht?

Leon: Now, look here, lady . . .

Mrs. Jenkins: I am looking and I don't care for what I see. Why don't you mind your own business, you conceited, dictatorial, misbegotten, trouble-maker . . .

Annie: You tell him, Mrs. Jenkins!

The women surround Leon.

Leon: I'm not making any trouble –

Jeering – Oh no? Etc.

Mrs. Brodie: What did you write yon deft book for, if not to meke trouble? Teking the bread out of the working woman's mouths?

Judy: *Planting herself in front of him.* You'd like to see us all fired, wouldn't you?

Leon: Well, I'd like to see you all happy wives and mothers . . .

Mrs. Jenkins: Well, I'm an 'appy wife and mother, and I don't need *you* to tell me my duty.

Leon: If you had any womanly feeling in you, you'd understand my book. You'd thank me for writing it . . .

Judy: Thank you! That's *good!* *She slaps him.* There's my thanks.

Leon: *Grabbing her by the shoulders.* You darn little fool! What you need is a good spanking just to teach you manners – *He shakes her.*

Annie: You take your hands off her!

Mrs. Jenkins: *Whacking at him with her umbrella.* Take that, you little 'itler, you!

General scrimmage. They all go for Leon, except Kay who

138

tries to pull them off.

Mrs. Brodie: "Back to the Kitchen" is it? You're going back to the hospital!

Kay: Don't hit him! It isn't fair! It's five to one . . .

More women arrive, shouting, "It's Leon Hunter;" "Come on Lilly;" "They've got that Leon Hunter!"

Judy: Hold him Annie! Give him one for me!

Mrs. Jenkins: I'm giving 'im one for all of us!

Fighting and protesting Leon is forced off to the right. Kay is pushed out of the crowd and stands holding her wrist. Mary Godwin, with her little black bag, comes down the street from the left.

Mary: Kay . . . for Heaven's sake . . . what is it? Are you hurt?

Kay: Never mind me . . . it's Leon Hunter. I think they're killing him this time.

Mary hurries off. Kay limps after her. The uproar continues. A policeman's whistle is heard. Gradually the tumult and the shouting dies.

The curtain goes up on Leon's office. He is lying on the couch, with a large piece of sticking plaster on his forehead. Mary sits beside him, a glass of milky liquid in her hand.

Leon: *Groaning as he comes to.* Ohhhhhhhhhhhhh!

Mary: *Soothingly.* All right – just take it easy.

Leon: Mmmmmmmmmrrrrrrrrr . . . my head . . .

Mary: Don't worry . . . it's not a bad cut.

Leon: What happened? I don't seem to remember . . .

Mary: Somebody slugged you with an umbrella. They chased you home, knocked you down, and you passed out when you hit your head on the doorstep.

Leon: Were you . . . part of the mob?

Mary: No, no. I just happened to the passing. I got the policeman to carry you in here.

Leon: Policeman? It must have been quite a riot . . .

Mary: Biggest man-hunt since *Uncle Tom's Cabin*. Now sit up and drink this.

Leon: *Suspiciously.* What is it?

Mary: Sel volatile. Wonderful for a hang-over.

He drinks it.

> *She puts her hand on his forehead.* You're a little feverish.

Leon: Your hand is beautifully cool.

Mary: I'll get you a cold compress . . .

Leon: *Catching her hand.* No! No, don't go anywhere. Just stay here and talk to me . . . quietly. You're the only girl that's talked quietly to me . . . for such a long time.

Mary: So I understand.

Leon: I guess you . . . know who I am?

Mary: J. Leon Hunter, the Boycott Boy.

He groans.

> Woman hater number one.

Leon: But I don't . . . I don't hate women at all. I only want them to be happy.

Mary: You want them to be happy *your* way, and they'd rather be unhappy . . . in their own way. Isn't it queer . . . human beings are like that. Will you tell me something?

Leon: Anything.

Mary: What kind of small boy did you used to be?

Leon: Oh . . . now why rake that up?

Mary: Because I want to know.

Leon: My childhood is something I try to forget.

Mary: Why?

Leon: Because I hated it. My Aunt Geraldine brought me up. She was an awful old battle-axe.

Mary: Of course – Judge Geraldine Hunter, I remember her.

Leon: Sure. She was a police magistrate. She ran for parliament, and she made my life a hell on earth.

Mary: So that's what you've been doing. Sticking your tongue out at Aunt Geraldine.

Leon: Please – don't get psychological on me!

Mary: I'm not. I'm just trying to understand you.

Leon: *Like a desert traveller seeing water.* You're trying to understand?

Mary: Yes, your aunt was a great woman, but . . .

Leon: But an old battle-axe just the same!

Mary: Well, she was a fighter. Her generation had to fight. She bossed you around and *Andromache* was your way

141

of getting back.

Leon: *More interested in Mary than her words.* Why aren't you like the others?

Mary: What others?

Leon: Don't you want to hit me with the typewriter? They all did.

She shakes her head.

You're not angry?

Mary: No.

Leon: That's wonderful. You're the only one who has tried to understand why I wrote my book. Do you believe . . . I wanted to do something for the human race?

Mary: Yes, I can believe that.

Leon: I saw so many people – so unhappy. *Hastily.* Aunt Geraldine wasn't really happy, either . . . even when she won an election. And all the girls I saw on the street, in the subway – always in a hurry. Their faces strained – worried . . .

Mary: I know.

Leon: So I thought . . . this is all wrong. Women don't belong in this kind of world. They ought to go back . . .

Mary: Back where?

Leon: Back to quietness. Gardens and warm kitchens – copper pans shining in the sun . . .

Mary: But that world isn't there anymore – for most people. And none of us can go back – *ever.* Oh, I agree this racketing rattling world isn't fit for women to live in! But

142

it isn't fit for men, either. We've got to go on, both men and women –

Leon: You haven't told me your name.

Mary: Mary Godwin

Leon: *Liking it.* Mary Godwin. All women with cool hands and low voices should be called "Mary."

Mary: *Smiling.* That's a nice line. I'll look for that speech in your next book.

Leon: I'm not going to write another book.

Mary: Oh yes you are! A real book about real people. Now you've got Aunt Geraldine out of your system, you can see straighter.

Leon: Mary, you mustn't go away. You keep on understanding me, and I'll try to understand you, and maybe we'll understand about things.

Mary: *Getting up.* I'll have to go . . . for a while. And you'd better get some rest. *She spreads the rug over him.* When you get ready to go home, call a taxi. Walking is bad for your health.

Leon: Don't I know it!

Mary: I'll try to drop in and see you this evening.

Leon: 18 Riverside. Come for supper. I make wonderful omelettes.

Mary: *Putting on her hat.* I scramble a mean egg myself.

Leon: I knew it! The minute I saw you sitting there, I said to myself – "There's a girl who can scramble eggs." Mary, you've got to come. I may have a relapse. After all, when you save a man's life, that makes you responsible for his future.

Mary: Does it? *Smiling.* But you said once I was unfit for the burden of responsibility.

Leon: I said *what*?

Mary: *Picking up her little bag and settling it on the table.* I'll send you some tablets from the hospital. *Pointedly.* St. Luke's Children's Hospital. I work there.

Leon: *Staring at the bag.* The hospital . . . Mary Godwin! Are you the . . . ?

Mary: *Sweetly.* Yes, I am. After my appointment you wrote such a nice piece about my emotional instability.

Leon: But Mary . . . I didn't know . . . I didn't mean it . . .

Mary: *At the door.* Perhaps you didn't realize that in saving your life I did a very professional job. Good-bye!

Leon: Mary, listen . . .

But she is gone.
He subsides, his head in his hands. Oh damn the luck!! The only girl . . .
Abruptly the door opens – Mary is back.

Mary: What does the J. stand for?

Leon: Huh?

Mary: What's your first name?

Leon: Oh – John.

Mary: Thank Heavens! John Hunter sounds like a man. Did you say 18 Riverside?

144

Leon: At seven o'clock!

Mary: Seven o'clock. Good-bye, John!

She goes.

Leon: *Beaming.* Ahhhhhhhh!

He lies back, settles the rug over him and shuts his eyes. But something under his head bothers him. Beneath the cushion he finds a copy of Andromache. *He flings it away. It falls in the wastebasket, but he doesn't seem to notice. Pounding the cushion into a comfortable shape, he settles down very cosily as the curtain falls.*

The End

The Last Caveman

Betty Shaw as Mrs. Davy, Harry Conroy as Jim Bryan, Jim Richardson as Herb Johnstone, Arthur Martin as Bill Carson, Les Pilcher as Mr. Davy, Steve McEachern as Denzil, Edmonton Little Theatre, Masonic Temple, 1938.

THE LAST CAVEMAN: *INTERVIEW*

Day: There appears to have been a strong socialist/pacifist streak in your own work. When did you become politically radicalized and what motivated it?

EPG: Well, I became a left winger in my first year at Varsity when I took economics. And then I went out to teach near Grande Prairie. And I was complaining that I had nothing to read, and one of the neighbors said "Oh I've got lots of those little Julius Handeman books." They were little blue-covered papers – sayings – that sold for 25 cents. Very left-wing writing, like Marx, Engels, and Mencken and so on. American radicals. I can see him riding up through the gate with a flour sack full of books on his saddle. And I used to sit on the wood pile outside in the afternoon and read them. But that, combined with the University courses, radicalized my thinking.

But *The Last Caveman* is really a plea for international law. The last caveman is the last guy that takes a shotgun and club to defend his two-by-four piece of land.

Day: Emphasis on provincial thinking.

EPG: Yes. Well, anyway. We had this chunk of land out at the cottage and our neighbors about half a mile down the shore were a family called Jones. As a matter of fact, the land we owned had originally been theirs, and they had lost it for not paying their taxes. And they were convinced that their leading citizen was out to get their land: the man who owned the fish house, and owned the store and owned the post office and was the chairman of the school board. You know the type?

Day: Oh yes.

EPG: Well anyway. These "poor white trash," the Jones family, were convinced he was trying to get their land, so they proceeded to arm themselves. They got a pile of stones, a club and a fierce dog and a Boer War shotgun and they were going to defend their land. And nobody could tell them that they would be far better off to go to law.

What happened in the play really happened after we had come home from the cottage. We read in the paper that Mrs. Jones and her son, Albert, had been arrested for attacking these two surveyors. Albert got six months.

Day: So in real life it didn't end too happily.

EPG: But that was the origin of *The Last Caveman*. And we were talking about international law. And this was in the thirties when the League of Nations was still a viable organization. And my husband said to me: "Well, there you are. There's an example of what the national states do. The national sovereign state thinks it has a right to take to violence." So it was really Ted who nagged me into doing it.

Day: Someone compared Denison's backwoodsmen with yours. Were Merrill Denison's plays an influence on your drawing of the Davys?

EPG: I don't know his plays very well. But I was taking these people absolutely off the originals. They're just exactly the way they are in the play. This half-witted boy, Denzil was very superstitious. But they were nice, loveable people. And they liked each other. They were very proud of each other, the Jones' were. They came from Devonshire – way down – and the people in the play couldn't do Devonshire so we changed to Lancashire.

Day: *Caveman* seems to have been more subtle and less outspoken in its politics than plays like *The Giant Killer*, *The Unknown Soldier Speaks, Glorious and Free* and The *House in Toad Lane*. Was your experience with doing *You Can't Do That!* an influence on your expressing politics or serious ideas in a comic form?

EPG: Well you see, Bill Irvine, who was a member of Parliament had written one play called *The Brains We Trust*. And it had been produced, but it hadn't got a very great reception. And he'd written this other one and he'd called it *Clean Water*. And my friends in the CCF began phoning me and saying, "Can you do anything about that play of Bill's? Because it has great ideas, but the dialogue is awful!" So I contacted Bill, and he agreed that we would collaborate, which meant that I took the play home and rewrote it from stem to stern, so that *You Can't Do That !*, as it was renamed, is his story and his characters and my dialogue. And it was produced at the Masonic Temple in . .

Day: 1936, I think.

EPG: Anyway, Mr. Roper, former mayor of Edmonton, who would be editor of *The People's Weekly*, put out a special edition that carried the news story described in the play. It was supposed to be the newspaper's coverage of this great experiment in national credit. And as soon as the curtain fell on the end of Act II, newsboys came roaring into the place yelling, "Extra! Extra! Read all about it!" The audience were shocked! They thought the war had broken out!

Day: Marvellous!

EPG: Then we took it around the country. We went to Wetaskiwin. And we went to Fort Saskatchewan. And we went to Springfield, a little community on the way to Lake Wabamun. We usually had a big fight wherever we went because, you see, the play advocates national credit and everywhere we went, we ran into rabid Social Crediters.

Day: Most of the early plays up to that point are very straight.

EPG: Well, this was supposed to be a comedy – and it *did* entertain people. The scene where the cabinet ministers woke up in their sleeping bags was always very funny.

Day: What other literary or dramatic models did you draw on?

EPG: Well, I told you. I was going to write like George Bernard Shaw. *The Last Caveman* is just vaguely Shavian in that it's a comedy about a serious subject – slip them an idea while they're laughing.

But it doesn't work, of course. I don't think Shaw's plays have had any effect, and I don't think it's successful to try to present a theoretical idea on any social question through a play. If you try to be too subtle about it, they miss the point completely. And if you spell it all out in economic language it bores them. People go to the theatre to be entertained, and if they are entertained they like it, and if they are not entertained they . . .

Day: Block it out.

EPG: Yes.

Day: Was the play actually commissioned for the Edmonton Little Theatre season of 1938?

EPG: Yes. It was one of the major plays.

Day: Oh good. Did they pay you for it?

EPG: Yes. Twenty-five dollars. Canadian playwrights had a sort of gentleman's agreement that we would never allow our work to be done without a royalty.

In the first version, Mr. Potter was Mrs. Potter's husband. And I decided it would be more fun [in 1946] to have a young guy who would be courting Miranda, so there would be a little suspense there.

The first production produced a marriage, you know. The two young leads, Alan Macdonald and Mickey Clifton, fell in love and got married. And Alan Macdonald who was playing the hero had a brother who was in the Canadian Peacekeeping force in Cyprus. So every now and then I would phone him up and say, "How's the peacekeeping force getting on?" Direct connection there!

Day: You also talked about . . .

EPG: I was going to say that *The Last Caveman* was done by the Everyman Theatre right across Western Canada and it was done over radio on Stage 51 by Andrew Allan. It was being broadcast while the Dominion Drama Festival was in progress in Calgary, so nobody in the theatre heard it.

Day: How about the Everyman production? How did Sydney Risk come up to pick it up?

EPG: Well, you see, he was working here for the Extension Department. And we became close personal friends. "Uncle Sydney" came for Sunday dinner every Sunday.

Day: Had he seen the original production?

EPG: No, he was just in favor of Canadian plays.

Day: And he asked if you had one?

EPG: Yes. It was very much better, of course, because they were professional kids. They did it in repertory with *The Importance of Being Earnest* and *The Marriage Proposal*. But it was a terrible strenuous thing. When they got here they were absolutely exhausted. They started out in Vancouver in a van and they travelled on the CPR all the way through the mountains.

I saw them in Calgary. In Calgary, they gave up the van and took the train through and across Saskatchewan where they were stopped for 24 hours in a blizzard. They got to Winnipeg, then they came back on the CPR again, and when they got here they were absolutely whacked because of this business of travelling all the time, doing their own scenery – they did their own building and junk. They were worn right out.

Sydney just worked the guts out of them. And he hoped, you know, that they would stay together as a company . . . but of course they didn't. They all went where the work was. The boy who played the surveyor, Murray Westgate, is the ESSO service station man on CBC. And of course, Denzil – played by Ted Follows, the father of the now famous Megan Follows – went to Halifax for awhile and then to Stratford. And the boy who played Howard, Arthur Hill, has gone on to be in the top ranks; he was in the original production of *Who's Afraid of Virginia Wolf* in New York.

Day: Quite a stellar cast!

EPG: Yes. They're all scattered to the winds now.

Day: Even the first production of *Caveman* appears to have been something of a lost opportunity. At the very least, it seems to have opened the door to the kind of Merrill Denison-Hart House Theatre collaboration between a local playwright working with a local theatre. Why was the opportunity missed?

EPG: Because I moved on to CBC! Writing stage plays was an interesting hobby, but the radio play was where the money was. What I liked best about it was that I could sell all my stuff. Dr. Johnson said "Only a fool writes without getting paid." That's where the prestige was, where the audience was. I was pushed into radio work because that's where the market was. That's where there was a demand!

THE LAST CAVEMAN: *FIRST PERFORMANCE*

The Last Caveman was first performed by the Edmonton Little Theatre at the Masonic Temple, 4 February, 1938, under the direction of William R. Wallace with the following cast:

Ben Davy – *Les Pilcher*
Stacia Davy – *Betty Shaw*
Denzil Davy – *Steve McEachern*
John Duncan – *Alan Macdonald*
Miranda Fortescue – *Marguerite Clifton*
Mrs. Potter – *Agnes Bradley*
Howard Potter – *Seymour Bushe*
Jim Bryan – *Harry Conroy*
Herb Johnson – *Jim Richardson*
Bill Sears – *Arthur Martin*
Colonel Hector Fortescue – *E. Maldwyn Jones*

A revised version of *The Last Cavemen* was toured by Everyman Theatre 18 November, 1946, to 17 May, 1947, directed by Sydney Risk with the following cast:

Ben Davy – *David Major*
Stacia Davy – *Esther Nelson* and *Lois McLean*
Denzil Davy – *Ted Follows*
John Duncan – *Floyd Caza*
Miranda Fortescue – *Peggy Hassard* and *Shirley Kerr*
Mrs. Potter – *Esther Nelson* and *Hilda Nual*
Howard Potter – *Andrew Johnston* and *Arthur Hill*
Jim Bryan – *Murray Westgate* and *Ronald Rosvold*
Herb Johnson – *Murray Westgate*
Bill Sears – *Edward McNamara*
Colonel Hector Fortescue – *Drew Thompson* and *Sydney Risk*

THE LAST CAVEMAN

Characters:

Ben Davy, a fisherman-farmer
Stacia Davy, Ben Davy's wife
Denzil Davy, Ben and Stacia's son, about 17, but none too
    bright
John Duncan, a veteran, about 32
Miranda Fortescue, about 25, poised, thoughtful
Mrs. Potter, a fluttery matron, fair and fortyish
Howard Potter, a young businessman, Rotarian
Jim Bryan, a young engineering student on survey
Herb Johnson, a hard-boiled surveyor
Bill Sears, the local big-shot of a small village
Colonel Hector Fortescue, OBE, DSO

Setting:

Time:
1946.

Place:
Lake Minnetaska, Alberta.

ACT I

SCENE 1

The clearing in front of Ben Davy's shack, just back from the shore of Lake Minnetaska. A crude pole fence runs across the back of the clearing, but the bars of the gate are down. There are a rough table and broken chair on the right, towards the house (which is out of sight). A few nondescript boxes and old "broody coops" clutter up the yard.
 Mr. and Mrs. Ben Davy come through the gate carrying a fish net which they drape along the fence to dry. Davy is a sturdy man between 50 and 60, cheerful, independent. His wife is shapeless and vigorous, with very few teeth. Both have traces of Somerset in their speech.

Davy: Eh, that's a great hole, Ma. Happen a whale went by.

Mrs. Davy: Be there whales in the lake, Ben?

Davy: *Hopefully.* Never saw none yet, Ma.

Mrs. Davy: Don't ye get swallowed then.

Davy: Book says Jonah came up again.

Mrs. Davy: I wouldn't be tempting the Lord twice, Ben!
 Calling. Denzil . . . Denzil!

Denzil: *From the left.* Coming, Ma. I'm coming.

Mrs. Davy: Hurry, then.

Denzil appears from beyond the gate. A thin, weedy boy, he might be anywhere from 15 to 18. He wears dirty overalls, a battered felt hat, enormous boots, and carries a gutted fish.

Mrs. Davy: Did you clean the fish?

Denzil: Sure. I cleaned it good, Ma. *With satisfaction.* It
  was a female.

Mrs. Davy: You mind your language. Put her in water and come help your Pa with the net.

Denzil: Okay, Ma.

They fall quietly to work. Mrs. Davy mends an old coat at the table. Denzil, when he comes back, helps mend the net with string. Ben begins humming "In the Sweet Bye and Bye."

Mrs. Davy: *Taking it up.*

We shall meet on the beautiful shore.

All: In the sweet . . .

Davy: In the sweet . . .

All: Bye and Bye . . .

Denzil: Bye and Bye . . .

All: We shall meet on the bee-yew-ti-ful shore!

Mrs. Davy: You got a real nice voice, Ben.

Davy: Guess I ain't no opry singer, Ma.

Denzil: Bet you could of been if you'd wanted to, eh Pa?

Davy: Never thought on it, Denzil, never thought on it.

Denzil: What's an opry, Pa? Did you ever see one?

Davy: Sure, I seen one, time I went up to London with my father, when I was a young lad. Kind of play acting it was, but nought was said plain-like. It war all singing and shouting and hollering, and fiddles drowning the singing out. There war a devil in it, too.

Denzil: A real devil, Pa?

Davy: I doubt he war an imitation, Denzil. But he war surely a good singer. They couldn't drown *him* out.

Denzil: I guess you seen about everything, ain't you, Pa?

Davy: Well, I don't say I seen everything, but I been a traveller. I seen a dancing bear in Tolpuddle once, and I seen the Rocky Mountains, and the Atlantic Ocean. That's a lot of water, ain't it, Ma?

Denzil: More water'n our lake?

Mrs. Davy: What with fog and stormy seas, we was sailing for seven days and nights, Denzil.

Denzil: Gosh, I wisht I'd been there.

John Duncan comes down the path through the gate. John is about 32, well built, with a restless what-the-hell look about him. He wears dirty pants, and an old khaki shirt with sleeves rolled up. He carries a tiny bucket.

Davy: Good day, Johnny.

John: Afternoon. How's the fishing?

Mrs. Davy: The fishing's naught to do with you, Mr. Duncan. Must you cry fishing from the top of the hill?

John: Hey . . . I'm sorry! *Grins.* I'll swear your nets have been out of the water since Friday.

Davy: It's a cruel shame to tell a man he can fish one day a week, and his belly aching with hunger and the fish out there jumping up to laugh at him.

John: *Sits down and starts rolling a cigarette.* Well . . . that's the law . . .

Davy: "Law!" *Spits.* It's what they call "conserving the

159

natural resources." What about human beings? Ain't we natural resources, too?

Mrs. Davy: That's right, Ben. Us tries to be natural.

Davy: License for fishing, license for listening, license for carrying . . . it'll soon be a man can't – a man can't do a damn thing in this country without a license.

Mrs. Davy: *Taking up John's pail.* The chickens lays every day. That's one thing they can't stop. Will a dozen be right, Johnny?

John: Yes, fine; thanks.

Mrs. Davy goes out towards the house.

Davy: How's the book getting on, Johnny?

John: That's a long story.

Denzil: I can read. I been in the fourth grade.

John: Good for you, Denzil. I'll remember that.

Denzil: What's it going to be about, hunh?

John: *Taking a while to answer.* Oh . . . cops and robbers.

Davy: *Hesitating.* Ah . . . Joe Lambert up to the g'rage is looking for a handy man.

John: That's all right, Davy, I don't want a job.

Davy: No harm in mentioning it . . .

John: Sure, sure.

Davy: And Joe's boy, that was in the Navy, *he's* buying a farm with what the gov'ment paid him . . .

John: All the soldiers settling down to raise a crop of mortgages. Isn't that just dandy. *He gets up, strolls towards the house.* Nice patch of corn you got there.

Davy: Aye, it's doing fine. Us be real proud of that garden. There's a sight of work and sweat gone into that patch of ground.

John: How long you been on this place, Davy?

Davy: Twenty years come next March . . .

John: Weren't planning to sell, were you?

Davy: Sell our place? No!

Mrs. Davy has come in with the egg pail. She stops dead at John's question.

Mrs. Davy: Us'll never sell this place!

John: *Surprised at their vehemence.* Okay, okay . . . I guess I got it wrong.

They still look at him.

Something I heard in the beer parlor at Gainford last night.

Mrs. Davy: *Belligerent.* Who was talking about we at Gainford?

John: A surveyor – Johnson, I think his name was. He must have meant some other part of the lakeshore.

Davy: And what did he say?

John: Look . . . the guy had had five beers . . . what does it matter?

Davy: Us be asking you . . . what did he say?

John: Oh, he was talking about surveying a road through and building cottages somewhere . . .

Davy: Sears came smelling around about this land, year before the war.

Mrs. Davy: And he don't get it away from we!

John: Okay, if you don't want to sell, that's the end of it.

Davy: Happen it might not be. That Sears . . . he's a slippery customer.

John: *To Mrs. Davy.* How much? *He takes the eggs.*

Mrs. Davy: Eggs is 25. I put in a bit of Devonshire cream that's a present, and no charge.

John: Devonshire cream! Man, that's more'n I got in Devon . . .

Davy: *Eagerly.* Was you in Somerset? Lulcambe?

John: I spent a leave in the west country, when we were at Salisbury. Lulcambe – there's a pub there called the . . . the Drowning Man . . .

Davy: The Drowning Man! Many a pint of ale I've had at the Drowning Man when I was a young lad. That was many a year ago. Happen they've forgot Ben Davy in Lulcambe . . .

Mrs. Davy: It's a rare place, Somerset, when the hedges is white . . .

John: Why did you leave England, Ben?

Davy: *Slowly.* The reason I left England was to be my own man. In Lulcambe I was Squire's man. Live in Squire's cottage and plow Squire's field. Me and Ma had been married seven years then, ain't that right, Stacia?

Mrs. Davy: Seven year, Ben.

Davy: One day in Lulcambe post office I saw a picture the railway company put up. It was a picture of a yellow corn field. That's wheat, we call it now . . . and a house and two young 'uns riding a white horse down a field. "Come to Canada," it says. "Come to Canada and own your own farm." Well, me and Stacia looked at that picture for a long time. Every day for maybe six months we'd go into the post office and look at the house with the red roof.

Mrs. Davy: And them two young 'uns riding down the field . . .

Davy: End of it was, we sold our cows and bits of furniture – took ship and come.

John: Right here to Minnetaska?

Davy: No, we was on a homestead, north of Beaver Lake, them first years. It couldn't have been where the man painted that picture. Terrible lot of bush there was up there, and muskeg. I wasn't so handy building with logs as I was when we put up this place . . . and it was cold in the winters. That was when we lost Denzil's brother Albert and his little sister Gwladys. After that Ma didn't have no heart to stay on the homestead and we moved down here to this lake. And here we be, ever since.

John: All right. Don't sell it. Who wants a bunch of cottages – damn people all dressed up and civilized . . .

Mrs. Davy: Dressed up! They city people don't wear no clothes at all, you might say – running round blistering the hide off their selves. Even Colonel Fortescue, at his age.

John: *Interested.* Fortescue? Does he come out here?

Davy: That's his cottage at the end of the point – the little one with the flag pole . . .

Denzil: And the fancy fence around the backhouse.

Mrs. Davy: Denzil! You mind your manners!

John: Where's that dog of yours, Denzil?

Denzil: Tiger? We ain't seen him for five days.

John: What happened? Somebody took a shot at him?

Davy: Not that us knows of.

Denzil: Best dog I ever had. Bite the hand off a strange guy, quick as look at him.

John: *Drily.* Yeah, well . . . so long . . . *Starts to go.*

Denzil: G'bye, Johnny. . . .

John: Bring the milk down in the morning, will you?

Mrs. Davy: Denzil will fetch it. Good-bye. . . .

John: *Turning.* G'bye – thanks for the cream. *He goes.*

Mrs. Davy: *Looking after him.* Something be the matter with that boy. Reminds me of that barred rock hen that never knew if her was broody or if her wasn't . . .

Denzil: Aw, he's a bum.

Mrs. Davy: He was a captain in the army, wasn't he? I heard tell he won a medal . . .

Denzil: Any guy that lives like he does is a bum.

Davy: *Who has been sitting quietly.* Stacia . . .

Mrs. Davy: Yes, Ben . . .

Davy: We ain't never had a white horse. All the horses we had was kind of brown.

Mrs. Davy: They was good horses to work, Ben.

Davy: That's true. *Pause.* You bain't sorry we come from Lulcambe, be you, Ma?

Mrs. Davy: I bain't sorry. Us have had a interesting voyage. *Pause.* Her'd be . . . 25 years old, now.

Denzil: Who would, Ma?

Mrs. Davy: Your sister Gwladys. Her'd be a nice looking young lady. Maybe her'd took after your Pa's sister Jennie. Her had curly hair, too. . . .

Davy: *Suddenly intense.* Ma!

Mrs. Davy: Yes, Ben?

Davy: Something's come into my mind . . .

Denzil: Gee whiz, Pa!

Davy: Joe Lambert told me he seen two surveyors in Gainford, day before yesterday. And what Johnny heard about cottages . . . and the dog being gone – Bill Sears is trying to get this land!

Mrs. Davy: Ben!

Davy: That was his game afore – trying to prove the line of 53 runs west of my stakes. And the dog – that'd be the first step. Bill Sears knows no sneaking surveyor'd cross that fence without Tiger'd chew his leg off . . .

Denzil: *Excited and mystified.* Where's Tiger at, Pa?

Davy: He could be poisoned, Denzil. . . .

Denzil: Who done it?

Davy: Happen it were Bill Sears. . . .

Denzil: Well, the dirty bastard . . . !

Mrs. Davy: *Slapping him across the mouth.* Stop that! Us be going to fight, yes . . . but us be going to fight clean!

The two elder Davys stand shoulder to shoulder in an attitude of defiance as the lights dim and the curtain falls.

SCENE 2

As the curtain rises and the lights go up, we are looking at another part of the lakeshore, outside the present home of John Duncan. His shack, part cabin and part dug-out, is just out of sight on our left.

With his typewriter on an applebox, another up-ended box stacked with papers, John is trying to work, but not making much progress. He stops, lights a cigarette, gets up, and walks over to scowl at the lake. He comes back and scowls at the page in the typewriter.

Denzil Davy comes up the shore path on the right. He carries a quart bottle of milk and a small dead animal.

Denzil: Hi, Johnny.

John: Hello, Denzil. *He doesn't look up.*

Denzil: I brung the milk.

John: Good. Stick it in the creek, will you.

Denzil goes out to the left and comes back shortly without the milk.

John begins stabbing at the machine.

Denzil: I can write, too, but I don't need no machine. *He gets no answer and edges closer.* I got a boil on the back of my neck. It only come this morning

John pays no heed. Denzil gets very close.

I found this here gopher in a trap this morning, and I scrunched him with a stone. He just went *Eeeeeek!* an' then he died.

John: *Tense.* My god, isn't there enough pain in the world, without . . . *He looks at Denzil and realizes it is no use.*

Denzil: *Cheerfully.* I got four gophers last week an' two squirrels and one skunk.

John: That I can believe.

Denzil: And yesterday I got a meadow lark with my slingshot. Zing! Right on the head, first try.

John: Look, Denzil . . . didn't they teach you in the fourth grade to be kind to dumb animals?

Denzil: Aw, sure. Teacher was always talking about "Our feathered friends" and "Our little brown brothers of the woods." But heck, she was crazy. She didn't know nothing. That's why I quit school.

John: But what's the idea, anyway, murdering things . . . ?

Denzil: Well, gosh, it's right to kill gophers. They eat Pa's pertatoes and cabbages.

John: And the meadow lark?

Denzil: *Squirming.* Well . . . it'd took me all morning fixin'

167

the sling shot, and I had to see if it'd aim straight. *Whips the slingshot out of his back pocket.* Look it here. Ain't it a dandy, tho'?

John: *Flexing it.* Not a bad job. "A sling and a stone. With this weapon David slew Goliath. . . . "

Denzil: *Grabbing it.* He did not . . . this is brand new! *Importantly.* We're going to need this at our place pretty soon. I'm going to use it on something bigger than a meadow lark. Zing! Right on the ear! Pa and Ma are fixing a pile of rocks by our place right now.

John: Pile of rocks?

Denzil: And Pa's getting the shotgun oiled. We're getting ready. Just let that dirty double-crossing Bill Sears come around – he'll find out!

John: Denzil, I think you're crazy with the heat. Go take a jump in the lake.

Denzil: Who, me? Say, I got more sense than that! There's a sea-serpent in that lake. I seen it. Maybe you don't believe that.

John: Sure I believe it . . . every word you say. Now for the love of Pete, scram out of here. . . .

Denzil: You mean you don't want to talk no more?

John: That's the idea, chum.

Denzil: A'right, I was just going. G'bye, Johnny.

John: So long, sargeant.

Denzil goes.
 John pecks out a few words.
 Denzil returns.

Denzil: Don't blame me if you're swimming out there and it bites off your leg!

John: *What?*

Denzil: The sea serpent.

John: Get out!

Denzil goes.

Damn that boy. *John tries to work in grim earnest.*

A girl appears on the shore path. She is slight and blonde, wearing attractive but practical camp clothes. Her manner is cool, composed, but friendly. She is very clean. In a lull in the typing, she comes along the path, looking out at the lake. A clatter of typing takes her by surprise.

Miranda: *Turning.* Oh . . . !

John: *Not looking up.* I told you to get the hell out of here.

Miranda: Did you?

John: *Whirling.* Eh? – *Taking her in.* Well!

Miranda: I'm sorry . . .

John: *Turning back to work. Her clean poised look irritates him, conscious of his own unshaven chin.* It's all right. You're not trespassing. There's a public right of way along the shore.

Miranda: *Demurely.* Thank you. *She sees the cabin.* Oh! You've fixed up the cave!

John: *Grimly.* Yes. Isn't it cute?

Miranda: Howard and I used to play Indians in that dug-out.

John: I live here.

Miranda: Why not? The McGreevey's never *used* it for a chicken house.

John: *Startled.* Chicken house!

Miranda: That's what they made it for . . . cut out the bank and put those logs in front. But they lost the place for taxes, and moved away. Are you squatting?

John: Am I what?

Miranda: Are you squatting, or did you buy the place?

John: I'm renting from the municipality.

Miranda: That's nice. That makes you legitimate, doesn't it? *She starts to go.*

John: *In spite of himself, he yields to a need to talk to her. Getting up.* Ah . . . what's your hurry? Have a cigarette.

Miranda: No thanks.

John: *Takes it as a rebuff.* Sorry. Haven't any tailormades.

Miranda: I don't smoke.

John: You weren't in the services.

Miranda: No. *Smiles. She senses his loneliness.* What's the book about?

John: Who told you?

Miranda: Oh, I read the evidence. Young veteran, with a book in his system, finds a quiet place and digs himself in . . .

John: Where he can live on jackfish, boiled nettles, and spam. Correct, up to a point.

Miranda: Well?

John: That was some time ago. Now I know there won't be any book. *Harshly.* Go on, say it!

Miranda: Say what?

John: *Gushy.* "Oh, that's too bad. I'm sure it's very interesting."

Miranda: *Drily.* I think you've been eating too many jackfish.

John: I guess you're right at that. *Grins.* My name's Duncan . . . make it Johnny. What's yours?

Miranda: Miranda . . .

John: Come again?

Miranda: My name is Miranda. My parents saw *The Tempest* on their honeymoon.

John: *The Tempest.* That's the one where somebody says "Oh brave new world.". . . !

Miranda: Yes.

John: *With irony.* "Oh brave new world." *He goes and stares out at the lake.* My book was about the federation of mankind.

Miranda: *Quietly.* I'm listening.

John: The rule of law among nations and the control of armed force.

Miranda: By a league?

John: The League was a first attempt, but it sidestepped a fundamental cause of war.

Miranda: Which is?

John: Which is the obsolete idiocy of dividing one world into seventy bits and giving each the right – the divine right, mind you – to start shooting.

Miranda: In other words – national sovereignty.

John: *He nods.* I got the idea going back from Dieppe. I thought maybe enough men had died. Bravely. Needlessly. Oh, there's plenty of books, but not one written by and for the Joe on the landing barge. Why we get a job like that and why our fathers got it, and how we could change the pitch for our sons. Those of us who had any sons. *A pause. He moves.* I took a pretty good degree in law in '39 . . never practiced . . . figured on the foreign service. Well, I got a bellyful of foreign service. Five years army and six months occupation. But I thought – maybe we'll get it this time – law and decency. I kidded myself. The Atlantic Charter – San Francisco – the UNO – and maybe the book was the one thing I could give . . . *He makes a savage gesture.* Then I got back and I woke up. Nothing had changed. People forget. They want to forget. They talk peace but they won't give up the junk that stands in the way. They don't want to think. Don't want to fight for a new world. What scares me is that I don't want to fight myself any more. I turn on the radio and the greed and hate that come squawking out of it makes me sick to my stomach. I don't give a damn any more about the human race. I'm not even telling it to go to hell. It's doing that of its own accord. But fast.

There is a pause. Miranda too comes to look across the water.

Miranda: You see that cliff on the west shore?

John: Want me to chuck myself off it?

Miranda: That cliff looks mighty permanent. But it lay under water for ten thousand years – until one day deep rocks moved, and the face of the earth was changed.

John: I am not impressed by examples from evolution.

Miranda: Isn't that what your idea is – evolution? Caveman to tribe to city to nation state to one world . . .

John: What kind of a girl are you anyway?

Miranda: That's not what we're discussing at the moment.

John: And what did you come around here for?

Miranda: To make up my mind about something.

John: I'll say this for life in Europe. It simplified the woman problem.

Miranda: In what way?

John: If you can't speak a woman's language, you don't bother to talk to her. You cut the intellectual chit-chat, and kiss her first. Then if you don't get your face slapped . . .

Miranda: *Quite pleasantly.* And if you do get your face slapped? *She moves away.* I didn't fight in the war, Johnny. I was drafted to teach other students, because it seems we needed engineers and they had to know some geology. But I've studied how the earth was made. I know the story of mankind. And I believe in life and its

173

power to renew itself. I honestly think what you have here may be the next chapter . . .

John: *Forgetting himself, explodes into enthusiasm.* It's got to be the next chapter. It's one world or no world! All I'm asking is to get on with the inevitable.

Miranda: Who was going to publish this book – if you *had* written it?

John: I sent McDougall's the first six chapters. No dice.

Miranda: Did you try Fortescue?

John: That old fire-eater? He made a speech to our OTC once. Been in three wars and enjoyed them.

Miranda: He's a smart publisher.

John: Last man on earth to back this book. He believes that war is good for a nation. "Brings out the best that's in them, by God."

Miranda: To do him justice, he hasn't said that since 1940.

John: I hear he has a house out there on the point.

Miranda: Yes. Come tonight and I'll introduce you.

John: Hey . . . you sound as if you knew the old turkey buzzard.

Miranda: I do know him. He's my father.

John: But I've *seen* the man. It can't be true . . .

Miranda: We have documents to prove it, and our fingernails are identical.

John: Well, I'm not taking back a word. . . .

Miranda: You don't have to. But there's law and order in the family, too. My grandfather marched across the prairie in a scarlet coat when the West was young.

John: How did the old – how did the colonel ever get mixed up with books?

Miranda: My Uncle Thomas left them in his will. When he died, fifteen years ago, Father came back from the Peace River country and ran the company as if it were a regiment. He just might publish your book . . . the struggle would be to get him to *read* it.

John: *Grabbing her arms, rather roughly.* Don't give me a line! You think it has a chance? On the level. . . .

Miranda: On the level, I think it has.

John: *Still holding her.* And what did you come over here to make up your mind about?

Before she can answer, a clear soprano is heard from the shore path, singing the "Indian Love Call" from "Rose Marie."

Oh damn that woman!

Miranda: Who is it?

John: Mrs. Potter . . . can't you tell? She sneaked up on me one day it was 90 in the shade. Since then, she *sings*.

Mrs. Potter: *Off.* Captain Duncan . . . Oh, Captain Duncan.

John: Hello?

Miranda: *Sotto voce.* "Captain" she says!

Mrs. Potter: May I come in? *She appears on the path, a fluttery lady in her early forties.* Oh, good morning!

And Miranda dear – this is a pleasant surprise!

Miranda: Yes. I came down last night.

Mrs. Potter: And you know this interesting man. . . .

Miranda: Oh yes, we're old college friends.

John gapes.

Mrs. Potter: *Isn't* that lovely! There's nobody understands us like the people we went to school with, I always say. Isn't the lake perfectly beautiful this morning – so calm, so still, so unutterably peaceful. It must be a great inspiration in your work.

John: Terrific.

Mrs. Potter: Howard and I have been down to the village and I brought up your mail. Just this paper.

John: Thanks.

Mrs. Potter: Not that there's anything very pleasant in it. Strikes, and those men fighting over the peace conference, and that dreadful famine in Europe. We heard something about it on the radio last night – quite by accident of course. We were trying to get the Kelly Soup Program, and really, it made me feel quite upset. I mean, it's not as if there were anything more we could do. . . .

John: *Grimly, to Miranda.* In 1946 already yet.

Mrs. Potter: *By the path.* I wonder what can be keeping Howard. He went down to Davy's for the vegetables. Captain Duncan, you'll have supper with us this evening, won't you?

Miranda: Sorry, he's dated up. I asked him first.

John: Hey . . . did I promise . . . ?

Mrs. Potter: Oh, you'll get a good dinner at Miranda's. You may not think it to look at her, but she's a very good cook, besides being a doctor of genealogy.

Miranda: Geology, Mrs. Potter. Genealogy is family trees.

Mrs. Potter: Is it really? Well I wish you'd take a look at the trees at our house in town. The best nursery stock, and the way they die off is a scandal.

Miranda: *With mischief.* Are you doing any writing just now, Mrs. Potter?

Mrs. Potter: Nothing to speak of . . .

Miranda: Mrs. Potter is a highly successful poet. She comes out in all the women's magazines.

Mrs. Potter: *With a gay laugh.* Oh I don't suppose Captain Duncan ever reads them, Miranda. Just a few simple, homely little thoughts. . . . *Calling.* How-ard!

Howard: *Off.* Be right there.

Howard Potter comes along the path. He is a tall, fairly good looking boy, with a pleasant charm of manner, very little concerned about anything but himself, his job and his golf score. His slacks, sports shirt and ascot scarf make John irritatingly conscious of his own dirty trousers.

Mrs. Potter: You remember my nephew . . . He was out on the 24th of May. . . .

John: Yes, of course. . . .

Howard: Hello, Duncan . . . *Sees Miranda and is very delighted.* Well . . . how do you do? I didn't expect you till tomorrow.

Miranda: *Smiling slightly.* It was too hot in town. . . .

Howard: Plenty hot out here. Don't know why we can't get a road along this shore.

Mrs. Potter: The Colonel should speak to the government, Miranda.

Miranda: Father doesn't want a road. He says he comes out here for peace and quiet.

Howard: Well, that's darn selfish of him. Packing stuff along that track is killing me.

Mrs. Potter: Now, Howie, you know you walk further than that playing a round of golf.

Howard: What's going on down there at the Davy place, anyway? I went in for the potatoes. That half-witted boy yelled "Stay back of that fence" and nearly took my ear off with a sling shot.

John: The Davys seem to think there's dirty work at the crossroads.

Miranda: Oh?

John: They've got it in their heads Bill Sears is trying to pinch the farm.

Miranda: I wouldn't be surprised. Bill Sears is a crook.

Mrs. Potter: Oh, Miranda!

Howard: The post-master? Smart business man, I'd say. I guess he owns half the village now.

Miranda: And how did he get it? By giving credit in the Depression and foreclosing when they couldn't pay.

John: *Dryly.* Nice fella.

Howard: It wouldn't hurt if somebody cleaned up the lakeshore and built some neat cottages.

John: But dammit, that's the Davys' *home*. They don't want to sell.

Howard: Did you see their title deed? Poor white trash like that . . . probably squatting on the land . . .

Miranda: The Davys are not poor white trash!

Howard: What would you call them . . . God's chosen people?

Miranda: They're crazy . . . but I love them. *Smiles.* Denzil believes the heat wave will get you if you walk down the track at night. They're like something left over from primitive times. . . .

Howard: You said it. Before the invention of soap and water. Well, let's go. I don't want to miss the World Series. *To John.* I got a bet on the Cards to take New York. You coming, beautiful?

Miranda: My canoe's on the beach. But I can't take you. She leaks.

Howard: Too bad. Can't have Aunt Edna getting her . . . feet wet.

Mrs. Potter: Perhaps you'll come to supper some night next week, Captain.

John: Thank you very much.

Mrs. Potter: Howard will be fishing and we'll have some nice jackfish. Well, good-bye . . .

Miranda: Bet I beat you home!

Howard: I'll take that. *Looks at the lake.* The wind's against you. *To John.* Come over if you feel like sailing, Duncan.

John: Thanks. So long. *The Potters leave. John is standing tense, holding in his anger.* Those kind of people! It's those kind of people we're up against, kid. Soft. Selfish. Cushioned by their little bit of money and security. Mrs. Henry B. Potter . . . sticks her head in the sand and listens to the Kelly Soup programs. If she ever looked a fact in the face, she'd faint dead away. And that darn glamour boy . . . uses the right kind of shaving soap and keeps his pants pressed. He'd push the Davys in the lake and call it smart business . . .

Miranda: What do you care? You're through fighting for anybody.

John: *Suddenly remembering how Howard looked at her.* My god in heaven . . . he's not mixed up in your life?

Miranda: I expect you for supper at half past six. Wear a clean shirt, if you have one. Good-bye. *She goes.*

John: Miranda . . . *He stares after her.* Hey, Miranda –

Miranda by now is launching her canoe. She waves. He grins and answers with a wave gives a salute, then his face hardens. He comes back to the typewriter.

Mrs. Potter writes poetry, does she? She gets it published, does she? *He shoves paper in and types a heading. Remembering –*

"Deep rocks moved and the face of the earth was changed – "

He begins to type furiously, as the lights dim and the curtain comes down.

ACT II

The Davy place. The bars of the gate are up. There is a pile of rocks roughly the size of baseballs a little way inside the gate.

Mrs. Davy and Miranda come slowly in from the direction of the house. Mrs. Davy has a club, which she lays down on the rickety table. Miranda carries a paper bag, probably full of lettuce. She looks worried and annoyed.

Mrs. Davy: That's how it's been, Miranda, this whole week past. No work done, no fishing done. Him sitting here with the shotgun, like Sir Francis Drake on a monyimint, waiting for the Spanish Armada.

Miranda: I wish Mr. Davy would talk to Father. He was a magistrate in the North country.

Mrs. Davy: Eh, ye know what a man is when he's made up his mind. *With a look at her.* Or maybe ye don't know . . . yet.

Miranda: *Ignoring this.* You've worked so hard on this place. It used to be nothing but bush and slough from here to the lake. . . .

Mrs. Davy: It bain't much of a house . . . but it's all us has.

Miranda: Remember the day I fell off the roof and cut my knee open – and Mr. Davy carried me home. . . .

Mrs. Davy: *Laughing.* Eh, what a child ye were for climbing and jumping!

John appears suddenly behind the gate. He looks cleaner than when we saw him last. He carries a flat parcel, his manuscript.

John: Too bad she's changed, eh Mrs. Davy? *He looks at the*

181

gate. Hey, what's this, the Maginot line? *He leaps over it.*

Mrs. Davy: Bless me, Johnny, you came down that road quietly. . . .

John: Tomorrow I'll fire two rounds and send up a flare. No – I've been trying for a week to get this woman to climb up to the cliff with me – but will she go . . . ?

Mrs. Davy: No girl hereabouts walks up there with a man unless she's certain sure what she be going to say to him. They must come back to-gether – there's no path down the other side. Did ye see Ben on the track?

John: No.

Mrs. Davy: Happen they're down at the shore. He told me to watch this gate, but now there's two of ye, I'll go get my bread out of the oven.

John: What are we watching for?

Mrs. Davy: Any strange body.

John: Or the sea-serpent! Sure, we'll put salt on his tail.

Mrs. Davy goes off to the house.
When they are left alone there is evident tension between John and Miranda.

John: Hello.

Miranda: Hello.

John: I finished it. *Hands her the parcel.*

Miranda: Swell!

John: Typed the last chapter by candlelight. It was as good a way to waste an evening as any other. So that's why the gal won't go up the cliff with me. She's not certain what she's going to say –

Miranda: Are you and I sure about anything?

John: Yes, I am. I'm sure that nothing's changed since last Friday. The world's evil is no less. Man has still no comfort on the face of the earth. And yet when I'm with you . . . God, I want to believe that life could have some sort of meaning. Some beauty or dignity. . . .

Miranda: Why won't you believe it?

John: *Harshly.* Maybe it's the wrong setting. Look at this layout. Poverty. Ignorance. *He shakes the gate.* They're gunning for trouble all right.

Miranda: Well, why don't you help them?

John: Who – me?

Miranda: Davy likes you. He'd listen to you.

John: Thanks. I'm not sticking my neck out.

Miranda: Well, let's go talk to Bill Sears – find out what's back of it.

John: As if he'd tell us.

Miranda: *Turning away.* You're still all twisted inside, aren't you?

John: *With light bitterness.* Can't get rehabilitated. That's my trouble. They say there's nothing like the love of a good woman. . . .

Miranda: You finished the book. You did the one thing you could do to help "the world's evil." And it's good! But writing it hasn't helped you – because somewhere along the line you stopped believing in people – or liking them. Even the Joe on the landing barge . . . you don't really care about him. . . .

John: So Davy is Joe at the moment, is he?

Miranda: He could be. And you . . . *She hesitates.* You don't trust your feelings for me . . .

John: What would a nice little girl like you know about that?

Miranda: I know it didn't happen just because there's been a moon this week. It's more important than that. Or it could be – if you'd let it.

John: *Sincerely.* Miranda – for God's sake – I haven't anything . . .

Miranda: You've got courage. Or I thought you had. Some men came back from war with nothing inside their minds but a dreadful emptiness.

John: *Quickly.* Who, for instance?

Miranda: They threw away that whole experience. They won't think about it. They burrow down into their jobs and good times and pull the covers over their heads. But you were angry. And there's hope in your anger. Maybe it's the only hope we've got. And I could help you – if you didn't shut yourself away. If you'd come alive . . .

John: Now listen, my girl . . .

Davy and Denzil can be heard on the path.

Denzil: *Off.* Sure, I can carry it, Pa.

Mrs. Davy comes in quickly and takes up her club.

Mrs. Davy: Pa and Denzil is coming.

Miranda: I'm going. And Father's going to see this, Johnny.

John: He'll never publish it.

Miranda: Maybe not. But he'll look at it, if I have to feed it to him in his porridge! Look Mrs. Davy – I can still climb – when I want to! *She makes a neat job of the gate, and whips off down the path, turning to the right.*

Mrs. Davy: *Looking after her.* Eh, times have changed, since my young days.

John: Have they?

Mrs. Davy: I had two children, afore I was Miranda's age. But now that Howard's home and settled, happen it may be soon. *She takes up guard with her club.* Remember – us has been here constantly.

Davy and Denzil come along the path. Denzil carries a large stone. Davy has half a dozen more rolled in a gunny sack. Davy is very chirpy. He has an air of excited expectancy.

Davy: Well, Stacia . . .

Mrs. Davy: Well, Ben. Not a soul been by, except Miranda and Johnny here.

Davy puts down his stones, takes down the bars one by one. He and Denzil come through, and Davy puts the bars up again.

Denzil: Look what I brung, Ma.

Mrs. Davy: Eh, that's a purty one, Denzil.

Denzil: Think us can hoist it, Ma?

Mrs. Davy: Us'll have a try, Denzil. Us'll have a try.

The rock is added to the pile.

Davy: Well, Johnny – we hasn't seen you since many a day.

John: No. I've been sticking to my knitting. *Flips a coin to Denzil.* Here's the two bits for packing the milk.

Denzil: Gee, thanks.

Davy: Get the gun, Denzil.

Denzil: *Skipping out.* Yes, Pa!

Mrs. Davy: You'll have that gun wore out a-cleaning it, Ben.

Davy: Pooh – women doesn't understand fire-arms. Does they Johnny?

John: *Who is lounging against a box, rolling a cigarette.* Nope. Fundamental principle, Mrs. Davy – the artillery must be in perfect shape.

Davy: I know what I'm doing. I met Len Walters by the fish house this morning. Told me them two surveyors was in the post office last night. One old fellow and one young, kind of green, Len says.

Mrs. Davy: Well, us be three.

Davy: Aye, us be three. Len heard them say they'd finish the road just this morning, and you know what that signifies. Us be next.

Denzil brings back the shotgun, some oil and a rag.

Denzil: Can I clean her this time, Pa?

Davy: No, Denzil. I'll tend to her myself.

Denzil: *Looking at John with suspicion.* Pa – what about – him?

John: Don't mind me, Denzil. I'm strictly on the fence. *He* *goes and leans against the gate.*

Davy: Johnny knows a man's got to defend his home. That's what he was doing hisself, over in Europe. *To Denzil.* You go to work and fix another sling shot. One you make last week *is* all wore out.

Denzil: Okay! Boy, this'll murder them! *He starts work.*

Davy: *Davy cleans the gun.* Happen us'll get our name in the papers, Ma.

Mrs. Davy: What for, Pa?

Davy: McGreevey's was in when they had trouble about that liquor brewing.

Mrs. Davy: Notoriety is something I never crave for, Ben. *Thinking.* I hope they spells it proper, tho'. "Eustacia." T'aint a common name.

John: *After a glance behind him.* There's somebody coming from the track.

Davy jumps up. Denzil gets behind him.

Denzil: Is it them, Pa, is it them? *They watch.* Naw, it's only that crazy Potter woman.

Mrs. Davy: Don't talk that way about Mrs. Potter, now.

Denzil: Aw, she is too crazy.

Mrs. Davy: A nice kind woman, even if she be ignorant, poor soul.

Denzil: *Falsetto.* "Well, my little man, and how are you today?" She makes me tired.

Mrs. Davy: You mind your manners, now.

Mrs. Potter appears, with a bundle of magazines.

Mrs. Potter: Good afternoon, Mr. Davy!

Davy: Afternoon, ma'am.

He takes down one bar, and after some hesitation Mrs. Potter gets a leg over the other two and comes in.

Mrs. Potter: Thank you. Ah – thank you very much. Hello, Captain Duncan!

John: Hi.

Mrs. Potter: Oh, Mrs. Davy – what a fascinating pile of stones! Don't tell me you're going to make a rock garden?

Mrs Davy: Not persactly . . . we . . .

Mrs. Potter: With dear little creeping plants behind the stones! That will be charming. Well, young man, and how are you to-day?

Denzil: The boil on the back of my neck's getting bigger all the time.

Mrs. Davy: Show Mrs. Potter your boil, Denzil.

Mrs. Potter: *Hastily.* Some other time, some other time . . .

Davy: Didn't see two strange looking fellows on the track now, did you ma'am?

Mrs. Potter: No, Mr. Davy. Are you expecting company?

Davy: That I am.

Mrs. Potter: The hospitality of you country people is just wonderful, I always say. Mrs. Davy – I brought you a few magazines.

Mrs. Davy: *Taking the bundle.* Thank you kindly, I'm sure.

Mrs. Potter: I hope you liked the others I left with you?

Mrs. Davy: Oh yes indeed, papers comes in real handy. The thickest ones Pa used to paste on the chicken house walls –

Denzil: And the thinnest ones we . . .

Mrs. Davy: *Loudly.* Denzil! *To Mrs. Potter.* Yes, indeed, us used them all.

Denzil: Is there any funny papers in the bunch, Ma?

Mrs. Potter: No, Denzil, I'm afraid I don't approve of funny papers. So crude, so ugly. Giving young people such a distorted view of life. But there's a nice story about an Indian legend. Don't you like Indians, Denzil?

Denzil: Naw. All the Indians around here is lousy.

Mrs. Davy: *Firmly.* Take the paper, Denzil.

Denzil: *Reluctant.* Okay. *He takes it.*

John: *Who has been more and more irritated by Mrs. Potter.* Do *you* like Indians, Mrs. Potter?

Mrs. Potter: Well of course! We saw the parade at Banff this summer. So picturesque – so colourful! And their wonderful handicraft – I'm *very* interested.

John: *Savagely.* But do you know conditions among Canadian Indians? Do you know their TB rate – or why, as Denzil says, their children are likely to be lousy?

Mrs. Potter: *Taken aback.* Why, no – no –

John: Why no! It was a good show at Banff, but you don't really give a damn about them –

Mrs. Davy: Johnny! Mrs. Potter is a visitor to we.

John: Excuse me.

Mrs. Potter: *Bright and forgiving.* I did meet Miranda on the path just now. She told me that you had finished your book.

John: Yes.

Mrs. Potter: The Colonel is a very shrewd publisher. He put out such a good murder mystery last year, *The Body in the Beer Keg.*

Davy: Eh, that was a tragic thing.

Mrs. Potter: Did you read it, Mr. Davy?

Davy: Not I. I was thinking on the waste of good beer.

Mrs. Potter: I like a good thriller, I'm afraid. Because – well – there's so much won't stand thinking about in this world, isn't there – but a mystery always comes right in the end. What is your book called, Captain Duncan?

John: If you'll read it, Mrs. Potter, I'll call it "The Case of the Last Caveman."

Mrs. Potter: "The Case of the Last Caveman." Oh, that's very good! Is the Colonel going to publish it?

John: Off hand, I'd say it has as much chance as a snowflake in hell.

Mrs. Potter: That reminds me, I must see Mr. Walters about getting more ice. This hot weather, you know. Are you going that way, Captain Duncan?

John: No, I think I'll walk to the post office. Mrs. Potter, do me a favour, will you? Let's forget the "Captain," eh?

Mrs. Potter: Well of course if you . . . I only mean it as a compliment . . .

John: Yeah, yeah, I know. But I'm back in the ranks now.

Davy: I should think a man'd not want to forget an honour that come to him.

John: *Quietly.* I'll never forget why it came, and when. But let's drop the handle, shall we?

Mrs. Potter: Just as you say, Cap . . . ah, Mr. Duncan. After all if there should be another war – of course, there won't be, but we said that before, didn't we – but if there should – you might eventually be a *general!*

John: God forbid.

Davy has let down a bar and Mrs. Potter struggles over.

Mrs. Potter: Oh, thank you, Mr. Davy. Good-bye – good-bye Denzil.

Denzil: *Glum.* G'bye.

Mrs. Potter goes.

John: Every time I talk to that woman, I feel like shooting either her or myself.

Davy: *Drawing a bead.* Her back view makes a damn good target –

Denzil: Go on, Pop, shoot one off! Shoot one off just to scare the pants off her.

John: *Businesslike. Mrs. Potter has annoyed him out of his pose of indifference.* Look, Davy, you're a full grown man. Don't you think you've played with that shotgun long enough?

Davy: And who said I be playing?

John: Sure, sure – you're defending your home. But doing it with a gun won't land you anywhere except in jail.

Davy: They can't jail a man for shooting a thievin' scoundrel. . . .

John: Don't you think they wouldn't. A prosecution for manslaughter is no joke.

Davy: An Englishman's home is his castle. I'm an Englishman, I hope . . .

John: Yeah. But the Battle of Hastings was fought quite some time ago. You own this land, okay. Have you got a title deed?

Davy: *After a pause.* That's my business.

Mrs. Davy: Tell him, Ben. He's a good lad.

Davy: *Slowly.* I bought this piece from old man Jeffries and he give me a receipt, all made out proper.

John: Well, that's good enough! *He sees their glum looks.* Oh. Where is the receipt?

Davy: I figured it was in the tobacco jar with them grocery bills, but it ain't.

Mrs. Davy: I'd of swore it was in the Bible with my marriage lines. But it bain't there.

Denzil: I never seen it.

John: Well . . . where is old man Jeffries?

Mrs. Davy: Us don't know.

Davy: Old man Jeffries is dead.

Denzil: He fell off the cliff one night when he was liquored up and bust his head right open.

John: Listen – I'll be in town some day next week, I'll look up this section in the land titles office. . . .

Davy: Nothing in them books is going to stop a skunk like Bill Sears.

John: Oh for God's sake, use a little sense. . . .

Davy: Did Sears send you down here to cry us off?

John: Don't be a damn fool! It's nothing to me what you do. Only I'm telling you . . .

Denzil: You're a bum. What'd you know about it, anyway?

John: Not very much – but after all, I started out to be a lawyer. . . .

Mrs. Davy: *As if he had uttered an obscenity.* A lawyer! Us never knowed that about you.

Davy: My father always said he'd trust a Cornishman before he'd trust a Welshman. And a Welshman before he'd trust a lawyer. Now get away from here over that fence and keep your thumb out of my affairs.

John: Mrs. Davy – !

Mrs. Davy: You heard what Ben said.

Davy: Go on, git!

John: You're a stubborn, pig-headed fool, Ben Davy, and your own worst enemy. *He jumps the gate.* In fact, you're so darn human I can't help liking you. But remember . . . if that gun goes off . . . I'll have to tell the judge I warned you. So long. *He goes off, whistling a march.*

Mrs. Davy: *Sadly.* A lawyer. And I thought him a clean living lad like any other.

Denzil: He's a bum. I told you, any guy that lives like he does is a bum.

Davy: Don't pay it no mind, Stacia.

Mrs. Davy: Maybe us should take advice in the matter, Ben. The Colonel be gentry. He'd know the way of it. . . .

Davy: I need no gentry nor colonels to teach me my duty. Right is right and no fancy talk can change it. Denzil, come and hold the gun while I go after the cows.

Denzil: *Thrilled.* Can I, Pa?

Mrs. Davy: Denzil could go after the cows.

Davy: I'd rather go myself. I might spy something out. I'll go round by the shore and come back by the track. *He gives Denzil the gun.* You keep watch now.

Denzil: Sure.

Mrs. Davy: I think I seen the cows heading east this morning.

Davy: I'll find 'em. *He goes out past the house.*

Denzil: Ma.

Mrs. Davy: Aye?

Denzil: What does surveyors look like, Ma?

Mrs. Davy: They looks like men for the most part, Denzil.

Denzil: Will I shoot them in the head, Ma, or shoot them in the belly?

Mrs. Davy: Shoot them in the legs. Then they can't run away.

Denzil: I wisht they'd get here while Pa's gone.

Mrs. Davy: I doubt they'll be here before supper. Sun's getting around.

Denzil: What are we going to have for supper, Ma? Fish?

Mrs. Davy: And where would I get a fish, you and your Pa being too busy with they weapons to get out on the lake? There's eggs, and I'll take up some turnips afore the worms gets to them.

Denzil: You could go now, Ma. I'll keep watch.

Mrs. Davy: Maybe I'll do that. Then we can eat when your Pa gets back. *She starts out.* Don't you let no strange body cross that gate!

Denzil: Don't you worry, Ma.

Mrs. Davy goes out toward the house. Denzil has a good time with the gun. He examines it all over, takes out the cartridges, puts them back, looks down the muzzle once or twice, and draws a bead on various points.

Mrs. Davy: *Off, yelling.* Den-zil! Denzil! The pigs is in the garden!

Denzil: *Leaping to his feet.* Will I bring the gun, Ma?

Mrs. Davy: Head 'em off! Run around the house and head them off. They're making for the bush!

Denzil puts down the gun and runs out. From behind the house comes yelling and grunting which fades as the pigs escape into the bush. For a moment the yard is empty.
Herb Johnson and Jim Bryan appear beyond the gate.

195

Herb is about 50, short, weatherbeaten and hard-boiled. Jim is an easy-going youngster of twenty. He carries a surveyor's transit.

Herb: *Pushing back his hat.* There y'are, Jim. That's 53 over beyond them trees.

Jim: Boy, what a lay-out! You mean people *live* in there?

Herb: Sure, that's the Davy place. Swect looking joint, ain't it? They say it's a wonder the house don't get up and walk away. Don't seem to be anybody home.

Jim: There's one of the kids over in the bush. . . .

Herb: There's only one kid and he's only half there, Bill says. Ignorant as hell, the whole outfit. Funny thing, too – they ain't Hunk or Ukes. Some kind of God-forsaken English. Well, guess we'll run a line from here. . . .

Denzil comes tearing around the corner of the house. He sees the men and stops dead, staring, then he rushes out, yelling.

Denzil: Ma! – Ma! They're here! I seen them – Ma!

Jim: Hey, what's the matter with him?

Herb: Aw, don't pay no attention. Gone to tell his mother we're here. Maybe they're going to serve tea. Set up the transit, will you?

Jim: Okay.

The transit is swung over the gate and set up in the yard. While they adjust it, Mrs. Davy rushes in and snatches up the shotgun.

Mrs. Davy: You get out of here! You get back over that fence or I'll shoot you dead!

Herb: Afternoon, Mrs. Davy. My name's Johnson and I'm . . .

Mrs. Davy: I know who ye be and who sent ye here. You get back over that fence, quick.

Denzil: Go, Ma. Shoot 'em! Shoot 'em in the legs!

Herb: All we're trying to do, lady, is . . .

Mrs. Davy: You're trying to get this place away from we!

Herb: Bill Sears hired us to run a line across here to . . .

Mrs. Davy: Well, he ain't running nothing across it. It ain't his land. Ye go back and tell him that.

Herb: Sister, if you'd only listen to reason . . .

Mrs. Davy: Go, git!

Herb: *Shrugs.* You run into this in our business, Jim. Guess we'll wait till the old man gets here.

Mrs. Davy: You take that infernal contraption out of our yard, or us'll knock it into bits!

Herb: Take it out for now, Jim.

The transit is swung back over the gate, Mrs. Davy covering the move with the shotgun.

The surveyors have a short conference and Herb goes off down the road. Mrs. Davy watches this manoeuvre suspiciously.

Mrs. Davy: Denzil –

Denzil: Yes, Ma?

Mrs. Davy: Hold the gun.

197

Denzil: Yes, Ma!

Mrs. Davy: If that young fellow comes across the fence, you shoot, d'ye hear?

Denzil: Bet your life, Ma.

Mrs. Davy: I'm going for your Pa.

She goes out right. Denzil squats on the rock pile, keeping the gun trained on Jim who lounges by the gate. Silence. Jim takes a cigarette. As he reaches out to strike his match on the gate, Denzil waves the gun.

Jim: Take it easy, brother.

Denzil: Don't you make no false moves.

Jim: Okay, bud.

Silence again.

Denzil: Anyway, I ain't your brother.

Jim: Kinda too bad.

Denzil: Why is it too bad?

Jim: If I was, we'd be on the same side of the fence. I could sit down on that box and rest my feet.

Denzil: You can set down on the ground.

Jim: It looks kind of damp right here.

Denzil: All city guys is sissies.

Silence.

What do you want to come round here making trouble for?

Jim: I'm not making any trouble.

Denzil: You are too.

Jim: Did I ask to get mixed up in any war? I need the money or I wouldn't be here.

Silence.

Denzil: What do you need the money for?

Jim: Well if it's any of your business, Superman, I pay my fees at Tech.

Denzil: What's Tech?

Jim: It's a college.

Denzil: I don't need to go to no college. Only sissies go there.

Jim: Get in a rugby game and you'll find out. I broke my leg last fall.

Denzil: I got a boil on the back of my neck.

Jim: *Clicking his tongue ironically.* Tck-tck-tck-tck . . . !

Denzil: Bet it hurts worse'n a busted leg.

Jim: I bet it don't.

Denzil: It does too. It's as big as a mountain.

Silence.

What's that game you were playing?

Jim: Rugby?

Denzil: Yeah. What is it?

Jim: It's a football game.

Denzil: Bet I could play it.

Jim: You gotta know the rules to play it.

Denzil: Why?

Jim: If you don't, the referee takes you off the field. Say, don't you see any movies?

Denzil: No.

Jim: *Studies Denzil.* It's amazing! Well, like I said, the referee is the boss of the game.

Denzil: Do you know the rules?

Jim: Do I? I was quarterback.

Denzil: You could tell them to me now.

Jim: Not from here, I couldn't. Have to sit down and draw lines on the ground.

Denzil: *Denzil considers this; he is tempted.* Ma and Pa might get here.

Jim: There's no harm in drawing lines. Anyway, we could hear them coming.

Denzil: Will you get back of the fence then?

Jim: Damn tooting I will.

Denzil: Okay. *He lays down the gun and carries a box near the gate.*

Jim: Thanks, Bud. *He vaults over, sits down, stretches his legs.* Feels kind of good to sit down. Now, gimme that little stick. *He draws lines on the ground.* Now, here's the playing field. There's a goal at each end. The idea is to get the ball past the other fellow's back line. Catch on?

Denzil: Sure.

Jim: Well, first they kick off in the middle, then they catch the ball and run it back here.

Denzil: Heck, that's easy.

Jim: Yeah, but while you're running the other side tackle. That's how I got my leg broken.

Denzil: *Unimpressed.* Uh-hunh. What's tackle?

Jim: Well now, I'll show you. *He looks round for something to use for a ball, sees Mrs. Davy's gunny sack by the rock pile and starts for it.*

Like a flash Denzil is ahead of him and has snatched the gun.

Denzil: You get back there! You get back . . .

Jim: Now what's biting you?

Denzil: Thought you'd fool me, didn't you? Thought you'd be smart and get the gun.

Jim: Aw, go chase yourself. I gotta have something for a ball. And put that damn gun away. It makes me nervous. *He picks up the gunny sack, wads it together, and ties it round with a bit of string.*

Denzil slowly puts the gun down on the table.

Now, the other guys line up behind the quarterback and he yells out signals, and then passes the ball. When I pass you this, you make a touchdown between the posts, understand?

Denzil: What's a touchdown?

Jim: It's the best play in the game. All you got to do is get the sack over the line and fall on it. Now – get behind me and kind of crouch over. Are you ready?

Denzil: Sure.

Jim: 47 – 23 – 19 – 38 – 52 – Hike!

Denzil gets the sack and whips across the yard and lands on his stomach under the gate.

Denzil: Did I do it? Did I do it?

Jim: *Laughing.* Oh man, if the coach could see this! Okay, we'll do it again, and this time I'll tackle. All set?

Denzil: *Very pleased with himself.* Okay, bud.

Jim: 19 – 38 – 52 – 47 – 23 – Hike!

Denzil starts off, Jim tackles expertly, they land in a heap.

Denzil: *Denzil very astonished and howling.* You lemme up! You get offen me. Ma – Ma!

Jim: That's the game, don't you understand it? Shut up, you dumb kid . . .

While Denzil howls, his parents arrive. Davy takes up the gun. Mrs. Davy beats Jim with her fists.

Mrs. Davy: Get off my boy! You get off my boy.

Jim: Listen, lady, this is all a mistake . . .

Davy: You put your hands up! You put your hands up, young feller, and keep them there.

Denzil: He threw me down! He threw me down and stomped on me!

Mrs. Davy: *Punching him.* Murderer! Murderer!

Jim: I wasn't trying to hurt the kid. I was showing him rugby – it's a game.

Davy: Go on, you get over that fence!

Jim: Don't worry, I'm going –

He vaults the fence, as Herb, Bill Sears and John arrive down the path. Sears is the local big shot. Outwardly smooth and plausible, he is actually quite unscrupulous and enjoys the power he holds over his neighbors.

Sears: Now then, what's going on here?

Davy: You ought to know, Bill Sears, you started this.

Sears: What happened, Jim?

Jim: I was showing Li'l Abner how to play rugby when hell busted loose around the place . . .

Mrs. Davy: Hell's going to keep on busting loose if you don't get away from here quick.

Sears: Now listen, folks, all I want is for the boys here to run a line . . .

Davy: You ain't running nothing on my land! I paid for it in money once and we been paying for it in work and sweat ever since.

Sears: If you paid for it, that can be proved at the proper time. I'm sure it's to the advantage of all of us to know exactly where we stand . . .

Davy: I'm standing in front of a damned swindling scoundrel, and if you move one step I'll shoot ye between the eyes.

John: You're not getting anywhere, Sears. If you're as smart as I think you are, you'll call this whole thing off. . . .

Sears: I'm hiring these men by the day. I'll have the job done now . . .

John: I've stood beside other fellows that talked big like that. Two minutes later they were awfully dead pigeons.

Sears: Are you encouraging these fools to use violence?

John: *Getting sore.* I'm asking somebody to use a little common sense!

Sears: Let me tell you, there's law and order in this country. You young veterans will have to learn we no longer settle our affairs at the point of a gun.

John: Damn right! If you really believe this survey's crooked, lay your information in the proper place.

Sears: I'm satisfied I'm acting for the good of the community.

Herb: Aw, what are we waiting for? I been bluffed before this.

Sears: I refuse to be intimidated. Bryan, take your instrument across . . .

John: Dammit man, leave the thing alone!

Sears: Who do you think you are giving orders? The war's over . . .

John: The war's not over as long as a cheap little Mussolini is walking through the country . . .

Denzil: *With a sudden wail.* My boil! Ma – he busted my boil! *Sobbing with rage he rushes for his slingshot.*

Jim: I wasn't trying to hurt the kid – it's a game –

Davy: *Raising the gun.* Us knows your game. . . .

John: *Jumping into the yard and advancing on Davy.* Davy . . . put that shotgun down . . .

Denzil's stone catches Jim on the ear.

Jim: *Starting for Denzil.* You dirty little so-and-so!

John: Stay out of here!

But it is too late. Herb and Sears follow Jim into the yard and the battle breaks out in real earnest. Jim grabs Denzil, and he falls howling. Mrs. Davy goes for Herb with a club. John tries to wrest the gun from Davy. Davy lets him have it, and goes for Sears with his fists. A blow from Mrs. Davy's club catches John and he goes down. On a scene of active and ruthless warfare, the curtain falls.

ACT III

On another part of the shore, outside the summer cottage of Colonel Hector Fortescue, DSO, OBE. At the back, on our right, is a trellis fence with a few poppies and marigolds growing against it. The little clearing is set out with attractive beach canvas furniture. It is about seven in the evening. Miranda, in a bright summer dress, is sitting composedly in a deck chair. Colonel Fortescue, an active choleric gentleman in his late 60's, is pacing restlessly about. He wears a pair of shorts, an open-necked shirt, and a deep tan. On the table beside Miranda lies John's manuscript, in a bright blue folder.

Miranda: You haven't told me yet why you won't read it.

Colonel: Because I've heard all that poppycock before, that's why. Disarmament – League of Nations –

Miranda: The book isn't about the League of Nations.

Colonel: What is it, then? Brotherly love – sweetness and light – the drivel we get from that female next door?

Miranda: Careful! She may be on the porch.

Colonel: No, she's not. *Looks at his watch.* 7:05. She's listening to Kelly's Soup.

Miranda: He tried to explain his point the other night, but you were too busy fighting the African campaign.

Colonel: Can't understand the fellow. His army record's good enough.

Miranda: Doesn't it occur to you that some young men, who have been through hell once, want to stop it happening again?

Colonel: You can't stop war, Miranda . . . because you can't change human nature.

Miranda: There hasn't been a war between New York and Pennsylvania for generations. And human nature was very human, when I was there last.

Colonel: What the devil has Pennsylvania got to do with it?

Miranda: Suppose they had a dust-up – not being sovereign states, neither of them claims the right to be judge and jury in their own case, and to settle the dispute by mass murder.

Colonel: Don't be ridiculous! They're part of a federal union.

Miranda: But they haven't always been! Only a hundred and fifty years ago – as long as the life of one of the big trees in the canyon – they were little, quarrelling states, complete with customs barriers and local militia. . . .

Colonel: Since when did you become so damned historical, may I ask?

Miranda: Since I read "The Union of the Free" by John Duncan.

Colonel: By God, it's just occurred to me. You're in love with the fellow!

Miranda: I thought it was women who always get personal in an argument.

Colonel: Now don't change the subject! You're too – too theoretical, Miranda. It's all this blasted science – evolution – high-brow humbug. If you'd settle down with some decent chap – like Howard Potter –

Miranda: Do you really want me to marry Howard?

Colonel: Why not? Steady fellow. Good job in the bank. She's only his aunt by marriage. . . .

Miranda: I believe it's quite the thing right now for girls my age to grab a man, but fast.

Colonel: Well, after a war . . . men are in a marrying mood. I'm not a young fellow, m'dear. I'd like to see you happily settled, with some reasonable security . . .

Miranda: There is no security for any of us, in a world of anarchy.

Colonel: Free peoples will not give up the right to defend themselves . . .

Miranda: You mean the right to make war. Pennsylvania gave it up.

Colonel: To hell with Pennsylvania!

A shot sounds in the distance.

Miranda: What was that?

Colonel: What was what?

Miranda: It sounded like shooting.

Another shot.

Colonel: By Jupiter, you're right. If those damn villagers are after ducks out of season, I'll have them prosecuted! Now what were we talking about?

Miranda: Duncan's book.

Colonel: You've never cared tuppence what I publish. If you're not in love with the blighter, why are you so interested?

Miranda: Because I'm tired of living in a world without freedom.

He tries to speak but she goes on.

> I don't call it freedom when we're all afraid. Deep down in ourselves, even when we're doing happy things – sailing the boat, working at our jobs, dancing and laughing – somewhere inside us we know it's only a breathing spell. The horror will come back. Bombs will fall, children scream, boys will die in flames. All for something called "National Sovereignty." All because of the stupid, criminal humbug of dividing the world – which *is* one world – into seventy pieces, and giving them all the divine right to start killing.

Colonel: And what about patriotism? What about loyalty?

Miranda: I've got a high enough opinion of the human race to believe we could extend our loyalty to a federation of mankind. *She smiles.* I know why you won't read this book.

Colonel: Oh indeed?

Miranda: You're afraid it might convince you. You know that what I've been saying is true – because underneath all that bluster and bombast, you've got a logical mind and an honest heart . . .

Colonel: That's a damn lie!

Howard: *Off to the right.* Hello! Ahoy there . . .

Miranda: It's Howard. *Calling.* Hello . . .

Howard: May I come in? *He strolls on from down right.* Good evening, sir.

Colonel: Evening, Howard.

Howard: Hot enough to suit you?

Colonel: It's not hot. Why do you wear so damn many clothes?

Miranda: Not everyone has your progressive ideas, Father.

Colonel: Hrphm.

Howard: Hear the golf final this afternoon, Colonel?

Colonel: No –

Howard: Higgins took Woywitka, four and three.

Colonel: Good game?

Howard: He did all right for a Ukrainian – but not quite good enough. Aunt Ede sent me over to organize some bridge.

Colonel: I don't mind – if you'll play with her.

Howard: She's out in the back kitchen fixing a drink.

Colonel: A collins?

Howard nods.

My God, she puts so much sugar in it, it turns my stomach. *He starts out.* Set up the chairs, Miranda. We'll play here, it's cooler. *He hurries out toward Potter's.*

Howard and Miranda arrange chairs for bridge.

Howard: That's pretty. Have I seen it before?

Miranda: No. *She smiles.* Thank you.

Howard: I heard from the boss, Miranda. He can get me a house.

Miranda: Where?

Howard: Sherwood Crescent.

Miranda: *Impressed.* Wow!

Howard: I got to call him in the morning.

Miranda: I see.

Howard: Well? *Silence.* What do I tell him? Look, beautiful, you can stall me for a couple of ice ages, but we can't stall a real estate agent.

Miranda: I don't know. Honest to Pete, Howard, I don't know . . .

Howard: Would it be out of place to inquire just when you will know? I'm not sticking around for the berry picking. I figured we'd get this thing lined up a week ago.

Miranda: *Unhappily.* I did, too. Common sense tells me I'm a dope. I ought to slip the handcuffs on you so fast . . .

Howard: Well – what's got us stymied? This is what we been waiting for, isn't it?

Miranda: Yes.

Howard: The war's over, my job's okay, we find a house . . .

Miranda: *Sadly.* And we live happily ever after. You're a sweet guy, Howard. But every now and then . . . we seem to be standing miles apart. I'm on the cliff and you're at the other end of the lake . . .

Howard: That's fancy talk. For instance?

Miranda: For instance – what you said about Woywitka.

Howard: Are you turning me down because a guy lost a golf game?

Miranda: But you called him a Ukrainian. Sure, I'll bet he's proud of it. But – you label people in your mind . . .

Howard: Hey! This sounds like our unshaven chum on the north shore. Has Duncan been beating my time?

She doesn't answer.

What would a bird like that have to offer a girl?

Miranda: He's got nothing to offer anybody except his anger and his courage. You don't want to fight any more, do

211

you, Howard? You'll jog along in the bank, getting a raise every year, getting a little balder . . .

Howard: Raising my kids the best I can and leading a normal human life. That's what you want, too, if you'd come in out of the moonlight and get wise to yourself. Damn right I don't want to fight any more. There's been too much fighting now . . .

There is a shot, closer than last time.

Good lord, what's that?

Miranda: I heard it before . . .

They listen. There is sound of angry voices.

Howard: Sounds like trouble towards the village . . .

Miranda: Howard! The Davys had a shotgun!

Howard: Nuts. That happens in the Kaintucky mountains . . .

Miranda: They're coming, whoever it is . . .

The angry voices are louder. The Colonel bounces back in indignantly, Mrs. Potter on his heels.

Colonel: What the devil is all that row at this time of night?

Howard: Don't know, sir . . .

Mrs. Potter: Maybe it's a wedding. You know – they make a noise to keep people awake all night. A shivaree they call it . . .

Sears, John and Davy appear on the path from the beach. Sears carries the gun, Davy's hands are tied behind him. John's shirt is ripped off one shoulder, he looks as if he had been rolling in the Davys' yard.

212

Howard: *Amused.* I don't think it's a wedding.

Miranda: Johnny – !

John: *Grinning.* Well – I fell off the fence. Here I am.

Mrs. Davy arrives, her arms tied with strips of her own apron. Denzil trots along beside her snivelling. Jim and Herb bring up the rear. Herb has a black eye.

Davy: *Trying to be social.* Good evening, Colonel.

Colonel: May I ask what in blazes is the meaning of this? Duncan – are you drunk?

John: There's been a slight dust-up in the village, sir . . .

Sears: I am on my way to Gainford to lay charges of assault, with violence and intention to do grievous bodily harm.

John: I persuaded Mr. Sears to take your advice before going any further.

Colonel: *My* advice?

Sears: He said you was a magistrate.

Mrs. Davy: Us was willing to come. Us knowed we'd get justice from you, Colonel.

Colonel: I see no reason whatever why my privacy should be invaded . . .

Mrs. Potter: Oh please, Colonel – "Blessed are the peacemakers," you know.

Howard: Might get into the papers, sir. If we could stop it right here . . .

Colonel: *Weakening.* Well . . . *His eye falls on Denzil.* Dammit, boy, take your hat off!

Denzil: T'ain't my hat. It's an old one of Pa's . . .

Colonel: Take it off, confound you! There are ladies present.

Denzil: Gee whiz! *He takes off the old hat and stands turning and twisting it.*

Colonel: Bring a lamp, Miranda. Untie that woman's arms, one of you.

Herb: Do you think it's safe, Bill?

Mrs. Davy: I wouldn't soil my hands with ye, ye blackguard!

John undoes Mrs. Davy's bonds.

Colonel: *Sitting down.* Now then, what's all this?

Sears, Mrs. Davy, Davy, Herb, and Jim all speak in unison.

Sears: Right now I want it understood that the only reason I came here was to . . .

Mrs. Davy: These here are the villains, sir, that came breaking into our place, murdering Denzil and . . .

Davy: We was defending our land, Colonel, that's all we was doing. We're British subjects and we got the right . . .

Herb: This afternoon we goes down to the Davy place, simply in the course of business, and before we could . . .

Jim: All I know about it is that this bunch of wild cats blames me busting the kid's boil . . .

Colonel: *Shouting them all down.* Stop it! By Christopher, I come out here for peace and quiet and I'm going to have it! If you can't control your tempers, you can get off my property!

Davy: *To Sears.* There, you hear that? *To the Colonel.* Just

214

what I said to him Colonel.

Sears: The corner of 16 ain't your property!

Davy: It is too!

Sears: You can't prove it . . .

Mrs. Davy: Us paid taxes for near twenty years . . .

Sears: You've paid no taxes for the last three years, as I know, being reeve of the district. The land is still on the books under the name of Harold B. Jeffries. *To the Colonel.* Shiftless and improvident people, Colonel, a drawback to the community.

Mrs. Davy: Liar. Murdering liar.

Sears: *Ignoring this.* The land therefore reverts to the municipality. My idea is to buy it, subdivide it into building lots, and put up cottages. I had employed Mr. Johnson and Bryan to survey the ground, when they were attacked with malice aforethought.

Herb: And with this here club. *He lays it on the table.* That's what the old dame tried to use on me.

Howard: Looks like she made a birdie, too.

Herb: I dunno who you are, mister, but keep out of this, see?

Howard: Sorry.

Jim: And here's the slingshot Li'l Abner used on me.

Denzil: You throwed me down and jumped on me!

Jim: Aw shut up!

Colonel: Did you attack the boy, Bryan?

Jim: No, sir. We were talking by ourselves and he asked me to teach him rugby. I showed him a tackle and then his folks got back and the shooting started.

John: Here's the shotgun. *He lays it on the table beside the other weapons.* I warned Davy this afternoon that the law takes a serious view of violence with fire arms.

Davy: They was trespassing! Us told them to stay out. Us has a right to defend our land . . .

Colonel: You've no right to endanger human life by taking the law into your own hands! *Breaks gun.* This thing's loaded!

Davy: Sure it's loaded.

Sears: It went off where I dropped it on the track back there a piece. . . .

Davy: Eh, slippery customer!

John: It was fired twice during the scrap at Davy's fence.

Miranda: *Setting a lamp on the table.* We heard it, didn't we, Father? While we were talking about Pennsylvania.

Colonel: Hrmph!

John: The Davys are simple minded people, sir . . .

Mrs. Davy: Now there's a Judas for you!

John: They've lived on that land for a long time, cleared it, improved it, and although they cannot prove title of ownership, they surely have some claim in equity . . .

Colonel: Is that true, Davy?

Davy: I can't prove nothing – except that I'll fight for what's mine!

A slip of paper falls from the lining of Denzil's hat which he still twists in his hands.

Denzil: Dam' right we will!

Colonel: *Glaring.* Be quiet, boy!

John: Since they believed themselves about to be attacked, they fortified their property and got ready with these weapons . . .

Colonel: Fortified, rubbish! Dammit, the Royal North West Mounted Police put an end to that sort of nonsense in 1874.

Davy: Was we to sit still and let him walk all over us? It's more than human nature could stand . . .

Colonel: Human nature has nothing to do with it. Let me remind you this province is no longer in a state of anarchy.

Davy: I'm a free man! That's why I come to your bloody Canada . . .

Colonel: If you're free, it's because there's a law in this country, sir, a law that protects human life and property! By resorting to armed force you make yourself the aggressor and become liable to trial and punishment. If this were a court of law, you'd go to jail . . .

Sears: Come on, boys. Thank you very much, colonel, that's all I wanted to know. *He starts out.*

John: Just a minute. There's something I don't understand . . .

Sears: You heard what the Colonel said . . .

John: Davy . . . you paid your taxes for 17 years?

Davy nods.

Why did you stop paying them?

Sears: What does it matter why the half-witted old fool . . .

Colonel: Answer the question, Davy!

Davy: *Dogged.* Us stopped because Sears told me us didn't have to pay after Denzil stopped going to school.

General sensation.

Colonel: Aha!

Mrs. Potter: *Pained.* Oh, Mr. Sears . . .

Denzil: *Alarmed.* I don't have to go to school! I don't have to go to school no more! I can read – lissen! *He snatches up the paper which fell from his hat.* "Ministik, March 5, 1924. Received from Benjamin Davy the sum of forty five dollars, being pay-ment for all that part of the east half of section 16, township 53, Range 5, west of the fifth mer – mer –

John: *Softly.* Meridian.

Denzil: The fifth – what he said. "Sit-u-ated between the CNR right of way and the shores of Lake Ministik, comp – comp-rising five acres more or less, signed Harold B. Jeffries." *Silence.* Jeez, old man Jeffries was a funny writer.

Dead silence.

John: *Gently.* Where did you get that paper, Denzil?

Denzil: On the ground. It fell out of my hat when he made me take it off.

John takes the paper to the Colonel. They examine it, John

218

goes back and cuts the rope on Davy's hands.

Colonel: *Quietly.* I recognize old Mr. Jeffries' signature. It corresponds with my receipt for this property. The law will defend your ownership, Davy.

Mrs. Davy: *In a sudden loud sobbing cry of relief.* Oh, Pa . . .

Davy: *Putting his arms round her.* There, there. Stacia – there, there, lass . . .

Mrs. Davy: Does it mean us be safe, Ben, after all?

Davy: Aye, us be safe. The house and the pigs and the garden and the fishing boat on the shore.

Sears: Oh well, in that case . . .

Colonel: Wait a minute, I've got something to say to you.

Sears: Some other time, Colonel . . .

Colonel: I know your kind – hiding behind the law. Using it to cheat and bamboozle these poor devils out of all they have in the world . . .

Sears: I don't have to listen to this!

Jim: *Grabbing his arm.* Oh yes you do, mister!

Herb: *Closing in on the other side.* Getting me and Jim mixed up in your dirty business – spoilin' our reputations –

Colonel: You don't need money. You've got this village sewed up now with your fish house and your store and your post office. It's power you want. Power to bully and brow-beat your neighbors. Dammit, sir, you're a fascist, that's what you are! If I hear any more of it, by

Jupiter . . . *He picks up the gun, looks at it, lays it down.* I'll have you in court for extortion, malfeasance, and skullduggery!

Herb: That's telling him!

They turn Sears round and head him down the path.

Sears: You'll be sorry for this, Johnson . . .

Herb: *Shoving him.* Aw beat it! Go jump in the lake twice and come out once! *He comes back dusting off his hands.*

Mrs. Davy: Well, Pa – us best be getting home.

Davy: Aye, the cow ain't milked . . .

Denzil: And them pigs'll be clear to Spruceville by now.

Davy: Good-night, Colonel – and thank you.

Colonel: *Brusque.* Quite all right – quite all right.

John: You'd better take this – and don't lose, it, hunh?

Mrs. Davy: *Taking the receipt.* Us'll keep it safe. *She looks at him.* I'm sorry I spoke harsh to you, Johnny. You're a good lad . . .

John: Even if I once was a lawyer?

Mrs. Davy: Eh, somebody has to do it, as I say to Pa when we cleans the chicken house. Come Denzil . . .

Denzil: Okay. Can I put my hat on now?

Miranda: Yes, you can put it on now.

Denzil puts his hat on with a flourish and goes off swaggering.

Davy: Good-night, Johnny . . . G'night all. . . .

Amid general good-nights the Davys leave.
The Colonel strolls to the end of the path watching them.

Herb: I want you folks to understand me and Jim had no idea this wasn't strictly on the level.

John: That's all right, Herb. Many a good man gets killed in a bad cause.

Mrs. Potter: Oh, Mr. Johnson – it *is* Mr. Johnson, isn't it?

Herb: Yes, ma'am.

Mrs. Potter: I have a nice piece of beefsteak in my ice box – – just the thing to take the swelling out of your eye . . .

Herb: Well –

Howard: There's a long cold drink on the kitchen table. How about it, Bryan?

Jim: Man, lead me to it!

Herb: Now you're talking!

Mrs. Potter: I take it our bridge game is off, Colonel?

Colonel: *From the end of the path.* If you don't mind.

Mrs. Potter: Oh, it's been a very interesting evening! What you said, Colonel – about anarchy – and . . . well, freedom – and the Mounted Police – it certainly makes you think, doesn't it? *She thinks for a moment, then recovers herself.* Well . . . come along, boys – the beefsteak!

She goes off, followed by Herb, Jim and Howard. There is silence.
The Colonel comes slowly to the table, tired. John and

221

Miranda are in shadow, but the light shines full on the Colonel as he stands looking at John's book.

Colonel: I think I'll go in, Miranda.

Miranda: Yes, Father.

Colonel: Duncan . . . you brought those damn people here on purpose, didn't you?

John: Yes, sir.

Colonel: I realize that. Still, it was an admissible piece of strategy! *He slowly takes up the manuscript and the lamp.* I'll take this with me – might read for a while. Do you want this lamp? *He looks at them.* No, I see you don't need this light. *Near the house he turns, barking again.* Not that I promise anything, remember!

John: I quite understand. Good-night.

The Colonel goes.

Softly. By God, he took it!

Miranda: He talked himself into taking it. . . .

John: I won't change the world overnight. But I did it. And doing it has changed me. . .

Miranda: What changed you was getting your shirt ripped off and your face pushed in the dirt. Getting back in the fight.

John: Anyway, I'll be all right. I'm in the clear . . .

Howard: *Off, calling.* Miranda!

Miranda: I'm here –

Howard: *Coming back.* Aren't you coming? Got one

poured for you – *He takes a good look at them.* Oh –!

Miranda: No. No, thank you. And Howard . . . call the agent. Not Sherwood Crescent. Not anywhere . . .

Howard: *After a moment.* I see. Going to live in a hole in the ground, are you?

Miranda: I'm going to live – in the world as it really is. Terrifying – but real.

Howard: I don't get it. But if that's how you want it. . . . G'night!

Miranda: Good-bye, Howard.

He goes.

John: Will you come up to the cliff with me, Miranda?

Miranda: It's a climb . . . you've had a hard day . . .

John: I feel like climbing. *He folds his arms around her shoulders and smiles at her.* Sure?

Miranda: Certain sure.

He kisses her, taking his time.

Miranda: All right. We'll climb.

The moonlight is full on them as they go up the slope together. And the play ends.

The End

The High Green Gate

CKUA Players 1935-36. Sheila Marryat, Dick Allen, Leslie Pilcher, Frances Garness, Fred McNeil, Jack Delaney, Farnum Howarth, Delbert Rogers (on piano), Dick MacDonald, Francis Taylor (on lap), Harry Taylor, Audrey Stutchbury, and Donald MacDonald (seated on floor). Many of the actors here performed in the initial broadcast of *The Building of Canada* series in 1937. Sheila Marryat commissioned *New Lamps for Old* and *The Building of Canada*.

Day: In "The Girl Who Is Out of Step" you said that you had made up your mind that you never intended to marry because of the stifling effect it had on many women. You obviously changed your mind. Can you talk about Dr. Gowan and your marriage?

EPG: Well, when I was a girl I had in front of me the example of my mother whom I thought had a very dull life. She had too much work to do – too much housework – and I thought to myself, I'm never going to get married if that's what marriage does to people!

   After I grew up and left home and my horizons widened a bit, I had a lot of gentlemen friends, but Ted Gowan was the one with whom I was the best friends, you know? And by this time it had been made obvious to me that I was technically a "highbrow" because I was determined to go to university and find people who spoke my language. And Ted Gowan was by far the most intelligent of all the young chaps I knew.

   We met first when I was teaching at Marlboro, right out in the bush, and we used to spend Sunday afternoons hiking into some spot in the neighboring landscape. Then when he won the Rhodes Scholarship that fall, I thought, "That's the end of that. He'll go on to Oxford." But when he came back from Oxford – he came back in '29 – I was in my last year at university. So we just picked up where we left off. We were married in '33 and never got tired of each other. "Go thou and do likewise."

Day: Yes! Both you and Gwen Ringwood suggested that

marriage was a mixed blessing to a woman's writing career. I think what Ringwood said is that on one hand she found marriage better than a Canada Council grant and a lot more fun – but then the domestic things got in the way of it too.

EPG: Well yes, Gwen and I were both really subsidized by our husbands.

Day: In the essay you wrote on women in the twentieth century you said it was a catch-22 because on one hand financially it freed you to write. On the other hand, it was hard to be taken seriously if you were married. It was seen as a hobby.

EPG: Yes. Well, it wasn't a hobby. But it wasn't easy, you know, to combine it with one's responsibilities to one's husband and his position. We entertained a lot. And my husband was totally in favor of me having "a writing career" – in quotes – but just the same he expected me to entertain his friends and students. I'm laughing. I'm reading a book by Sheila Hailey, the wife of Arthur Hailey. And it's the same thing; he expected his coffee on the table promptly at 8:30.

    If you want to write, you have to have your priorities, and every day, as I remember it, was a kind of battle between, "Will I put my day in on this side of the fence or the other." You haven't researched Gowan unless you've read "The Freedom of Mrs. Radway!"

Day: How did you manage with your own son and writing while he was growing up?

EPG: Well, we always had someone living with us. After the airforce couple passed on, we had other people. Homeless ladies, women who were glad to do a little housework and look after the little boy while I was pounding the typewriter.

Day: In many ways, *The High Green Gate* seems a darker more troubled play than many of your earlier ones about the role of women in public life. In *The Hungry Spirit* and *Back to the Kitchen* there seems to be this real faith that education was a key to female advancement and that the war had changed things in such a way that women, working or not, would be playing an increasingly assertive and important role along side men in the public sphere. In The *High Green Gate* you seem to be unsure.

EPG: Well, *Back to the Kitchen* was intended as a comedy. And there is a serious idea behind it I suppose, but it was really written for entertainment. This was written as the sort of thought-provoking series which would have some elements of entertainment in the dramatic situations, but it was intended to provoke thought – socially desirable thought.

Day: What can you tell me about the circumstances surrounding the writing and production of *The High Green Gate*?

EPG: Well, you see, these topics were assigned to me. I was working under assignment from the Department of Talks and Public Affairs. So that I didn't choose it. It was simply one of the topics on the list.

But I went out to see what we had in Edmonton, and what we had in Edmonton at that time was pitiful. It was one little daycare centre and it had a high green gate – that's where the title came from. It had been set up by benevolent ladies. We had a wonderful woman in Edmonton called Muriel Dick who was quite well off and she had a terrific community conscience. She believed that a person in her position should do good works. So she and her friends had organized this daycare centre with the high green gate and I went down there and listened to them.

They took microphones down to the children's daycare in Toronto and got the kids saying "See the little hands go clap, clap clap!"

Day: Were the women based on real life people or cases?

EPG: Yes, they were to a certain extent. It seemed to me that there were three reasons for daycare. There was the woman with the career. The Frances woman who's interested in plant science. For Frances, I was really thinking of Dr. Silver Keeping[1] who died just a short time ago.

Day: Yes. I'd heard of her.

EPG: Now she was a woman who carried on her research in spite of all sorts of discouragement and neglect.

Then there is the poor little immature kid that shouldn't be married at all, you know, and believes all the moonlight and roses stuff, and she's not really a good parent and she needs a daycare centre. And then, of course, there is the poor woman who was absolutely on the edge of survival and *has* to work and *has* to have a daycare centre.

Day: I was wondering why you left an open-ended finish to this play.

EPG: Well, I just wanted to leave it to the listener to evaluate the three cases or say whether they needed daycare at all. And of course to my mind I would have chosen Frances. But I knew damned well it should go to the third one, the working woman.

Day: Did that actually happen with the little girl?

EPG: Well, I'd heard of some case where the child was being abused, you know. Just locked in her room and this sort of thing. Just because daycare wasn't regarded as a community service. It was a private racket.

Day: And so there wasn't much quality.

EPG: No.

Day: To what extent does the alderman in the play represent male or civic resistance to the idea of daycare?

EPG: Well, the alderman was a composite figure of all the resisters and all the people who say, you know, a woman's place is in the home. Look after your own kids and why should the taxpayer pay for somebody else's kids to be kept off the streets? Which is exactly what they said before public schools were invented!

Day: Did men feel differently than women on the subject?

EPG: Well, men for the most part didn't see it at all, you know. At that time, they just didn't see it.

Day: By the forties and fifties, your attitudes seem to have become a lot more complex.

EPG: Well, you can't stay 25 forever!

Day: I was wondering if you wanted to discuss that change and the move to radio series. *The Town Grows Up* series was slotted under CBC's talks for women?

EPG: *The Town Grows Up* was commissioned by a wonderful little woman named Elizabeth Long who was the head of Women's Talks programs. And she and Marjorie – I don't remember Marjorie's . . . she was a

Winspear. Anyway these two women were back of this series and they were very proud of the fact that the executive was a woman, the director was a woman – Kay Stevenson – and the writer was a woman – me!

Day: Were the other two series dealing with the family court and social services – *Judge For Yourself* and *Down Our Street Today* – also seen as more attractive to women audiences?

EPG: Well, I can't answer that. *The Judge For Yourself* was instigated by Ken Crockett, a young lawyer here in town. And he made it possible for me to get access to government files. Cases which had come up in family court.

Then, I was very fortunate in having the advice of a good social worker, a friend who was head of the family bureau here in Edmonton. Kathleen. Anyway, she took me around with her when she went to visit some of her clients.

Day: Oh really.

EPG: And it was an eye opener! Oh brother! Places that we . . . the women that we met who were trying to hold a family together in some awful shack. Good Lord! This woman was living in a sort of chicken coop thing out in what was Jasper Place then.

Day: Really bad, eh?

EPG: Yeah. Awful things. Awful cases of abuse. The most heartbreaking thing I ever saw was the story of the little boy I called *The Second Son*, about this horrible old militaristic father that used to beat up this kid – and the kid couldn't do anything to please him. The child had run away from home. And he came home on Christmas

Day and the father marched him straight down to the police station.

Day: That's really ...

EPG: Yeah. . . . Well, in dealing with things, like teenage pregnancy and so on, the scripts weren't nearly so outspoken, but I don't think they were any the worse for that. They got the idea across without using language or things that would offend people. No use turning the audience off, you know.

I like *The High Green Gate.* I think it's viable – that it says what it's supposed to say.

---

1. Dr. Eleanor Silver Keeping (1902-1991), a noted mycologist (specialist in the study of fungi), served as one of the University of Alberta's first woman lecturers in the Sciences (outside of nursing) after her graduation with an MSc in 1924. Her promising career, including studies abroad and the acquiring of a PhD from the University of Maniboba, initially appeared at an end when she married Dr. Frank Keeping, since her status as a faculty wife prevented her from receiving a salary. With his support and encouragement, however, she continued her research on her own until Dr. Rankin, Dean of Medicine, hired her in 1933. She went on to establish one of the first medical mycology laboratories in the Commonwealth before "retiring" in 1954 to become an honourary research associate in the Departments of Medical Bacteriology, Botany and Genetics for the next two decades. (See "Gone But Far From Forgotten: The University Loses Three of its Best," *New Trail* 46 (Summer, 1991), 13-15).

THE HIGH GREEN GATE: *FIRST PERFORMANCE*

An Interpretation of the Day Nursery in a Canadian City

Broadcast over CBC 2 December, 1952, as Chapter Three of
"Down Our Street . . . Today" Series

THE HIGH GREEN GATE

Characters

Kathleen Kirby, director of Family Welfare Bureau
Alderman Bassett, hard headed, he'd have you know
Peggy Webster, pretty, blonde, immature
Stan Webster, a mother's boy, a good natured lug
Frances McKeever B.Sc., intelligent, 26
Tom McKeever, a mature, civilized guy
Yvonne Leveque, a working woman of 35, slight accent
Paul Leveque, small, 40, a mechanic ill at ease in the
    mechanical world
Suzanne, 4 or 5, a badly frightened child
Voices of: Fran's father; Adding Machine; Foreman doubled at
    the producer's discretion

Setting:

Time:
1952

Place:
A growing Canadian city.

Announcer: Down Our Street – To-day.

Music. Series theme up big.

> Down Our Street – Today . . . another dramatic report on
> Canada's families in 1952. Marriage is an institution
> we've had with us for some time – in one form or
> another. To-night three marriages come under the
> scrutiny of a professional woman who is concerned with
> our problems in living to-gether. Maybe you remember

Miss Kathleen Kirby, Director of the Family Welfare Bureau in a growing Canadian city. Here she is to tell a story we call . . . *The High Green Gate.*

Music up and out.

Kirby: This morning I held three cards in my hand – three cards from one of the files in my office. Let's not get over-dramatic and say I held three children's lives in my hand, but I *did* have to make a choice. There are a hundred and fifty more names where these came from – our records of the families who ask to have a child admitted to the City Creche and Day Nursery. I know these children – and their mothers –

Peggy: Marlene – that's my little girl – I gave her a permanent last week and does she ever look *cute*! *Clouding up.* Stan doesn't care about her – or about me either. He's not the way he was when I married him – he's not the same guy at all! That's why I can't live with him. . . . I can't live with him any more!

Music. "Blue Heaven." Gone Sour.

Kirby: Marlene Webster, whose parents don't love each other any more. A broken home. Then the next card . . .

Frances: David is a quiet little boy – it would do him good to have other children to play with. If I knew he was happy and well looked after – *I* could get out. *With intense frustration.* I could get out of that box myself.

Music. Frustration in B flat minor.

Kirby: David McKeever – the child of a woman in conflict with herself. And my third card . . .

Yvonne: To ask for help – that's not *what* I want to do. To

235

work in the garment factory is not what I want to do either. But that woman – when I tell you what she is doing to my Suzanne – to a little child four years old. . . .

Music. "Vive la Canadienne" fighting mad.

Kirby: Suzanne Leveque – who lives in two rooms of a house on Waterloo Street, while her father works in a machine shop – when he's well enough – and her mother in a garment factory. Lively Suzanne – quiet David – and Marlene – with the permanent – I have a place for one of you, my dears, a place for *one* of you. There might be room for more if it weren't for Alderman Bassett. . . .

Music. A Hard Headed Man.

Kirby: Alderman Bassett came to inspect the premises of the City Creche and Day Nursery Society – that is, after they moved to where they are now in the converted garage when the old property was condemned. We showed him the high green fence – the play-ground with the sand-boxes and the Jungle Gym; showed him the bright painted lockers, the rocking-horses, the bathroom with its knee-high fixtures. We listened to the children singing in the kindergarten room . . .

Sound of small children singing:

> See the little hands go clap clap clap
> See the little feet go tap tap tap.
> This is what I say to you
> "Here is my hand how do you do?"
> See the little hands go clap clap clap
> See the little feet go tap tap tap!

Bassett: It's – a little close in here. . . . Could we move along. . . .

Kirby: Yes, of course.

236

Sound of door cuts off kindergarten.

Bassett: Well, they look happy enough. But I'll never believe that any small child isn't better off in his own home with his own mother. After the war, I hoped we'd get back to normal. But these young women nowadays – all they think about is the high wages they can get.

Kirby: The families are carefully screened, Mr. Bassett. No child comes here except in case of absolute need. And they pay something . . .

Bassett: Seventy-five cents a day – doesn't begin to cover the cost. That's what I said when the city council agreed to pay rent and utilities for this place. Why should the taxpayer who is looking after his own family, pay to look after other people's children?

Kirby: Well . . . of course. They're citizens of the future. A personality is often formed in these years . . .

Bassett: You can't tell me a place like this is any substitute for a good home!

Kirby: Social workers don't think a day nursery is a substitute for a home.

Bassett: I'm glad to hear you say so!

Kirby: But if the possibilities of home life are not complete then the nursery can help. You see, here the community can join forces with parents to give a child the good secure feeling he needs at the centre of his life.

Bassett: What do you mean – "possibilities of home life."

Kirby: The physical things to begin with, of course. Decent housing . . . enough money for an adequate standard of living . . .

Bassett: They want too much, these young married couples. Radios – refrigerators – all the latest gadgets . . .

Kirby: What a child needs most are mature parents – people who find it just as satisfying to watch a child develop as it is – to own a new car, shall we say.

Bassett: Exactly. If a woman's not willing to stay home and look after her children, she's got no business having children. They're agitating for another day nursery in Parkside. Council won't give in on that one if *I* can help it.

Music. Stern stuff. Stiff.

Kirby: Mr. Bassett is the manager of a wholesale drug and cosmetic company. They may have handled the mascara that 21 year old Peggy Webster wiped off her face as she told me why Marlene needed the day nursery . . .

Music. "Blue Heaven." A little queer. Out for,

Peggy: So then he walked out on me – walked right out and went to the hockey game. Just because he was mad at me for buying the fur coat. I sat there waiting for him to come home – and then wondering if he was coming home at all. I heard the end of the game – then I turned the radio off. All I could get was that darn song – "Wish You Were Here – Wish you were Home." That's a swell thing to throw at a girl when her guy walks out and slams the door!

Music. Mocking "Wish You Were Here."

Then I thought I'd straighten up the joint, just to be doing something. Under the chesterfield was a box of stuff Marlene had been playing with. Souvenirs – pictures I cut out of magazines right after we were married, when I was going to make a scrap book of my dream house. My dream house – that's a laugh! At the bottom of the box was a big round piece of cardboard – and I'm telling you, that really broke me down. Left over from when I was 17. From one night we were dancing . . .

Music. Sneaking schmaltzy waltz. Hold in background with,

Stan had on a new suit that night . . . I remember thinking he looked like Van Johnson. It was the big romantic stuff like in the movies. He was going to marry me – take care of me. What a line the guy had . . . what a line . . .

Stan: *Close.* See that moon up there, baby? Say the word and I'll get it for you – right out of the sky . . .

Peggy: *Music. "Alone for a Moment."* He did, too. Before the lights came on he climbed up and grabbed the blue paper moon. Stan was a clown . . . but he was a lot of fun . . .

Music. Waltz ends on sour note.

None of it worked out. None of it came true. Y'know – how a girl kind of dreams about being married . . . oh, not like at *home.* We never had much fun when I was a kid. . . . Mom was one of those demon housekeepers. . . . My Dad was a quiet person – cared more about the garden than he did about us. But Stan and me – that was going to be sweet and wonderful. *Harsh.* Why does a guy have to change so much . . . just because you're married to him?

Music. Three quick chords of question.

Stan: *Off a little.* Pete's sake – Peggy! What's all this stuff in the bath tub?

Peggy: It's the baby's wash. I didn't get around to it this afternoon.

Stan: *Mild grumble.* What the heck were you doing . . . Out window shopping again?

Peggy: I was making over my green dress. Look, isn't it going to be something?

Stan: Sure, swell.

Peggy: You're not looking at it. You don't care how I look.

Stan: *Off again.* Hey . . . have I got a clean shirt?

Peggy: The laundry didn't come, and a good thing. I'm out of money.

Stan: Oh for gosh sakes . . .

Peggy: I paid the installment on the refrigerator!

Stan: You'd have money if you knew how to keep house.

Peggy: Like your mother I suppose.

Stan: Okay, like my mother. She got along with an ice box.

Peggy: Maybe it's too bad you left home. Maybe you should have stayed where somebody would wait on you hand and foot – pick up your pyjamas where you drop them on the floor . . .

Stan: My mother doesn't spend her time reading sloppy love stories or listening to that malarkey on the radio . . .

Sound of baby crying. Take down to background with,

My lord, does that kid have to cry *all* the time?

Peggy: *Heavy sarcasm.* I'm sorry. I'll call the butler to move her crib into the sun room.

Stan: *Please* . . . let's not have wit and humour . . .

Peggy: Oh no – that's *your* department! You're the funny one. *Her face crumbles.* Good old Stan – the life of every party . . . !

Stan: Hey . . . Peg! Look, Baby – don't cry. This place is getting on our nerves. We ought to get out more, that's what it is. We ought to get out more . . .

Music. Tag of cock-eyed "Blue Heaven."

Peggy: Stan certainly got out . . . in the next three years. He was in and out of several jobs – we just got by with the installments. Maybe I shouldn't have bought the fur coat. I didn't mean to when I tried it on. Oh, it's not real good fur – but soft and warm – kind of protecting – as if somebody loved you and thought you were wonderful. Then when I got it home . . .

Stan: *Furious.* Take it back! Come on – back in the box . . .

Peggy: I *won't* take it back!

Stan: A hundred and eighty nine dollars for a hunk of rabbit . . .

Peggy: It's beautiful – I want it. You've got money for what you want. Short wave radio – and liquor – and prize fight tickets –

Stan: It's my money.

Peggy: Alright . . . I'll go to work.

Stan: Sure you will!

Peggy: I can get my job back in the store.

Stan: And what about Marlene?

Peggy: What about her? As if you cared . . .

Stan: You're spoiling the kid anyway – giving her everything she wants just because she screams for it . . .

Peggy: At least she'll remember that I loved her!

Stan: Maybe you think my mother is going to take over . . .

Peggy: Your mother would like nothing better! But don't worry . . . Marlene's my child. I'll look after her. Poor kid. She didn't get a *man* for a father! All she got is Mrs. Webster's little boy!

Sound of door slamming. Silence.

Peggy: I waited up till 5 o'clock, but he didn't come home. Next day I found out he was living with his mother. I haven't seen him for a month and that's all right with me. He's not the man I married four years ago . . . and I can't live with him. I can't live with him any more!

Music. "Blue Heaven" comes to a bad end.

Kirby: Marlene Webster, aged 3. Her parents were certainly unprepared for the realities of married life. I wonder if Alderman Bassett could be convinced that our society has any responsibility for the lies we permitted to be told to a young girl; the false, over-glamorized picture we sold her in our glossy advertisements, our movies and radio? Then what about the homes Peggy and Stan came from? The parents who gave their daughter so little affection she rushed into marriage at 17? Stan's mother, who couldn't let her son grow up – sent him into life "a boy under the skin?" It's a commonplace story. Immature parents and a broken home. But here is Marlene. Does the community owe her the protection of our day nursery? She won't get what she wants by screaming for it there! She'll be set in a quiet place to cool off, while business goes on . . .

Sound of small children reciting:

> I look to the right
> And I look to the left
> Before I cross the street.
> I use my *eyes* – and I use my *ears* –
> Before I use my *feet!*

Kirby: *Dry.* Child might even learn, what her mother never did, to look where she's going!

Music. Transition.

Frances McKeever came into my office wearing a handsome tweed suit and English brogues . . .

Fran: I'm not sure that I'm a Welfare case at all, Miss Kirby. It's not money I need as much as help – help with David.

Kirby: Believe it or not, my dear, there are just as many family problems on one side of the tracks as there are on the other.

Fran: I dunno . . . I see girls my age on the bus – girls with thin coats and two or three spindly little children – and I wonder what right *I've* got to be unhappy. Then I get home and the door closes behind me . . . and I'm back where I started. . . . *Very tense.* Inside that box!!

Music. Frustration in B flat minor.

Poor Tom . . . he's too nice a fellow to have a woman like

243

me happen to him! My husband's an engineer. We were in university at the same time. *Grins.* I got a higher mark than he did in a physics course once – just once! Oh I was a smart girl. I've always been a smart girl. Maybe that's my trouble. Back in high school it was fun to be smart. My father was proud of me . . .

Father: This is a very good report, Frankie. Very good. I think we'll be able to afford college in a year or two. Plenty of opportunity for girls in the professions nowadays. Yes indeed, the bars are down. Just make up your mind, when the time comes. . . .

Fran: When the time came I took a B.Sc. in the biology pattern. Dr. Rigby was my special prof – you know, the man who does research in wheat rust? They said his work was worth millions to Canadian agriculture. Those were the days when the world was my oyster! Getting engaged to Tom – working on Student's Council. The night before I graduated I made a speech to our women's fraternity . . .

Music. Phrase of "Gaudeamus igitur," symphonic.

Public speaking. And so to-morrow as these gates close behind us and we go out to take our places in Canadian life, we will always be aware of the obligation laid upon us. The modern world has given us freedom and opportunity our grandmothers never knew. It will be our task to prove that women can play a full part, not only as wives and mothers, but in education, in science, art, and public life, as citizens in a free society!

Sound of applause. Fade with.

I worked in Dr. Rigby's lab for six months before I was married and then up until just before David was born.

For a couple of years biology was a strictly private affair – but he's going on four now – really at the tinker toy stage. David and I see a lot of each other from eight in the morning until he goes to bed at seven. Then after I get the kitchen straightened up . . .

Tom: *On a yawn.* Want to go someplace to-night?

Fran: *A little hopeful.* Why . . . do you? I *think* I could get a sitter . . .

Tom: Tell the truth I'd just as soon put my feet up. They're unloading steel, I'll have to be out there at 7 to-morrow. *Yawns.* Wha'd you do to-day?

Fran: *Precise.* It was Tuesday, dear. I ironed. *Fake bright.* We've got a new milkman!

Tom: That's nice.

Fran: His name is Torvald Iverson and his folks live in Seattle. *With an edge.* It's nice to talk to somebody . . . *different.*

Tom: Get your face on, woman. You're going out of this house before the fuses blow . . . !

Fran: Tom . . . sit down! I'm sorry. Sounded kind of bitchy, didn't I.

Tom: Yeah.

Fran: What's the matter with me, will you tell me? I'm married to a swell fella. David's the cutest little number that ever fell off a tricycle. I'm lucky! So what's eating me? I thought I was a normal woman . . .

Tom: Well, if you want my evidence. . . .

Fran: *Affectionately.* Shut up that's not what I mean. Why am I so darn lonely all day long – lonely for a little adult conversation? I wash. I cook. I clean house. I ride herd on Davie – all by myself. Is that natural for a human being? Didn't we start out living in tribes . . .

Tom: There's Mary Parker two houses down . . .

Fran: Mary came over yesterday to borrow a book. By the time we stopped her Peter from climbing into the fireplace, lifted her Susie out of your liquor cabinet, pried her Joe and my David apart . . . adult conversation my foot! *Pause.* There's a joker in the deck somewhere. If this was to be my life, why wasn't I getting ready for it? Why did everybody pretend I was going somewhere else? *Up.* It's stupid – it's wasteful –

Tom: I had lunch at the hotel to-day. Ran into Dr. Rigby.

Fran: *Flat.* Did you. How is he.

Tom: Fine. They're starting a new project. In plant rust.

Fran: Oh.

Tom: He wants you, Fran.

Fran: No . . .

Tom: Said he hasn't had a man in the lab in five years who could touch the calibre of your work.

Fran: *Very moved. On a whisper.* What a guy, what a guy . . .

Tom: Well, he's the top in his field . . .

Fran: Not the professor, you idiot . . . you! You told me.

Tom: What should I do . . . beat my manly chest at the idea of my wife working?

246

Fran: You think I should – go back?

Tom: It's up to you. I want you to be yourself. My girlfriend was a biologist. She was a lot of fun . . .

Fran: I'm not much fun to live with in my present state of mind. I don't even know if I'm good for Davie. He's too quiet. *Warming.* If I knew he was safe and happy . . . but who'd take care of Davie?

Tom: When my mother used to teach school, Grandma McKeever lived with us. I dunno where we'd put a Grandma in this caboose – even if we had one . . .

Fran: There's a day nursery somewhere in town . . .

Tom: Behind City Hall. I pass it when I'm going to pay the taxes. A high green fence and a green gate . . .

Fran: *With deep feeling.* I'll always remember this, Tom. You understood – you told me . . .

Tom: *Smile matching Fran's mood.* Oh well – Doc Rigby's going to call you up anyway . . .

Music runs up to a question.

Kirby: The second card, David McKeever. If we open the high green gate for Davie, we allow his mother to spend several hours each day among her colleagues, doing socially useful work. Our society encouraged her to prepare for that work. We gave her many years of expensive training. Is it reasonable that the community give Frances some help now, in fulfilling the goals she set herself? And Davie. When you hear the healthy hullabaloo behind the green fence, in free play period . . .

Sound of joyous noise of children in playground. Down for.

. . . you wonder if a quiet little boy might learn to take
it . . . climbing with the other Tarzans in the Jungle
Gym . . .

Sound of playground up full into:

*Music. Conclude Fran's chapter. Whiff of "Vive la
Canadienne."*

New tone. For Yvonne Leveque there is no free choice.
She sits at a machine in a factory for seven hours a day.
That is dictated to Mrs. Leveque by the cost of living.
Still a pretty woman at 35 – her body settling into
matronly curves – and in her brown eyes, the fighting
spirit that stopped the Iroquois . . .

Yvonne: *Snappy.* Figure it out for yourself, Miss Kirby.
When Paul is not sick – when his back does not bother
him – he makes forty dollars a week. Five people cannot
live on that much money. Also we have a debt of 600
dollars to the hospital and the doctor. I have the family
allowance – but my two boys, Wilfred and Louis, they're
like young calves, they could drink up that money in
milk alone! They're such good boys. They make the
beds for me, and take turns after school to call for
Suzanne at the house where I am boarding her. So I
think we're getting along alright – until it begins – in the
night . . .

Music up into nightmare. Out with.

Suzanne: *Screaming and crying.* Mamma – mamma –
mamma –

Yvonne: *Soothing.* Suzanne – Suzanne – my goodness –
what's the matter with my girl –

Suzanne: The dog, mamma . . . the dog . . . it will eat me . . .
Cries.

Paul: Somebody's having a bad dream!

Yvonne: Ttt-tt-tt . . . you see . . . you have wakened Papa.

Suzanne: It was coming after me. It was going to bite me . . .

Yvonne: There's no dog here. Mamma will put the quilt over you. Go to sleep.

Suzanne: Yes Mamma. Will you leave on the light?

Yvonne: For a little while. Shut your eyes.

Suzanne: *On a sigh.* Bad dog. *Drifting off.* Bad dog – bad dog –

Music. Vague lullaby. Out with.

Paul: *Quietly as he lies awake.* Yvonne – ?

Yvonne: *Yawns.* Well – ?

Paul: It would be nice – if we had a dog.

Yvonne: *Affectionate irony.* I think so too. Meat is so cheap.

Paul: When I was her age there was a big black dog. His name was Lolo. He could bring the cows by himself.

Yvonne: Now who is dreaming?

Paul: It was another world. My grandfather had his own land. When you have land, you're safe. But when a man has nothing but two hands to work – and the pay cheque every week . . .

Yvonne: What's the use of that talk. Go to sleep.

Paul: *Pause.* There's no dog at this house where Suzanne is boarding?

Yvonne: Mrs. Johnson wouldn't have *any* animals. She's too clean!

Paul: Not like that other *dirty* place. Or the one before that, where Suzanne was hungry.

Yvonne: The woman on the machine next to me – she leaves her boy at the creche.

Paul: I don't like it – asking help from strangers.

Yvonne: It's not charity – she pays –

Paul: We should take care of our own children. The good Lord gave them to *us* . . .

Music. Uneasy.

Yvonne: In the morning, Suzanne did not want to get up. She said she was sick, but she had no fever. The boys talked and laughed with her, so she forgot she was sick and went away with Papa at half past 8. But that night . . .

Music. Roll up the nightmare and hold through.

Suzanne: *Screaming.* Mamma – the dog – the dog – the dog!

Music. Wipe it out.

Yvonne: The next day at work my mind would not keep up with my machine. If Suzanne is sick I should take her to the doctor, but that costs money. Wilfred needs a new coat this winter, and Louis' shoes are too small for him. In my head the prices of all that go adding up – adding up.

Adding Machine: *Mechanical.* Doctor, $5.00 – coat, $12.95 – shoes, $6.00 – total, $25.95. For the rent this week

$12.50 – to pay on hospital bill $10.00 – grocery $18.25 – total – $40.75 . . .

Yvonne: Paul should get his teeth fixed – maybe we could move to where the rent is not so high . . .

Adding Machine: *Getting faster.* Rent this month, 50 – dentist, 15 – coat-15 – shoes, 6 – total, $84.00. Hospital – doctor – grocery – rent – butcher – shoes – coat – hospital – doctor – grocery – rent – butcher – shoes – coat.

Music picks this up into squeal of jammed machine.

Yvonne: So it happens. My machine is jammed and breaks down. When the foreman comes to fix it . . .

Foreman: This doesn't look like my best operator! What's the matter, Mis' Leveque? Don't you feel so well?

Yvonne: No – I have a headache. I seem to be so clumsy. . . .

Foreman: It's four o'clock. Why don't you check out.

Yvonne: It would be alright?

Foreman: Sure, go on home. Forget about stitching pants for the rest of the day.

Music. Phrase of happy release.

Yvonne: That's why I went to bring Suzanne home myself. Out in the street I feel happy again. It's nice to be outside so early. I walk along, thinking to-night I will have time to make a meatloaf – the boys like that, and it lasts for two days. I go up the steps of Mrs. Johnson's house and knock . . .

Sound knock. Pause. Knock again. Door open with.

Yvonne: I try the door – it's not locked. I go into the front hall . . .

Sound door close.

Yvonne: *Calling.* Hel-lo! Is anybody at home? *Pause.* The house is so quiet – no sound anywhere. I go into the front room. All the photographs are staring at me. Mr. Johnson who is dead now and their two children when they are small. The paper flowers – the ornaments on the piano – everything wrong with that room! Nothing could be alive in such a place. It is quiet as the grave! I go back to the hallway . . .

Sound of quick footsteps.

Yvonne: *Up.* Suzanne – ? Suzanne!

Suzanne. *Far off.* Mamma – mamma –

Yvonne: Suzanne! . . . where are you?

Sound of running up stairs.

Suzanne: *Off.* Mamma . . .

Yvonne: *Desperate.* Where are you – where are you – ?

Music. Sneak in the nightmare and build with.

I throw open three doors but she is not there. At the end of the hall a door is locked. I can hear Suzanne pounding on the other side of it. I struggle and shake the door – then I see the key hanging on a nail high up – I open the door and catch the screaming child in my arms . . .

Suzanne: *Crying.* The dog, mamma – the dog – the dog!

Music. Out in smash.

Yvonne: *Quietly.* It was a china dog with grinning teeth and staring eyes. Suzanne had knocked it down and broken it. For punishment she was locked in that dark room with the pieces of the dog staring at her. They left her alone in the house. If there had been a fire she would have no chance at all. So now even Paul has changed his mind about the City Creche. Will you have room there for my Suzanne?

Music. Restates the question.

Kirby: This morning I held three cards in my hand. I looked at the end result of many problems in economics, in housing, in education and psychology, in what we like to call our "way of life." As Alderman Bassett is fond of saying when people ask awkward questions at election meetings:

Bassett: These matters are beyond the scope of the municipal authority. They must be approached at the Federal level.

Kirby: At the *world* level, you could say, Mr. Bassett. The ideas that the billboards of our civilization hold before young people – ideas that do nothing to prepare them for the realities of marriage . . .

Peggy: It was the big romantic stuff, like in the movies; the pictures I cut out to make a scrap book of my dream house . . . *Harsh.* . . . my *dream* house!

Music. Three sardonic chords.

Kirby. The contradiction in the goals we set before our young women . . .

Fran: If this was to be my life, why wasn't I getting ready for it? Why did everybody pretend I was going somewhere else?

Music. Three frustrated chords.

Kirby: The cost of food, rent, medical care – in Canada under a boom economy . . .

Yvonne: When Paul is not sick he makes 40 dollars a week. Five people cannot live on that much money.

Music. Three chords of "Oh Canada."

Kirby: But while we slowly and painfully search for the answers to these adult problems, children need care and protection – to-day. Suzanne – David – and Marlene – with the permanent – they need the underlying control, the experience of group belonging, the care for health and safety in a good day nursery.

Which of them did I send there? Our space is so inadequate, I could send only the one whose need is greatest – to the child's world inside the high green gate.

Sound of small children singing:

> See the little hands go clap clap clap
> See the little feet go tap tap tap.
> This is what I say to you
> "Here is my hand how do you do?"
> See the little hands go clap clap clap
> See the little feet go tap tap tap!

Music. Pick up tune of children's song and take to finale.

The End

Breeches from
Bond Street

Bethoe Thompson as Clarissa Black, Jim Scott as Slivers Johnson, Grant Strate as
Charlie Curtis, Gary Gordon as Brooks, Studio Theatre, 1949.

BREECHES FROM BOND STREET: *INTERVIEW*

Day: Many women who ended up pursuing a writing career initially took a degree in English. You went into History, traditionally one of the more "masculine" of the arts disciplines. What prompted your choice and what impact did your history training have on your radio writing?

EPG: The reason I became a history teacher – took an honours degree in history – was that history was my favorite subject in high school. My history teacher, Mary Crawford, was a dynamic little person. And she made history so relevant and interesting, or maybe I just liked it anyway! And then, of course, at university I fell into the hands of Professor Burt who was a very good teacher and a very fine lecturer.

Day: You mentioned that you had to quit the teaching because it was expected that if you married . . .

EPG: Way back in '33 when I married there was no question of going on teaching; it just didn't occur to people.

Day: . . . and one of the reasons you went into writing was to keep yourself from going crazy.

EPG: Well, yes. Because I had an honours history degree and I had been using my brains for . . . you know. And here I was in a house and expected to be satisfied with just . . . doing the housework!
It was through my history training that I was asked to become a radio writer in the first place. I see it as a pageant, you know, a cavalcade of the centuries. I think

my series *The Building of Canada* established my reputation with CBC. I think it was damned good and they ought to do it over again!

Day: I notice that *Breeches* was written at a time when there was a real interest in rediscovering and dramatizing Alberta history and folklore: the Gard project, Ringwood's *Stampede*, the *This Is Our Story* series. To what extent did this movement affect the genesis and relatively frequent early productions and reworkings of the play?

EPG: Well, you see, it was written for CJCA, which is a private station and, very unusually, they had a young man working there who was interested in doing Canadiana. He got the idea for this series called *This Is Our Story*. They were only 15 minutes long, but the idea was that each story concentrated on some outstanding character in Alberta's history. And some people were real characters, like Nellie McClung and the buffalo. I wrote a story about the buffalo in Alberta being saved when they found a little herd in Montana and brought it up here.

I always felt that the remittance man never had a fair share, that everybody assumed the man would be a drunken bum, an active no-good. And I wanted a situation in which a remittance man would be involved. I was reading a book by a dear old man, Mr. Higginbotham – he was the first Alberta druggist. He and his brother bought a great box of cosmetics and things out from Ontario, and in McLeod, Alberta, set this thing up in the Mounties' fort and started selling drugs. And in his reminiscences he told about how this mountie had sent for a girl. There were ads in the paper called "Heart and Hand" from Chicago, but when she arrived he decided he didn't like her and he gave his orderly a hundred dollars to give her to go home. I thought this was a situation in which a remittance man could be involved. But I changed the mountie because it was such a dirty trick that we couldn't pin *that* on one of our heroes!

Day: No.

EPG: And you know the painter, Charlie Russell?

Day: Yes.

EPG: Well, in one of his drawings he's got a hold-up, and there's a whole row of people being held up in a stagecoach. In among them there was a frightened-looking little girl with an 1885 costume and a gambler with a fancy waistcoat and a bowler hat and a cigar. So I decided to use the gambler for my villain and the little girl became my heroine.

Day: Right.

EPG: Well then, that was the 15 minute short radio play. Then I decided to expand it into a half an hour radio play which was sold to Buckingham theatre. And then I wrote it as a television play. And then a stage play.

It's been my most popular dramatic idea. There is a certain Alberta atmosphere of the period but it's not really a history play. The whole point is that the two principal characters have been rejected: Brooksy by England and Liza by her so-called fiancé. It's a funny play and yet people respond to it; they've all been lonely or felt rejected. It's the *Anne of Green Gables* syndrome.

Day: It seems to me there are traces of Clarabel, the feisty gun-packing heroine of *The Argonauts* in the spinster character of *Breeches*. Are the two related? You seem to have ambiguous feelings about the strong pioneer woman. On one hand, in the historical plays, she's this figure of enormous strength, but in *The Ghost of Grandma Fraser* in the *Down Our Street* series, you suggest you can create a myth of superhuman self-sacrifice and domesticity that few modern women want to follow.

EPG: Well, I just wrote women that I could understand. And I never wrote a "Yes, John," wife in my life! All my heroines are self-assertive people. Well, they've all got a good slice of the old . . . of myself in them. So they more or less behave as I might have under the circumstances.

Day: You mentioned that one of the reasons you thought it was popular was because it also had publication possibilities that a lot of your plays didn't.

EPG: I accidentally ran into a very influential American dramatist, Percival Wilde, when we were travelling in England. And we became good friends. I showed him the script of *Breeches from Bond Street* and he said, "French's will take this." So he sent it to French's and said, "You're publishing this." So they did!

Day: Well, it went through all sorts of variations. Which of the versions did you like the best?

EPG: Oh, I like the straight stage play best. Although in the television and in the radio we could open it up and have different places. Of course, on radio we started with Slivers and Eliza riding from Calgary to McLeod and talking away; the exposition gets in there. But I don't think it improves it any. Yes, I think I like the stage play best. I've seen it very, very often.

Day: I notice that the play was one of three opening the

Studio Theatre at the University of Alberta in 1949.

EPG: Well, it was Bob Orchard, you see. He was the head of the Drama Department and he was arranging the program. There was *The White Man On The Mountain*, which he wrote. It was a kind of poetic affair. And there was *Breeches* and . . . what was the third one?

Day: *Box and Cox*, I think.

EPG: Oh, yes! *Box and Cox.*

Day: What do you remember of the production?

EPG: Oh, the production was very good. The men were particularly good. The boy who played Slivers, Jim Scott was the kind of strong actor that if we had been together longer, I would have begun writing plays for him, you know. And young Gay Gordon played Breeches.
      The cast on the Canadian TV was interesting. The boy who played Breeches, Charles Jarrett, went on to become quite a distinguished director in film, and I see his name in the English *Listener*. And *their* picture was in *The Listener*.

Day: So, this one made it overseas as well.

EPG: Oh well, *Breeches from Bond Street* was part of a series called *On Camera* which CBC was doing, I think it was in 1952 or 3. It would have been very early television days. Anyways it was picked up by the BBC. So they printed this picture of *Breeches from Bond Street* in *The Listener.*

Day: So, that's another one that made it internationally, like some of your radio series – *The Barlows of Beaver Street*, for instance.

EPG: Yes, indeed! I would like to have another idea that was as good!

Day: While some writers, like Len Peterson, managed the transition from radio to the professional stage, a number of amateur era playwrights like you, Gwen Pharis Ringwood, and Robertson Davies appear to have had great hopes for stage production in the post-war era, and even wrote full-length plays that were professionally produced, but then nothing comes of it. Why?

EPG: Well, one reason, of course, is that after my husband's death, I had to have a job to bring in some ready cash. The kind of writing I did required so much research that I couldn't earn a living. I mean, I couldn't live at the same standard I had been living, after Ted died. And the school board invited me to come and teach at Ross Shepherd. And I said, "I'm not an English teacher. I'm a History teacher."

And they said, "Well, you've been a writer, you know." So I did. The theory was that I'd do my own writing in the evening. And you can imagine how well *that* worked out!

So that from 1958 on, I was out of the picture as far as dramatic writing was concerned. Except for the *Jasper Story*; I don't really see how anybody else could do a better job on the Jasper Valley and all this 200 years of history! And the Dried Meat Pageant for the Crees – Treaty Number 6 – which was my final run at historical drama.

Day: 1977.

EPG: 1977, yes. It was a strange thing that I was 70 years old when I . . . I think that day at Dried Meat Lake was the top of my life as a playwright. It was such a perfect day and here was this enormous hill, and here was this horizon all around. Alberta's horizon. And the circular sky and people coming in thousands. On every road there were people coming, you know, and the Indian teepees were set up. And the Indians running around in the most gorgeous outfits you ever saw.

And I said to myself, "This is it! I can die now!"

BREECHES FROM BOND STREET:
FIRST PERFORMANCE

Breeches from Bond Street in its stage version was first performed by the Provincial Players in Hut C as part of the inaugural program of Studio Theatre, University of Alberta, 4 March, 1949, Bob Orchard, director, with the following cast:

Eliza Spenser – *Carolyn Barnes*
Trader Black – *John Bracco*
Neville Brooks – *Gary Gordon*
Slivers Johnson – *Jim Scott*
Charlie Curtis – *Grant Strate*
Clarissa Black – *Bethoe Thompson*

BREECHES FROM BOND STREET

Characters

Clarissa Black, co-proprietor of the hotel, tall, angular, no-nonsense, 50

Charlie Curtis, a "reformed" gambler, heavy-set, 35

Neville Brooks, a remittance man, a bad chip off the ancestral oak, young, genial, ne-er-do-well

Trader Black, hotel proprietor, stout, easygoing

Slivers, stagecoach driver, small, wiry, trace of Texan accent

Eliza Spenser, a mail-order bride, small, plain but spirited, 27

Time: 1884

Place: A back yard behind Trader Black's hotel in a southern town in what is now Alberta.

The back door is slightly left centre, and has a couple of broad flat steps before it. There is a pail of water at the end of the lowest step. At left is a long bench, or garden seat, with a young man asleep on it, his hat over his face. A neat new board fence, with a gate in it, runs from the corner of the hotel out of sight at right. On this side of the fence, a few small seedling trees, not more than eight inches high, are trying to grow. Above the fence, the blue Alberta sky. It is late afternoon in summer.

Clarissa Black, a tall angular woman of about 50, is sitting on the top step reading a newspaper. Her dress is plain, her speech is plain, there is no nonsense about her anywhere. Charlie Curtis is standing near the fence, looking off through binoculars. He is a big, heavy set fellow of about 35, dressed a little too flashily to look as respectable as he

thinks he is. There is peace and silence.
Clarissa snorts at something she has read; turns a page.
Charlie seems to focus on something. He gets excited.

Charlie: I got him! He's moving! It is a coyote! *He looks at the binoculars.* Wonderful invention. Care to try them, Sister Black?

Clarissa: Thanks, Charlie. Right now I don't need no spy glasses to see a coyote. And don't you "sister" me, you hypocrite. My name's Clarissa, and damn well you know it.

Charlie: *Wounded.* Hypocrite. There's a hard word. Just because a man has seen the error of his ways –

Clarissa: Uh-huh.

Charlie: I'm through with gambling, Clarissa. No more poker for me, nor faro, nor black-jack.

Clarissa: If you've quit gambling, it's because you've figured out a smarter way to be crooked. What's it going to be? Real estate or mining stock?

Charlie: I'm a changed man, and I'll prove it to you. Just wait and see.

Trader Black appears in the hotel door. In shirt sleeves with his vest open. Trader is enjoying a free afternoon. Stout, easy going, Trader is a very relaxed character. He is amused by human nature, but hopeful about it.

Trader: Howdy, Charlie!

Charlie: Hello, Trader!

Trader: *Tongue in cheek.* Warm day. Can I offer you a drink?

Charlie: *Hastily.* No, no! Not any more! Nothing like that.

Clarissa: Don't get excited, Brother. Trader was talking about the bucket of water he brings out here to water the trees.

Charlie: Trees? What trees?

Clarissa: That's them against the fence. Just be careful how you step around there. Trader's fixing to have a garden here in the back yard.

Charlie: *Looks at the seedlings with some contempt.* If the Lord had intended trees to grow here, he'd have grown them.

Trader: *Drily.* You can leave the Lord out of it, Charlie. Contributing 200 dollars to building a church don't put you on speaking terms with the Almighty yet.

Clarissa: Especially when the 200 was poker winnings.

Charlie: You won't tell Mrs. Pearson that, Clarissa?

Clarissa: I never speak to Mrs. Pearson if I can help it. She's the kind of old biddy I came West to get away from.

Trader: Clarissa don't like women much, Charlie.

Clarissa: Not female women. But they're catching up to me.

Charlie: I wouldn't say that. They're not so plentiful. There ain't three unmarried women between High River and the Border.

Trader: You sound like you had them all counted, Charlie. Where you going with the telescopes? Never heard tell of you hunting or rounding up cattle.

Charlie: I got my reasons. *Looks at his gold watch.* Three thirty. Stage should be in soon.

Trader: Yep. Slivers'll be crossing the river about now. You expecting some freight, Charlie?

Charlie: You could put it that way. Well, see you later.

Trader: *With a lazy gesture.* Adios!

Charlie goes out through the gate, Trader watching him.

What's the matter with him anyway? He's as jumpy as a six-year kid that has to go. *Watching.* If he's meeting the stage, he's headed the wrong way.

Clarissa: Where'd he get the fancy spy glasses?

Trader: Won them off his Lordship, at Tony's place a few weeks back. *He goes over and looks at the young fellow on the bench.* Brooksy's been mighty broke this last little while. Sold everything he owns, except his saddle.

Clarissa: Ain't this the day his remittance is due?

Trader: That's right. He told me to wake him up when the stage gets in. *He sits on the steps and lights a cigar.*

Clarissa: You shouldn't have sold him that drink before dinner. He ought to be sober two days a year. *She goes over and shakes the sleeper.* Brooksy!

Trader: No sir, they didn't break up the game last night till going on three.

Clarissa: *Shaking him roughly.* Hey Brooksy! *No result.* Well, there's nothing else for it.

She gets a small dipper of water from the pail and sloshes it on his face. He sits up fighting and spluttering.

Brooks: Aaaaaaaaayaaaaa! Stop it! *Shakes his head, gets his eyes open.* Clarissa, you she-devil! Is that any way to treat a friend?

Clarissa: Come on. Get up. You just got time to shave.

Brooks: Shave? What time is it? *Yawns.*

Trader: Going on four.

Brooks: Right you are. *But he makes no move to get up.*

Clarissa: I don't see how you figure what day a letter gets here all the way from England.

Brooks: *His manner to her is affectionate banter.* My dear Clarissa, you don't know old Twitchley, the family solicitor. Regular as clockwork, on the appointed day, he bangs off the old bank draft and then forgets all about me for another six months. I suppose they've all forgotten me. Even Molly.

Clarissa: Molly. Was that your sweetheart?

Brooks: A beauty! What legs she had! I could do anything with Molly.

Clarissa: Well! No wonder they shipped you out of the country.

Trader: *Laughing.* Don't be so slow on the draw, Clarissa. Molly was a horse.

Clarissa: A horse?

Brooks: Irish hunter. Only creature that ever understood me.

Trader: Slivers says you're a good hand with animals, Brooksy. And he's tired of driving stage. Still looking for a partner to go raising horses for the police.

Clarissa: Nobody can be partners with Slivers and with Johnny Walker at the same time.

Brooks: Now, Clarissa, a man must have some distractions in this savage wilderness.

Clarissa: This ain't a wilderness. Getting too damn civilized. Nobody's been shot for the past six months, and they're selling face cream in Higginbotham's store.

Trader: Why don't you take Slivers up on the proposition, Brooks?

Brooks: I've considered it, old boy. " A sober, righteous and godly life." But on the other hand, why in blazes should I?

Loud voices and singing inside the hotel indicate that the stage is probably in.

Clarissa: Stage is in, Trader. Ain't you going in the bar?

Trader: My day off. Pete can handle them.

Brooks: *Starting up the steps.* Allowing half an hour to sort the mail, I'll do it nicely. Any warm water on the stove?

Clarissa: I don't heat water for shaving.

Brooks: *Turning on the charm.* Oh, come now, Duchess –

Clarissa: And stay out of my kitchen!

Brooks: Special occasion, Clarissa. You want me to look my best, you know you do. Must I go to meet my solicitor with a two-day beard?

Clarissa: *Giving in but still tart.* You put your clean pants on. They're hanging in your room. Try if you can look like a Christian for half a day.

Brooks: A Christian? My good woman, those breeches were made in Bond Street for a gentleman. Did you sew the buttons on?

Clarissa: Why in blazes should I?

Trader: She sewed them on.

Brooks: Thank you, my darling! *He goes into the hotel.*

Trader: Horses and women. He sure has a way with him.

Clarissa: Worthless good for nothing!

Trader: *Takes a dipper of water to his trees.* He gives us just what we expect of him, Clarissa.

Clarissa: And who expects him to be a drunken gambler?

Trader: Everybody in the country. A remittance man. The boy was branded the minute he stepped off the CPR. And that's the way Brooksy played it.

Clarissa: You shouldn't water plants in the heat of the day. Not that them seedlings'll ever amount to anything. Them's Ontario trees.

Trader: Earth is earth. Water is water. If there's anything in these twigs wants to grow, the Alberta sun will bring it out.

Clarissa: If it don't shrivel them up and kill them dead. Here's Slivers now!

A thin, wiry little man has come hurrying through the gate. Slivers is dressed in Western style, and has a touch of Texas in his voice. He is excited right now, and upset as he comes to her at steps.

Slivers: Clarissa, am I glad to see you!

Trader: Well, Slivers, you've been pushing those ponies!

Slivers: Howdy, Trader! Clarissa, you got to help me!

Clarissa: What's the matter?

Slivers: She's standing out there in front of the hotel, looking like a prairie chicken in a pack of wolves.

Clarissa: Who is?

Slivers: The girl.

Clarissa: What girl?

Slivers: The girl I just brought in.

Clarissa: Why Slivers Johnson at your age!

Slivers: Don't look at me! It's none of my doing. She came here to marry Charlie Curtis.

Clarissa: Well! So that's why the old buzzard had his fancy waistcoat on!

Slivers: She rid from Calgary with me on the hurricane deck. Telling me all about it. How she loves the prairie and how proud she'll be to be a rancher's wife.

Trader: Rancher? Charlie never was a rancher.

Slivers: She don't know that. She ain't seen Charlie yet.

Clarissa: But you just said –

Slivers: Don't you understand? It was a mail order proposition.

Clarissa: Mail order!

Slivers: Eliza that's her name, Eliza Spenser. She answered an ad in the matrimonial column of *Heart and Hand* ye know, that Chicago paper the boys been passing around. And Charlie sent her the money to come out here.

Clarissa: Well, didn't he meet the stage? Where is he now?

Slivers: I don't know, Clarissa. And what she don't know, is that Charlie took a look at her through some opery glasses off the livery stable roof. And he decided he don't want her.

Trader: *Really shocked.* Slivers!

Clarissa: Don't want her! My God, the low down . . .

Slivers: He sent over a hundred bucks for me to give her to go back home. And you got to let me bring her back here, Clarissa, so you can tell her.

Clarissa: *Stepping back fast. Me* tell her?

Slivers: It's a job for a woman.

Clarissa: No thank you! My shoulders wasn't made for little dollies to cry on. Go find the Reverend Beggs, or the Mounted Police.

Slivers: The boys tell me the Reverend is out of town.

Trader: And the Constable rode over to the Reserve and won't be back till tomorrow.

Clarissa: Then tell her yourself!

Slivers: Clarissa, I ain't got the courage. Never knowed I was a coward. I've faced stampeding steers, down in Texas. But there's something about that girl's eyes.

Clarissa: What's the matter with her eyes?

Slivers: Nothing the matter. They're mighty pretty. But it's like she had a dream in them. A picture she's made of how things are going to be. I – I couldn't face the look in her eyes when the mirage blows away!

Clarissa: Oh, stuff and nonsense.

Brooks: *Appears in the doorway, his face covered with lather, shaving brush in one hand and mug in the other. He has on the clean breeches and his undervest. He is highly amused.* My word, Slivers you are in a hole, eh?

Slivers: You been listening, have you?

Brooks: Heard every word, old boy, couldn't help it. What sort of girl is she?   Not quite . . . well, not *quite* I suppose?

Clarissa: *Dangerously.* Not quite what?

Brooks: Well, I mean to say, girls who answer matrimonial advertisements –

Clarissa: And why shouldn't a woman take a chance like the rest of you? You're gambling your life away.

Brooks: Oh, but look here, that's different.

Clarissa: If one of us has to break the bad news to this girl I know who's going to do it. *Pointing. Brooksy!*

Brooks: Oh, I say, Duchess . . .

Slivers: *Leaping for him.* Clarissa you're a genius!

Brooks: *Backing away.* Me talk to her? Not a chance!

Slivers: *Grabbing his arm.* You got such nice manners and a smooth lines of words. Why didn't I think of it? We been partners, haven't we? You'll do this for me, Brooksy?

Brooks: Leave me alone, dammit!

Clarissa: *Grabbing his other arm.* Come on, get your shirt on!

Brooks: Trader, for God's sake, call these idiots off!

Trader: I dunno, Brooksy. You sure get around Clarissa.

Slivers: Any other man tried to shave in that kitchen, she'd run him out with the carving knife.

Clarissa: She's nearly as far from home as you are, Brooksy, and she's had a crooked deal.

Slivers: *Takes roll of money from his pocket. Stuffing a roll in Brooks' pocket.* All you got to do is convince her she's better off without Charlie and give her this to go home on.

Brooks: But I don't *like* strange young women . . .

Trader: Not scared to do it, are you, Brooks? I've met plenty of green Englishmen. I never heard tell of one that was *yellow.*

Brooks: *Stung by this.* Oh, confound you, Trader.

Clarissa: You get the girl around here. I'll take him in and pretty him up.

Brooks: Oh, but Clarissa listen to reason –

He is still protesting as she drags him indoors.

Slivers: Think he'll do it, Trader?

Trader: It wouldn't surprise me.

Slivers: Well, here goes. *He takes off his hat and mops his forehead.* I'd rather ride herd on a hundred broncs than one filly, wearing a skirt. *He puts on his hat and hurries out the gate.*

Trader lingers by the steps, held by curiosity.

Slivers comes back with Eliza Spenser. She is a small girl, not flashily pretty; neatly dressed in a travelling costume of the 80s.

Opening the gate. Just step in, Eliza.

Eliza: Thank you. *She comes through and stops dead at the sight of Trader.*

Slivers: Ah, Miss Spenser, this is Mr. Black, proprietor of the hotel.

Eliza: *Relieved.* Oh!

Trader: *Coming to meet her.* Afternoon, ma'am.

Eliza: *Shaking hands.* Mr. Black? Are you the famous Trader Black?

Trader: That's what they call me.

Eliza: I've heard about you. You used to drive ox teams from Montana.

Trader: *Laughs, hoisting his belt.* That was before I carried so much weight myself! So you like the West, eh?

Eliza: Oh, I love it!

Trader: Changing fast.

Eliza: Yes, everything changes. Even Calgary might some day be like Toronto. Though, I don't see how it could, with all this sunshine.

Trader: *Dry.* The human race will do to this country just what they've done to the rest of the world.

Eliza: But it's wonderful to be here now when it's all new!

Trader: And take a hand in how it changes?

Eliza: Yes, maybe!

Trader: No maybe about it. *Smiles.* Looking at you, ma'am, I feel mighty hopeful. We don't have many ladies stopping here, but my wife would be glad to find you accommodation.

Eliza: Oh, thank you. Charlie took a room for me at Mrs. Pearson's.

Slivers: Just around the corner. And she'll be going over there right away.

Eliza: Charlie thinks of everything.

Slivers: He certainly does!

Trader: Well, just make yourself at home. *He starts toward gate.*

Slivers: *Sorry to lose him.* Ain't you tending bar today, Trader?

Trader: No. *He looks at Eliza, sizing her up, and smiles.* Figure I'll do an errand at the post office. See you later. *He goes out by the gate.*

Eliza: Do you know Mrs. Pearson, Slivers?

Slivers: Well, we don't exactly ride for the same outfit. The old b — ah, the old lady is strictly TT, if you follow me. Now just sit down, Eliza.

Eliza: *Sitting on the garden bench left.* My, you've been nice to me.

Slivers: *Stung.* Don't say that!

276

Eliza: When Charlie and me are settled on our ranch, you'll come and visit us, won't you?

Slivers: Now everything's going to be all right. Don't you worry.

Eliza: *Nervously.* I'm not worried.

Slivers: Everything's going to be fine. You enjoyed the trip, seeing the country and all?

Eliza: Yes. *As he edges away right.* Do you have to go?

Slivers: I sure do.

Eliza: Couldn't you stay till Charlie comes?

Slivers: No, sir! Now you see it's like this. I got my horses to tend to. You wouldn't want me to neglect my horse?

Eliza: Oh, no. No.

Slivers: You're a real sensible girl. You'll always do the sensible thing, won't you?

Eliza: *Puzzled.* I try to.

Slivers: Well, that's fine. You just keep on that way, and you'll *never* be sorry you came. *Suddenly he can't stand any more of it.* Good-bye Eliza.

Eliza: Good-bye, Slivers. And thank you.

He claps his hat on his head and rushes into the hotel.
Eliza has a bad moment of panic. She goes after Slivers as if to call him back; then pulls herself together, and sits down again on the bench. She takes a much-folded letter from her hand bag and reads it for the thousandth time. She brings a small mirror out, fluffs her front hair and bites her lips to give them colour. She is slipping the glass back into

her bag, when Brooks steps into the doorway. In his well-tailored clothes, clean and groomed, he is for this moment at least, the Hon. Neville Brooks of Brooklands, Derbyshire. He clears his throat. Eliza is almost afraid to look around. Then she does look, and gives a little gasp.

Eliza: *Rising.* Oh!

Brooks: *Coming down the steps.* Miss Spenser?

Unable to speak, she nods, looking at him with her soul in her eyes.

Miss Spenser, I – *Her eyes stop him.*

Eliza: *Coming slowly towards him.* Hello! *Relief and happiness surging up in her.* Hello, Charlie!

Brooks: *Flummoxed, backing away.* Oh, I say I'm awfully sorry, but you'll have to let me explain. You see . . .

Eliza: Oh, don't apologize for not being here to meet me. After all, when a man has three thousand head of cattle to look after . . .

Brooks: Miss Spenser, please listen. I . . .

Eliza: Don't you think you ought to call me Eliza? Start as you mean to go on, Mama used to say.

Brooks: You must have wondered why you've been kept waiting. Well . . .

Eliza: I didn't mind, I walked up and down in front of the hotel to stretch my legs. Of course, in Ontario we say "limbs" but I've been in the West for three whole days!

Brooks: Ah yes, but the fact is, that I'm not . . .

Eliza: I saw every man in town out there, I guess. But you're different. You're the only one I could possibly – *She breaks off in confusion.* I didn't know you were English.

Brooks: No.

Eliza: You are, aren't you?

Brooks: Oh, yes, I *am* English.

Eliza: Did you go to Oxford?

Brooks: Good God, no. Cambridge.

Eliza: *Apologizing.* Oh.

Brooks: One term. But that doesn't matter in the least, because . . .

Eliza: It's nice of you to say that. I finished high school before I started dressmaking. But I'm a good cook. You have to be to bring up a family.

Brooks: *Startled.* Family?

Eliza: My two brothers. I told you. I was only 17, when Mama died. But they're married now. And I haven't anybody but you. *She walks away from him.* There's something I must tell you. I think people ought to be honest, don't you?

Brooks: Oh, yes yes.

Eliza: Well, it wasn't true what I wrote about my age. I'm not 23, I'm 27. All my life I wanted to do something adventurous. I thought about it while I was sewing long seams in other people's trousseaus. Then when I read your advertisement "Lonely rancher wishes to correspond with young lady" I didn't sleep all that night. In the morning, I cut out the piece and put it in my needle case. And in the afternoon I answered it. Did you think I was bold?

Brooks: I didn't know anything about it. You see –

Eliza: *Laughs.* Of course, you didn't? We both took a chance. *She is now relaxed and happy.* I love the West, don't you? Everything's so big here. The mountains and the great wide beautiful sky! All new and different. And I think we can be new people too no matter what we were anywhere else.

Brooks: Yes, yes, one feels that at first.

Eliza: *Gently.* I'm sorry you were lonely in that big ranch house all alone. But I'll try to make it like home for you. I brought some of Mama's things – her dishes, and the teapot. It's not real silver, it's pewter but it's a pretty shape. And I have ten yards of curtains that I bought with my own money. *Pause.* I never expected to marry someone like you. I hope you won't be ashamed of me.

Brooks: *Desperately.* Eliza look here – before you say another word, there's something I really must . . .

Eliza: Yes. I know.

Brooks: You know?

Eliza: We're quite alone here. And, well you'll have to kiss me for the first time someplace, so . . .

She is evidently waiting to be kissed, and no Brooks ever let a lady down. After a moment's hesitation, he throws discretion to the winds, and kisses her softly.

Oh Charlie!

Brooks: *The name brings him back to reality with a jerk.*

Oh, my God we've got to get out of here!

Eliza: Could we find Mrs. Pearson's house now?

Brooks: Pearson's?

Eliza: Where I'm going to stay until, until we . . .

Brooks: Eliza, if I take you there now will you wait for me till I come back?

Eliza: Of course.

Brooks: You won't go out, or talk to anybody?

Eliza: No. But why?

Brooks: Never mind. Just promise.

Eliza: *Puzzled.* I promise.

Brooks: Good girl. Come along.

He gives her his arm and they sail out by the gate.
Slivers, with Clarissa behind him, peers out of the hotel door.

Slivers: Aw, dang it, they've gone. *He comes down the steps.* I shouldn't have waited for that drink. But I needed it.

Clarissa: Brooksy made me swear I wouldn't listen.

Slivers: You don't suppose he hurt the poor girl's feelings?

Clarissa: Don't worry. When he's got those britches on, he acts like the man they were made for.

Slivers: *Taking out a folded paper.* Wish he'd keep the pants on long enough for me to get his John Henry on this document.

Clarissa: What document?

281

Slivers: Lease on that land by the fork, at Willow Creek, first-class range. Got a spring of living water that never freezes. If Brooksy would use his remittance for a down payment, him and me could go raising horses.

Clarissa: Well, you know what happened the last time his money got here.

Slivers: *Sadly, folding away the paper.* Yup. I didn't know a fellow could stay drunk that long and remember his name when he come to.

Charlie: *Comes through the hotel.* Well, Slivers, you tended to that little matter, did you?

Slivers: How can you show your face around here today, Charlie?

Charlie: Aw, what's the difference? If she don't want to go home, anything in a petticoat can get a man in this country.

Clarissa: You lied to that girl, Charlie, telling her you had a big ranch.

Charlie: And she lied to me! Telling me she had red hair. I got no use for mousy little dames. Not but what I'm living respectable, mind you. But what I want is a big strong woman that wears bright colours. What would I do with a buttoned-up little schoolmarm?

Clarissa: I know what some schoolmarm should have done with you.

Slivers: She ain't a schoolmarm, she's a dressmaker.

Charlie: I like a woman to have some gumption.

Clarissa: If you had any guts yourself, you'd have met the girl, even if she turned out to have cross eyes and a wooden leg.

Charlie: No use creating a painful sitation, Clarissa. I took a gamble, and I paid for it.

Clarissa: Paid for it! What do you think a woman is – a consignment of five-inch nails? Does it ever occur to you a girl might have some pride and some feelings!

Charlie: That sounds kind of sentimental, coming from you. *He turns to go into the hotel.* Well, thanks, Slivers.

Brooks: *Comes hurrying in by the gate.* Just a minute, Curtis, could I speak to you on business?

Charlie: *Scenting money.* Business? Certainly. Man of capital, eh? Maybe we could step into Trader's back room –

Brooks: We'll settle this here. This is yours. *He shoves the roll of money into Charlie's hand, as if it burnt him.* Clarissa, you'll witness I'm returning to Curtis what he paid for Eliza's return fare.

Charlie: Eliza? *He looks at Slivers.* Whose errand boy are you, Brooksy?

Brooks: Never mind that –

Slivers: Where is Eliza at?

Brooks: I escorted her to Mrs. Pearson's front door.

Slivers: Did Mrs. Pearson see you?

Brooks: I don't know. I hardly think so.

Clarissa: Bet the old battle-axe was looking through her parlour curtains.

Charlie: Well, don't tell me your lordship is taking over the goods as delivered? *Laughs.* Mail order bride, eh? Second hand, too.

Brooks: I wouldn't talk that way, if I were you.

Slivers: Brooksy, don't do nothing rash!

Brooks: I'd rather not brawl with you, in front of Clarissa –

Clarissa: If you feel like fighting, boys, go ahead!

Charlie: Fighting? Not this delicate blossom. Might get his clothes mussed up.

Slivers: *Puzzled.* What did you aim to do, Brooksy?

Brooks: I'm trying to keep Eliza from being hurt by what's happened today.

Slivers: Oh, my God, you mean you ain't told her?

Brooks: She talked to me. You didn't exaggerate when you said she has remarkable eyes.

Clarissa: Must be quite a girl, if she's put the hex on both you fellows!

Brooks: She came here to meet a rancher. At the moment I can offer her nothing. *To Charlie.* But she's clear now of any obligation to you. If you'll keep out of the way until I get to the post office – have you that lease with you, Slivers?

Slivers: You mean it? *Holds out paper.* Right here, partner, right here!

Brooks: *Taking the paper and glancing over it.* Splendid! Lead the way, old boy. Clarissa, you're looking at the new owners of – *With a flash of pride* – of "Brooklands."

Clarissa: *Warning.* Get going Slivers!

Slivers: This is the happiest day of my life! I feel like doing what I ain't done these many years. I feel like yelling yippee! By Joshua, I will yell it! Yippeeee! Yippeeeee!

Waving his hat and heading for the gate, he bumps smack into Eliza. Her hair is loose, as if she had begun to take it down. A little red shawl or dressing sacque, is thrown over her shoulders. There is nothing mousy about her, as she blows in like a furious young tornado.

Why hello, Eliza, you looking for somebody?

Eliza: I am looking for the Honorable Mr. Neville Brooks!

Brooks: Eliza – I –

Eliza: *Driving him left in front of her.* Don't you speak to me! Don't you dare call me Eliza! You deceitful, low-down, cowardly, despicable hypocrite! Pretending to be a rancher! Pretending to be a man – !

Brooks: Miss Spenser – ! I did try to tell you – !

Eliza: Mrs. Pearson told me. How you spend your days in a barroom and your nights at a gambling table . . .

Slivers: Forgot to warn you, Brooksy. Ma Pearson's mighty thick with Charlie these days.

Eliza: So you're in this too, Slivers. This cruel joke. Oh, how could you? How could you do it? I suppose you planned it between you.

Brooks: I assure you – our intentions were of the best . . .

Eliza: *Slapping his face. That's* what I think of your intentions and your fancy clothes and your English accent! Where is he? What have you done with him?

Slivers: Done with who?

Eliza: Where is the real Charlie Curtis?

Slivers: *Stammering.* Charlie? Well, he – eh –

Charlie: *Steps forward, smiling and composed.* I believe I'm the party you're looking for, Miss.

Eliza: You're who?

Charlie: Curtis is the name. My friends call me Charlie.

Eliza: Oh, no! No, you couldn't be.

Charlie: Why couldn't I?

Eliza: Well – well – you don't look like a rancher.

Slivers: The only herd *he* ever rounded up was a stack of chips.

Eliza: *Desperately, clutching her dream.* The man I came to marry owns 3000 head of cattle.

Charlie: Well, maybe I did stretch it a bit. Who doesn't when he's courting a girl? For that matter, there might be a few things in these letters, that don't square exactly with the truth. *He take a bundle of letters from his pocket.* This your handwriting?

Eliza: *Looking at him.* Yes. Yes, it is. Oh, Slivers, please tell me honestly. Is this – ?

Slivers: That's him all right.

Charlie: I like a woman to have a little temper. Makes life interesting. So now we've had a good look at each other, maybe we could start in where these letters leave off.

Eliza: *Backing away.* What am I going to do?

Charlie: That's very simple, my dear, The Rev. Mr. Beggs will be here tomorrow. Meantime, we could take a walk through town – do a little shopping for something pretty.

Eliza: *Almost in tears.* I can't go back to Belleville. They'd laugh at me there, too.

Slivers: You mean you don't want Charlie after all?

Eliza: No!

Slivers: But he's the fellow –

Eliza: He's *not* the fellow – not now.

Brooks raises his head.

Charlie: Keep out of this, Slivers!

Slivers: You got no hold on Eliza.

Charlie: I'm taking up my option, that's all. A bargain is a bargain.

Slivers: Bargain! Why you double-crossing –

Clarissa: *Going into action, she thrusts the two men back with a swing of her arm.* Listen, Sister, when Biddy Pearson was in such a hurry to spill the beans on Brooksy, did she tell you anything about this rattler?

Eliza: No.

Clarissa: Alright. I'll let you have it straight. He saw you get off the stage today.

Eliza: He saw me? Then why –

Clarissa: He didn't claim the shipment, because he decided you was too ladylike for his purpose. He gave Slivers the money to send you back home, and we shanghaied Brooksy into breaking the news gently. That's the only

287

way he come to be mixed into it.

Charlie: *Furious, grabbing little Slivers by the shirtfront.* Couldn't you keep your mouth shut and do what you were told? Now every old goat in the country knows my business.

Clarissa: Old goat!

Brooks: *Stepping between them.* That's enough! Before I knock your block off, I'd like to say you're the most unmitigated blackguard I've met outside the Old Bailey.

Trader comes up behind the gate, with a letter in his hand and watches this scene with approval.

Charlie: Who's knocking whose block off?

Slivers: Brooksy! He killed a man in Montana.

Charlie: Why, you cast off hunk of worm-eaten family tree!

He takes a punch at Brooks and they fight.

Eliza: Stop them somebody, stop them!

Clarissa: Aw, let them enjoy themselves. The police is out of town.

Slivers: Watch his left, Brooksy, watch his left!

Brooks catches Charlie a clean one, and he goes down for the count.

Slivers: Well, I'll be damned, if them English schools ain't some good after all. If he was lying under a table, he'd look real natural.

Eliza: Is he dead?

Clarissa: Not him, sister, but he's out cold.

Eliza: Well, aren't you going to do something?

Clarissa: *Calmly.* Trader'll fix him up, when he gets around to it.

Trader: *Coming in.* Here's your letter, Brooks, all signed for. *He hands it to him and crosses to Charlie.* Yes, sir, it's been a lovely afternoon.

Trader, Clarissa and Slivers bend over the body.

Brooks: *Looks at the letter. He goes to Eliza.* Eliza – what they told you about me was quite true. You see, it didn't matter to anybody, how I lived. But you said – one can make a clean start here no matter what he was anywhere else . . .

Eliza: Yes.

Brooks: Slivers and I are taking up land. It's good range – I'll build you a ranch house, Eliza, and perhaps you'll pour my tea, from a pewter teapot. If you do me the honour to be my wife – I give you my word you won't be ashamed of me.

Eliza: It's still true – the other thing I said – that you were the only man I – *She raises her head and looks at him.* Oh, I'm sorry I hit you.

Brooks: Make it better! *He leans his cheek towards her and she kisses him.*

Eliza: Neville! *Hesitates.* That is how you say your name?

Brooks: Ah – yes.

Eliza: What did your mother call you?

Brooks: Well, as a matter of fact – she always called me "Bubbles." *Turning.* Coming, Slivers?

Slivers: Am I coming! We're lighting out of there before Charlie comes to. He might be hard to convince it was *bubbles* that hit *him*!

Slivers, Brooks and Eliza go out the gate.

Clarissa: *After a pause.* I wonder if Brooksy can stay with it.

Trader: Did you get a good look at that girl's face?

Clarissa: Yes. Yes, I did. *They smile at each other. Then she speaks as brusquely as ever.* Sun's getting around. Wouldn't do any harm to water them trees. Could be they make something of themselves after all.

Trader: *Chuckling as he takes up the water pail. There is very little water in it.* Always hope, in the West, if we got the spirit in us. Always hope. Even for you, Charlie. *He empties the water over Charlie.* Even for you.

Quick curtain.

The End

Woman in the
Twentieth Century

Honorary Chief Factor, Elsie Park Gowan, at Fort Edmonton, 17 May, 1979.

WOMAN IN THE TWENTIETH CENTURY:
FIRST PERFORMANCE

Lecture given to various groups in the mid 1930s.

WOMAN IN THE
TWENTIETH CENTURY *

It has been said that when Nora Helmer slammed the door of her doll's house, the bang re-echoed around the world. It announced a new age for woman – an age in which she ceased to be a chattel or a plaything; an age in which she escaped from bondage, achieved a position of freedom and equality. That was many years ago, but if any girl of today thinks the battle is over, let her think again and think hard. The doors are still banging, it is true. But they bang in our expectant faces quite as often as behind our triumphant backs.

This is a decade of reaction. The ideals which seemed so near achievement after the war are now farther away than ever. The ideal of internationalism is obscured by flaming national distrusts. Democracy has disappeared in some states and is tottering in others. Feminism, which seemed so splendidly justified by woman's war work and enfranchisement . . . feminism is blamed for every evil from unemployment onward.

As a result, the position of women in this century is completely illogical. From the first day a little girl goes to school, all her training is based on the assumption that her life will be the same as her brothers. She is taught the same things in public and high schools. If she shows promise of a keen mind she is encouraged to train for professional work. The world smiles on a bright little girl when she becomes a lawyer or a doctor or a first class business executive. She gets her picture in the paper and local citizens refer to her with pride.

Now let the bright little girl find a man with whom she would like to live. She affirms her intention to do so before the proper representatives of church and state. If she at the same time renounces all interest in her profession, the world smiles on her benignly. All is well lost for love in the good, old romantic Ethel M. Dell manner. But let her attempt to go on with her profession, and a howl of protest goes up. She is taking the bread out of some poor girl's mouth. She is undermining her husband's self-respect. She is neglecting her children or neglecting to have any. The smiling century which encouraged her to think like a man and work like a man says very firmly: "No, my dear, this will never do. After all, you are a woman, and woman's place is in the home."

The philosopher Henry Van Dyke has named the four best things which life can bring to anyone as work, love, play, rest. To know the joy of love is to live happily with one's mate; to know the joy of work is to spend the energies of one's life in an interesting job. As Van Dyke himself puts it:

> Let me but do my work from day to day
> In field or forest, at the desk or loom,
> In roaring market-place or tranquil room,
> Let me but find it in my heart to say
> When vagrant wishes beckon me astray,
> "This is my work; my blessing, not my doom,
> Of all who live, I am the one by whom
> This work can best be done in the right way."
>
> Then shall I see it not too great, nor small,
> To suit my spirit and to prove my powers,
> Then shall I cheerful turn, when the long shadows fall
> At eventide to play and love and rest,
> Because I know for me my work is best.[1]

If you are born into that half of the human race which uses hairpins, you take your choice of these two best things, work or love. Your brother has an unquestioned chance at them both. He chooses his profession and he establishes his home. The two best things are his by rights.

It must be pointed out that many women find the career of home-making a completely satisfactory outlet for their talents.

294

The cynical would say these hadn't any talents to distress them. The romantic would say they are in love, and the profound would explain that these clever women have escaped the world's "Be a man, little girl" propaganda. We will return to this point in a moment. For the time being we are concerned with the women who are sincerely enthusiastic about their profession, and who feel that profession to be their work in the best and truest sense.

The dilemma of the modern girl has been getting into print. Dorothy Dix devotes a column to it in her usual breezy style. This was the letter:

> Dear Miss Dix:
>
> I have practically everything a reasonable woman can desire, a loving husband, an attractive child, a cosy home, yet I am restless and discontented. Since I was a young girl I have been in a business office where new people with new ideas were coming in all the time and I was kept on my toes every minute. Going home at night was a diversion and I enjoyed it and doing my domestic chores.
>
> Now, since so many married women have been excluded from business offices, I have lost my job and I have to stay at home all the time and I am bored to tears. What I earned did not increase our income much. But I am so lonely and so bored. How am I to fill my days?

To this appeal Dorothy turned a sympathetic ear. After enumerating the blessings of economic independence to women, she said, "But for everything, we have to pay and a lot of women have to pay for their experience as business or professional women by having it totally unfit them for matrimony." A girl who held a high executive position in a big store married and went into housekeeping in a tiny apartment. I asked her how she like it and she frankly replied: "I'm miserable. I don't know what to do with myself. Putting me to run a little flat is like putting a thousand horsepower engine to do a one horsepower job."

Again, the *Forum and Century* a few years ago carried a pungent article called "The Educational Veil" pointing out that any young woman who goes in for teaching as a life job is expected to swear eternal celibacy.[2] Let us add here and now that even the possibility of marriage is a handicap in this as in other fields. A case occurred in this university so long ago that it can be safely referred to. A woman student in an honours course so far outshone the men in her class that the head of the department himself said, "she could run rings all round them." There was a vacancy on the staff in that faculty. Did she get the job? She did not. A man whom she had continuously outclassed was appointed, because she, being She, would probably marry and thus disqualify herself as a suitable lecturer. She is still teaching in a small country town.

The "Educational Veil" article pointed out that the woman teacher has three possible choices:

1. To put out of her life any idea of having a home of her own.

2. Clandestine affairs which are bound to be unsatisfactory to people of self-respect.

3. Marriage and resignation.

This assumes that the one term "Marriage" describes all legal relations between men and women and that all marriages are of the "family" type.

It ignores the fact that many young people of this century enter marriage for companionship in its most complete sense, but postponing the arrival of their children until the latter are wanted. The world does not approve of a partner in such a marriage being actively engaged in education. It may be remarked that in one small city of Alberta a married woman with an adolescent family held with great success the principalship of the high school. Her knowledge of life and human nature, added to a keen mind and professional interest, made her a tower of strength in the school. Her service to the community was made possible by the fortunate circumstance of her being a widow.

The illogical nature of woman's present status was neatly summed up by one Benge Atlee in *Maclean's* of September last. He wrote:

> The real proof of my contention that this is a man's world is the dissatisfactions which ambitious and intelligent women experience with regard to their lot in it. . . . If in business, she is all too conscious of the insecurity and ephemerality of her status. Not only is she the first to go when jobs are being cut down and often before men less efficient; not only is the work of her hand held at a constant discount as compared to her brothers. If she marries she must, in most cases, give up a career to which she has devoted earnest training and serious work, and retire to the home – which in a modern world has become more and more of a place in which merely to eat and sleep. She must leave in full flight a way of life for which she has ardently prepared herself, and commence another for which she has no training and to which she has been betrayed by her biologic urge.[3]

Two possible solutions present themselves, which may be roughly described as the Russian and German models. Whatever we may think of woman's position in these countries, it has at least the merit of consistency, which our muddleheaded methods have not. The Russian government has taken its women out of the home. Hitler would like his sisters to return to it. We will examine these alternatives in turn.

If we assume, as they do in Russia, that woman is in the industrial world to stay, the following radical reforms are necessary.

1. The organization of domestic work so as to relieve women of the worry and responsibility of two jobs. Let the kitchen be expanded to a central cooking establishment

controlled by expert dietitians. The meals will be delivered like the milk, ready for use. Anachronisms like furnaces and shovels will be abolished and houses be heated by turning a switch. Laundry and mending will be community enterprises. These things are the logical developments of the present tendency to centralization and large scale production.

2. The provision that maternity shall carry no disability for the professional or industrial worker. In Russia the mother is paid when, being with child, she can no longer work, and is so paid until she is fit to work again. When that time arrives, she finds provided by the factory or the farm a creche where her baby is cared for while she is on the job.

3. Women workers must be released from the disadvantages under which they labour at present. They must get equal pay for equal work, and their private lives be considered their own business. If however, she is engaged in a job which means more to her than merely a meal ticket, she must be permitted to carry on with it. If subsequently the quality of her work suffers, then and only then, her employer has a right to ask her to resign. It is up to the professional women of this century to prove that the quality of their work need not be impaired by marriage.

These recommendations are based on the assumption that women are in the industrial world to stay. Suppose however that the tide is now flowing in the opposite direction. Economic forces, rather than any choice of her own, brought women out of the home a century ago. The Russian philosophy of life arose from the Soviets' pressing need for workers, both men and women. In Russia's phase of development, every hand is needed to turn the lathes and wheels of industry, to produce the necessities and comforts of life. Is it not possible that this phase is now passed in Western civilization? The machine is now reducing the numbers of workers and the hours each must work. It may be that in the new social order to which our century is moving, the necessity for women in industry will no longer exist. It will no longer be necessary for women to be men. When that time comes, they will be relegated to domestic life again.

That purposely offensive word "relegated" sums up women's present discontent with the domestic career. Beneath its hypocritical palaver about the hand that rocks the cradle, the world despises home work. "A real job" is one which involves catching a car, punching a clock, and drawing a salary. The work of the little woman in the bungalow apron is regarded with a patronizing air by people who have real jobs. The little woman knows this and often feels she has sold her wage-earner's birthright for a mess of pots and pans. We will consider what is the matter with the domestic career that it leaves women discontented.

Firstly, domestic work is badly distributed. Some women have too much and others too little . . . a by-product of our present inequality of income. The poor man's wife, working without help and without conveniences, feels herself to be a slave. The woman of the more fortunate class is able to hire help, both human and mechanical. What is she to do with the time and energy thus saved?

1. She may become a writer, an artist, a musician. This group is a small one. Genius in the arts is scarce and few women have the force of character to fight down the smiling interference of a world which assumes she is just playing at the arts as a harmless way of filling time.

2. She can join women's clubs, reading groups, Little Theatres, Junior Leagues. These clubs give the married woman an outlet for her very human desire to shine before her peers. They provide an outlet for the brains and ambition stifling behind four walls. They provide the robust wage earning masculine world with a constant source of amusement.

Failing a creative vocation or a club, the great majority of married women drown themselves in a bridge-playing, tea drinking, gossiping existence which stultifies their own minds and makes the intelligent girl shy away from matrimony as she would from paralysis. "What," she says, "must I join this crowd of chattering idiots, all wrapped up in bridge-cloths, and scandal?" It is time-frittering woman who gives matrimony a bad name, but before we condemn her let us consider her history.

Which brings us to the second indictment of domestic work – that it is not worth training for. The time-fritterer was probably brought up to regard homemaking as something a girl learns casually in her spare time. It is possible that on her wedding day she has never cooked a complete meal or made herself a dress in her life. Of the sciences which lie behind preserving, laundering, choice of textiles, care of equipment, she knows nothing. Of physiology and psychology she has the haziest hand-me-down notions. Society regards this situation complacently. Brides' biscuits and burnt steaks are harmless little jokes. A young mother who reads child psychology is a high brow crank. She who says, "Daddy will spank you when he comes home" is a normal and natural young woman.

Remember we are describing here the great majority of women who step into domestic life from a store, office or factory. All her formal education has fitted her to live a man's life in a man's world. It is true that domestic science and technical schools do exist, but unless a girl makes a definite effort to get this training she will miss it. Will she likely seek it out as long as the student at a technical school bears the stigma of being too dull for other work? Even the University House-Eccer does not always escape this insinuation.

Not only is domestic work neglected from the standpoint of training, but industry conspires to reduce it to the fewest possible gestures. Patent foods, tinned vitamins and delicatessen salads tempt the housekeeper on every hand. Her doors are besieged by eager salesmen bearing every imaginable gadget designed to save her time. Time for what? Time for time-killing social activities with the gossiping sisterhood who meet to eat sticky messes and criticize each other's clothes.

The third and greatest disadvantage of domestic work is that it is badly paid. It entails a state of economic dependence. In more prosperous families where there is an income to divide, a woman's pride can be saved by arranging an allowance. In poorer homes the money question is the root of all evil. More often than ambition or boredom, it sends a married woman back into a paying job. It is significant that no one condemns such a woman more bitterly than those who cannot follow her example. This economic grievance is too well known to need further explanation here.

Mr. Atlee sums up the case against the domestic career:

> Those who . . . seek an outlet in philanthropic clubs become at best mere amateurs at life. Those who give themselves up frankly to the petty social round become killers of time, death-seekers. Those whose energies are entirely taken up with the household duty have the sense of being drudges. And finally all the band of married women, with the exception of a small group which is working in a man's world, . . . are economically dependent on man. In a state of society where money alone gives a real sense of independence, . . . their work is without wage. Is this enough? Is there no higher and securer destiny available to intelligence that can be as powerful and penetrating as [that] of the male? (49)

This is the indictment against home-making at the present time. If women are to be released from industrial life and are to find a soul-satisfying sphere of endeavour within the home, certain important changes must come about. Our philosophy, education, and social organization must change.

If home work is to be made a completely satisfactory career for women, it will have to be voluntary, respected and paid. Consider the last point first. There are many injustices in our present lack of economic system, and if precedent is any guide, woman's case may be the last remedied. But it may be, as many writers suggest, that in the saner state of the future, bearing the nation's children will be considered as important as bearing the nation's letters. This is not so revolutionary as it may seem. It is the principle behind the present Mother's Allowance, paid by Alberta to the widowed mothers of small children. It is the principle behind the bonuses for large families offered in Italy, Germany and Quebec. If the business of making a home and rearing a family is to be a satisfactory career, it must be rewarded by a claim on the goods and services of society. It must be a paid job.

Secondly, it must be a voluntary job. No happy worker is "relegated" to his work. The back-to-the-home movement must be voluntary and if a woman feels that she is happier in another profession she must be perfectly free to follow the other profession. It is absurd to assume that every girl child, simply because she is a girl child, is born with a predilection for food and textiles and will want to be a homemaker. Every boy does not want to be a policeman.

We have considered the retirement of women from industry. Nothing has been said of the retirement of women from the professions. Homemaking as a respected paying job will appeal to women at present employed in factories, stores, and offices. It will also appeal to many intelligent women who at present look down on it and feel they must prove their calibre by tackling "a man's job." But there will always be some women who are happier in another line of activity, particularly those professions which have to do with human beings . . . education, nursing, medicine, social service, political life. It must be made possible for such women to give their best energies to these high callings without enduring enforced celibacy and social censure.

Thirdly, if domestic work is to be respected and interesting, women must be trained for their jobs. We enjoy doing what we do well. We honour a profession which is considered worth an extensive training. Women will respect and enjoy the domestic career when they enter it equipped with a knowledge of food, textiles, hygiene, physiology and psychology which will raise their food from stupid drudgery, the aimless hit and miss business it is at present.

The thesis thus far has been that our civilization must decide whether or not women are to continue in industry. At present they are trained for work outside the home, and then thrust, unwilling and untrained, within its four walls. This illogical situation results in economic waste, discontent, an unsatisfactory life for half the population. If woman is to continue in industry she should be freed from the disabilities and injustices under which she labors at present. If the industrial revolution has come full circle, and is returning woman to domestic life, then housework should be made worthy of an active and intelligent human being.

This second view, that women should return to being women, is strongly held by Anthony Ludovici in *Lysistrata or Woman's Future and Future Woman.* A brief summary of the book is included lest the foregoing may not be sufficiently radical to goad all listeners into argument. *Lysistrata* contradicts so flatly most of our own cherished opinions that it stimulates us to re-examine our table of values. Indeed the book can be recommended for the pocket on cold mornings. A glance at any of this writer's conclusions is guaranteed to produce in the modern girl a state of red hot rage.

Ludovici traces all the ills of modern life to a contempt and slander of the body, the fact that physical depravity is uncondemned among us. Science is concerned with patching and repairing these second rate bodies of people willing to wear false teeth, glasses, all manner of artificial props which enable them to keep going. As a result we miss a great deal of the joy of life. Modern men and women can know only second rate ecstasies through their debilitated bodies. This acceptance of bodily depravity is uncondemned among us. This acceptance of bodily depravity has a serious effect on the

303

position of woman since she is the chief sufferer when corporeal equipment is defective. Not only is her mate lacking in natural vigor, but her own impaired efficiency has turned the joys and beauties of the natural life to pain and horror. Motherhood is regarded as an over-rated pleasure. The duties and virtues of the home are all connected with the body . . . sewing, cooking, the nurture of the young. These domestic arts are gradually being lost. The unmated woman worker and married woman disillusioned by the debility of modern man, combine to deny the value of love and the bodily experience it involves.Having estimated that there are 6,000,000 surplus women in Britain, he goes on:

> Owing to the degeneracy of modern man, a certain proportion of these 6,000,000 will of course, refrain from any attempt at marriage. Still faithful to the lost and antiquated values that once led people to respect and care for their bodies, they feel . . . they deserve something better than the mate the twentieth century can offer them; and although they may be fully and admirably equipped for happy motherhood this noble and small minority will turn nauseated away from it in order to become absorbed in interests that will help them to forget.[3]

If these present tendencies are allowed to continue, a very gloomy future awaits our civilization. The disaffected women will lure larger and larger numbers of girls away from bodily happiness. The domestic arts will be further neglected and our vices in food consequently aggravated. As women become the dominant force in industry, man will become superfluous. Extra-corporeal gestation will be perfected. Eventually, science will discover a means of determining the sex of the ovum, and only half of one percent of males will be raised each year. The population will then consist of sexless workers "looking around upon this cold hard and business-like world" in which industry will be the only activity. These female workers will ask themselves in increasing perplexity and distress, what purpose it all serves. "In their lives of stoic 'purity' and monotonous breadwinning alone, they are likely to discover that even waiting for the end is intolerable" (89).

From this Brave New World of triumphant feminism it is still possible to escape if we are willing to change our table of values. First we must destroy those body-despising values which condone physical depravity. Second, we must get rid of the idea that it is virtuous to sacrifice the greater for the less. At present, "Everything that is best in the nation, all those elements on which the successful survival of our race depends, are being penalized and sacrificed for the sake of the defective, the lunatic, the crippled, the incurable, the half-witted and the blind . . . This value must go" (97).

Thirdly, we must have a new ideal of masculinity. "We shall learn to expect from the manly man not only courage and proficiency in sport, but also will power, leadership, mastery over all the mysteries of life, and . . . intelligence sufficient to overshadow any female brain that is placed alongside of him . . . in fact, a man whose presence alone makes the claim of sexual equality a manifest and transparent absurdity" (98). It may be noted here that Ludovici refuses to recognize any improvement in woman's achievement in the last fifty years. It is not, he writes, that woman's mental capacity has been enhanced but that man's has been enfeebled.

If, therefore, our civilization is saved in the eleventh hour by a recovered joy in the bodily life, the woman of the future will be a gloriously happy being:

> The regeneration of man will immediately transform woman and her position; because her contempt for the male will vanish, she will recover both physically and spiritually the lost joy of *looking up* to her mate. Through the mastery he will introduce, her present very justifiable anxiety about the world will tend to disappear, and the serenity of a dependent existence be restored to her. Her life through being filled by a mate sufficiently versatile to supply her not

only with offspring, but also with every possible interest, will gradually lose the feverish restlessness of the modern woman, who is seeking constantly to forget the void both in her heart and in her existence.

With these changes, woman's claim to equality with man will gradually cease to be heard of . . . It is merely the fact that the claim is not *manifestly* absurd to-day that lends it for the time being a certain fatal plausibility.

But before woman is sound enough in mind and body to give birth to this new breed of masculine sons, . . . she [must] . . . learn to look at life from a very different standpoint. She will regenerate her own body before it is too late and recover the ease, if not the ecstasy of old, of all her own functions. She will learn to despise herself if she wears glasses, if she has false or bad teeth . . . if she cannot suckle her child. She will perceive the boastful levity of the present generation of women who concern themselves more and more with high-falutin' interests and matters of the soul, while all the while they are not masters of their own bodies. . . .

When once bodily normality is recovered . . ., she and her mate will attach a new value to . . . motherhood, domesticity, and marriage. All three will appear nobler and more desirable, not only because they have become more beautiful and more productive of beauty, but also because their responsibilities and annoyances *are endured for a man and for children who make them appear thoroughly worth while.* (104-106)

Surely the back-to-the-home movement will never find a more enthusiastic nor thorough-going champion than this! While we may agree that an improvement in our physical equipment is desirable, while we may see the force of his argument that marriage can never be a satisfactory career for women too debilitated to enjoy it, nevertheless, we must enter some objections to this analysis.

In the first place, is the body so universally despised as all that? Allowing for the fact that physical fitness is more difficult in crowded, industrial Britain than on these prairies, Olympic games and sun bathing are pretty universal phenomena. Our century is growingly aware of the importance of bodily health.

Secondly, the writer has followed the common tactic of taking from history only what suits his case. He assumes that the heroic mould of man existed before in Britain, and that all we have to do is reproduce the vigor of Elizabethan days. Have we any proof that the mariners of England who sailed the uncharted seas were a breed superior to the sky pilots of our own times? We have quoted his phrase, "Restore to women the serenity of a dependent life." Have we any evidence that the dependent life is necessarily serene?

Thirdly, while Ludovici censures the feminists for their sex hostility, he evidently feels not a little of that hostility himself. It appears in his contemptuous denial of woman's equality of intellect. It is an echo of the ferocious battle which went on in Britain between 1900 and 1914. The feminist of that day asserted her equality fiercely because it was so frequently denied. She fought a good fight did the suffragette of 1910, and the modern girl should not be misled by the absurdity of her garments to despise the worth of her achievement. But today there is less need to assert equality of opportunity – the opportunity of every human soul whether it be born male or female, to develop the talents which providence has given.

"What a piece of work is man," cried Hamlet, and for centuries the world echoed his admiration. To be a man was positive. It was to be the heir of strength, power, courage and opportunity.

"Frailty, thy name is woman," exclaimed the same Prince and for years they have been making us believe it. To be a woman was an unforgivable error in judgment. It was not a positive state, but a mere negative, passive condition of unmanliness. It stood for all the opprobrious qualities of weakness, timidity, deceit and vacillation. Small wonder that our great aunts, fighting their way out of the Doll's House, claimed equality and felt that to be free and self-respecting, they must be like men.

It is time now we made it known that to be a woman is not a negative condition of bad luck, but a positive good thing in itself. It is time we proved that courage, wisdom, and strength can go about, as they have done before, in feminine garments. All but the mentally adolescent among us have stopped worrying about our innate equality with man, or thinking of ourselves as his rivals in achievement. Comparisons are profitless. We are different, with different talents, powers and possibilities.

The challenge rests with us to make good our claim to the two best things. It was a challenge faced by Vera Brittain when she considered her approaching marriage. She writes:

> Marriage [I knew] would involve . . . a new fight against the tradition which identified wifehood with the imprisoning limitations of a kitchen and four walls, against the prejudices which still make success in any field more difficult for the married woman than for the spinster, and penalized motherhood by demanding from it the surrender of disinterested intelligence, the sacrifice of that vitalizing experience only to be found in the pursuit of an independent profession. I felt I must not shrink from that fight, not abandon in cowardice the attempt to prove, as no theories could ever prove without examples, that marriage and motherhood need never tame the mind, nor swamp and undermine ability and training, nor trammel and domesticize political perception and social judgment. To-day, as never before, it was urgent for individual women to show that life was enriched, mentally and spiritually, by marriage and children; that these experiences rendered . . . woman the more and not the less able to take the world's pulse . . . and play a definite hard-headed, hard-working part in furthering the constructive ends of a political civilization.[5]

A stiff job, that. But then, brains *are* a bother to a girl.

1. Henry Van Dyke, "Work," *Music and Other Poems* (New York: Charles Scribner's Sons, 1904) 49.

2. W.A. Trepanning, "The Educational Veil," *Forum and Century* 88 (October, 1932) 231-4.

3. Benge Atlee, "Should Women Be Men?" *Maclean's Magazine* 42 (September 15, 1934) 13.

4. Anthony Mario Ludovici, *Lysistrata: or Woman's Future and Future Women* (New York: E.P. Dutton, 1925) 36.

5. Vera Brittain, *Testament of Youth* (London: Victor Golloncz Ltd., 1933) 654.

The Freedom of Mrs. Radway

Elsie Park Gowan, 1971

THE FREEDOM OF MRS. RADWAY:
FIRST PERFORMANCE

Circa 1957. Broadcast over "Bernie Braden Tells A Story,"
CBC.

THE FREEDOM OF MRS. RADWAY

Mrs. Radway was one of those lucky women – the kind other women envy. She was married, had two children, but she also had a career. Maybe you remember the interview in the *News-Herald*, just after her book of short stories was published. "Constance Reid Radway," it said, "has successfully solved the problem of how to combine her career as a writer with that of a wife and mother."

In the interview, Mrs. Radway told how she did it. "Modern living," the paper quoted her as saying, "has set women free, given us time for creative work. I plan to be at my desk from nine to twelve every morning. The rest of my day belongs to my family."

Naturally, with Mrs. Radway's high ideals of citizenship and her concern for Native Peoples, she employed a Métis girl as household help. Sophie was the girl's name, and she'd been very happy there for almost a year, before the day Mrs. Radway made the headlines.

Thursday, the 28 of March, was a bright windy day, and Mrs. Radway got up early to wash her hair. With Dream-glo shampoo. She knew it was her duty as a wife to keep her good looks. For years, advertisements in every media had warned her what happens to women who neglect to be fragrant and streamlined.

While she rolled up her hair, the characters in the story she was writing began to whisper in her mind. Early Canada was Mrs. Radway's field, and she had the knack of bringing the past to life. Many people said her stories made them more *interested* in being Canadians.

At the moment her subject was Cunnebwahbam, an Indian girl whose portrait was painted by Paul Kane at Fort

Edmonton in 1847. What did Cunnebwahbam think about while the artist worked? Mrs. Radway decided that Paul Kane would be the first man to treat the Indian girl as a human being. Drudgery and slavery were a Cree woman's life, but Kane talked to her as if she were a person, with a mind and spirit. Yes, that would motivate the story for the modern reader. Mrs. Radway went down to breakfast.

George Radway was finishing his coffee. As his wife kissed him good-bye, she remarked he'd better play safe and wear his winter overcoat. Margaret, 10, and Wilfred, 8, were eating their cooked cereal. Their mother had just read a government bulletin about the importance of protein at every meal. Margaret and Wilfred refused to eat eggs for breakfast, but they looked healthy, so she tried not to worry about malnutrition.

At 8:47 Mrs. Radway went into her workroom and sharpened a pencil. At five minutes past nine, Sophie knocked on the study door and said something was wrong with the washing machine. Mrs. Radway went down to the laundry and struggled with the machine for twenty minutes before she phoned the repairman. The repairman said he would try to come on Saturday. He wasn't sure he could make it, but he'd try.

On her way back to the study, Mrs. Radway collected two letters from the mailbox – one for Sophie and one for herself from her father-in-law. At 67, Grandpa Radway was a semi-retired real estate man in Calgary. He wrote that he was coming to town on business, he hadn't seen the kids for ages, and could Connie put him up? Connie started a cordial note saying she'd be delighted to see him, when she heard a peculiar noise in the kitchen. It sounded like Sophie crying as if her heart would break.

Sophie's heart was broken because she'd just found out that her boyfriend had married a girl in the Peace River country. Mrs. Radway knew that a good employer would help poor Sophie over the crisis. They had a cup of coffee together and she gave Sophie a red head-scarf. After a while Sophie stopped crying and began to Take an Interest.

By this time it was almost noon. She'd been back with Paul Kane for half an hour, when Wilfie came bursting in the back door with the good news that Coopers were giving away their pups and he could get one free. When his mother looked doubtful Wilfie burst into loud sobs. He said if nobody adopted the pup, it would go to the pound, and did she want to be a murderer? That put Mrs. Radway on the spot. She'd read the books on child psychology and knew the importance of giving children emotional security. On the other hand, she knew who would be cast in the part of wet-nurse to the two-month-old pup.

At lunch time, young Margaret remembered that this was the night of her piano recital, and she'd want her white silk blouse clean and mended. "Of course, dear, I'll fix it," her mother said absently, because she'd just had a really good idea about Cunnebwahbam.

Thursday was Sophie's half day, and by one-thirty Mrs. Radway had the house to herself. She'd just started for her desk when the phone rang.

"Is that you, Connie? How are you, dear?"

It was her mother's voice, and by the tone of it, Connie realized what was expected of her. Proud of her independence, Mrs. Reid lived alone, but every so often she had what she called "one of my blue lonely days." Mrs. Radway knew how important it is that elderly people never feel themselves unwanted. Anyway, she was fond of her mother, so she invited her over for tea.

The doorbell rang twice in the early afternoon. Once it was a boy selling magazine subscriptions, and Mrs. Radway dealt with him gently. From her canvassing at election time, she knew how it felt to have a door slammed in one's face. Her second caller was from the Home and School, who wanted Mrs. Radway to take part in a round-table debate on

Education. "I know you're very busy," the caller said, "but we do look to people like you to give leadership – "

Mrs. Radway made a note on her calendar for a week Tuesday.

At half past four, his grandmother was just leaving when Wilfie arrived home, with the dog. He was carrying it inside his parka, kangaroo style, and he announced that Mrs. Cooper had named the pup "Puddles" which at once seemed an appropriate name.

From a reconstruction of March 28, it appears that the crisis developed rapidly. After school Margaret practiced her piano solo for an hour and ten minutes, George Radway was late getting home from the office. His wife kept back dinner for half an hour, but he said he didn't want any food. He had a very bad cold, he was going straight to bed, and would someone please bring him a hot whiskey with plenty of lemon.

After dinner, Wilfie went to a scout meeting, leaving the dog bedded down in the basement, on Wilfie's new sweater. When he left the house, his mother was upstairs reasoning with Margaret, who couldn't go to the recital because her blouse wasn't mended. While Mrs. Radway fixed the blouse, the dog began to howl, and her husband shouted from the bathroom asking where the devil was the aspirin?

The telephone rang while she found the aspirin, and she was slightly out of breath when she hurried downstairs to answer it. "This is TV Survey calling" said a voice like maple syrup. "What program are you watching, please?"

"We're not tuned in right now," Connie said politely, but she was wrong because upstairs George turned on a news bulletin.

Mrs. Radway stood in the hall with the telephone in her hand. The little dog howled in the basement. Margaret was playing the hard part on page six over and over. From upstairs the news of the day, all of it bad, rolled down like an ugly tide.

Mrs. Radway moved quickly in her well-organized way.

316

She brought George an extra blanket and took a bowl of warm milk down to the dog.

Then from George's work bench she picked out a heavy monkey wrench and wrapped it neatly in brown paper. She put on her coat and took the bus downtown, stepping off in front of the *News-Herald* Building. At 7:19 exactly, Constance Reid Radway threw the monkey wrench through the large plate glass window of the newspaper office – the very paper that had once printed her piece about how modern living has set women free. When the police came, she was doing a little war dance on the pavement.

Mrs. Radway is very happy where she is now. The doctors don't understand why she insists on *wearing* her blanket and having a feather in her hair. They don't understand, but they're working on it.

BIBLIOGRAPHY*

STAGE PLAYS

Homestead (alternate title *The Man Who Wouldn't Fight Back*), one-act, first produced: Edmonton Little Theatre, 31 March 1933.

The Giant-Killer, one-act, fp: Edmonton Little Theatre Experimental Division, Masonic Temple, 26 April 1934.

God Made the Country, one-act, fp: University of Alberta Dramatic Club, Alberta Regional DDF, Grand Theatre, Calgary, 7 February 1935.

The Royal Touch, one-act, in *Curtain Call* Vol 6 No 8, May 1935 and in *Canadian School Plays* EM Jones ed. Toronto: Ryerson 1948, fp: Lacombe High School Concert, 7 March 1935.

The Hungry Spirit, one-act, fp: Edmonton Little Theatre, Empire Theatre, 6 April 1935.

On the Romany Trail, one-act skit with music, fp: Llanarthney School for Girls, 1935.

The Unknown Soldier Speaks (written with Aubrey Proctor), one-act, fp: Women's International League for Peace and Freedom, Rialto Theatre, Edmonton, 10 November 1935.

You Can't Do That! (written with William Irvine), Toronto: Nelson 1936, three-act, fp: Commonwealth Youth Movement, Masonic Temple, Edmonton, 13 March 1936.

Glorious and Free, one-act, fp: Orange hall, Camrose, 14 April 1937.

The Last Caveman, three-act, in *Theatre History in Canada/Histoire du Théâtre au Canada* Vol 8 No 1, Spring 1987; fp: Edmonton Little Theatre, Masonic Temple, 4 February 1938.

A Toss for Father, one-act, and *Thumbleweed*, short comic sketch, fp: Edmonton Little Theatre, All Saint's Parish Hall, 23 February 1940.

The Shop in Toad Lane or Password to Liberty, one-act, Edmonton: Co-operative Wholesale Association, 1940 and in Co-op News [1940], fp: Olds School of Agriculture, 1940.

Back to the Kitchen, Woman!, one-act, Edmonton: Department of Extension, University of Alberta 1941, fp: Banff School of Fine Arts, 25 August 1941.

Airman's Forty-Eight (Written with Jean Duce), one-act, Edmonton: Department of Extension, University of Alberta 1942.

Maestro, one-act, Edmonton: Department of Extension. University of Alberta 1942 and in *Curtain Rising* WS Milne ed. Toronto: Longmans, Green 1958, fp: Banff School of Fine Arts, 26 August 1942.

The Princess Who Dreamed Too Much, one-act, Edmonton: Department of Extension, University of Alberta [1943] and Edmonton: Alberta Department of Culture nd, fp: Queen's University Summer School 1946.

Breeches from Bond Street, one-act, Toronto: Samuel French, 1952 and in *Prairie Performance* Diane Bessai ed. Edmonton: NeWest Press 1980, fp: Provincial Players, Studio Theatre, University of Alberta, 4 March 1949.

Who Builds a City, pageant, fp: Edmonton Gardens, 8 October 1954.

The Jasper Story, outdoor pageant, fp: Jasper, Alberta, July 1956.

Portrait of Alberta, outdoor pageant, fp: Edmonton Grandstand, 1956.

Cakes and Alumni, one-act, special mention in *21st Annual Canadian Playwriting Competition*, 1959.

Fame is the Spur, Stranger in the House, one-acts written for playwriting course, University of Alberta, 1971.

A Treaty for the Plains, outdoor pageant, fp: Dried Meat Hill, Alberta 1977.

A Song for Alberta, dramatic musical program written for Sunshine Singers of Strathcona Place, 1980.

RADIO PLAYS
Series

NEW LAMPS FOR OLD (co-written with Gwen Pharis Ringwood)

    CKUA Radio 1936-1937

    CBC Western Network 1937

    10 of 20 episodes, 30 min:

Includes: *The Coming of Power; Erasmus of Rotterdam; Mary Wollstonecraft; New Napoleon; The Story of Radium; Visions in Stone; Elizabeth Fry.*

THE BUILDING OF CANADA

    CKUA, CFRN, CRCN 1937

    CKUA, CBC 28 Sept 1938 - 8 Feb 1939

    20 episodes, 30 min:

Raleigh, Prophet of Empire; On This Rock; Kings of Acadia; He Was No Gentleman; Frontenac, the Fighting Governor; The Dragon from the Sea; Under One Flag; The Price of Loyalty; Grenville's Sword; The Silver Chief; Seven Oaks; The Patriots of '37; Radical Jack; The Eagle of Oregon; The Argonauts; The Figurehead; From Sea to Sea; Red Star in the West; Saddle and Plow; No More Heroes.

PLAYS OF OUR PROVINCE (Arranged by Elsie Park Gowan)

    CKUA, CFCN, CFRN [1940].

THE ALTAR OF THE MOON (Serial based on Francis Dickie's novel)

    CBC 8 Jan - 19 Feb 1941

    7 parts.

THE CALL TO HEALTH AND HAPPINESS CBC 4 Nov - 25 Nov 1942

    [Possibly re-broadcast May 1943]

    First 3 plays repeated as part of **THE HOPEFUL SIDE** series, 1946

    4 parts, 15 min:

*Laura Valadon; The Story of George Leonidas and his Indigestion;
Cancer of the Skin; Four Weapons Against Death.*

THE TOWN GROWS UP CBC 12 Nov 1943 - 25 Feb 1944

16 episodes, 30 min:

Includes: *The Story of the Town Waterworks; Six Cents for a Mule;
Gentlemen with Bright Buttons; Ramparts for Mary Jane;
Invitation to Lunch; Adventure in Liberty; Mystery Story; A Book
of Memory; Out of the Shadows.* Also plays on unemployment
insurance, social security and low rent housing.

THE PEOPLE NEXT DOOR – Series I

CBC 3 Nov 1944 - 2 Mar 1945

18 episodes, 15 min:

Little Girl Lost 3 Nov; *Transplanting Theresa* 10 Nov; *The Case of
the Unofficial Parents* 17 Nov; *The Case of Ann Grierson and the
Bogeyman* 24 Nov; *The Case of the Doubtful Bride* 15 Dec; *The
Case of the Unemployed Heart* 22 Dec; *The Case of the House
Divided* 29 Dec, 5 Jan; *Forgotten Melody* 12 Jan; *Shakespeare was
Eighteen* 19 Jan; *Navy Girl* 26 Jan; *Target for Tomorrow* 2 Feb;
Enemy on Maple Street 9 Feb; *Brides from Britain* 16 Feb; *The
Private War of Molly Barlow* 23 Feb; *Jack Barlow Comes Home* 2
Mar.

THE PEOPLE NEXT DOOR – Series II

CBC 5 Nov 1945 - 28 Jan 1946

13 episodes, 15 min:

Mary is a Person, Sergeant 5 Nov; *She's Nobody's Baby Now* 12
Nov; *The Unemployed Commando* 19 Nov; *Books After Battle* 26
Nov; *Marriage is for Adults Only* 3 Dec; *Flier Without Wings* 10
Dec; *Well, How You've Grown* 17 Dec; *Down to Earth . . . With a
Parachute* 24 Dec; *Janey's Last Chance* 31 Dec; *Bad Boy* 7 Jan;
Memo to an Editor From His Son 14 Jan; *Latchkeys and Old Lace*
21 Jan; *The Whistle Blows for Mother* 28 Jan.

THE BARLOWS OF BEAVER STREET CBC International Service

8 Nov 1948 - 27 June 1949

34 episodes, 30 min:

Includes *Easter Bonnet; Accent on Johnny; The Plow and the Second Hand Cars; Land of Milk and Honey; Susie says the Good Word; Gladys and the Great Outdoors; Operation Asparagus; Lazy by the Lake; Touch not a Single Bough; A Mind of Her Own; What Price Penelope; Week-end in Lower Five; A Letter to Louise; The Question of a House; The Question of a Holiday; Highway Going Home.*

DOWN OUR STREET . . . TODAY CJBC Dominion Network series
>18 Nov - 16 Dec 1952
>
>5 parts, 30 min:

The Ghost of Grandma Fraser 18 Nov; *Thirty Minutes Past Noon* 25 Nov; *The High Green Gate* 2 Dec; *The Reluctant King Wenceslaus* 9 Dec; *Sister Bridget and the Tramp* 16 Dec.

THE FERGUSON FAMILY CBC 26 Jan - 2 Mar 1954
>6 episodes, 30 min:

Includes: *Frank's Story; June's Story; Johnny's Story.*

JUDGE FOR YOURSELF CBC 28 Mar - 2 May 1955
>6 episodes, 30 min:

The Man Who Ran Away 28 Mar; *The Second Son* 4 Apr; *From Lillian . . . Without Love* 11 Apr; *The Girl From a Good Home* 18 Apr; *The Facts of the Case* 25 Apr; *To Break the Chain* 2 May.

Radio Plays Included In Other Series**

WINNIPEG DRAMA

Enter the Marquis 3 July 1939; *Clementine Steps In* [1939]

PROUD PROCESSION

North to Eldorado [1939-1940]

THEATRE TIME

Indians in Paris (Francis Dickie) 20 Mar 1940; *Raleigh, Prophet of Empire* (John Buchan) 24 June 1940; *The Pirate of Peace River* (Francis Dickie) 29 July 1940; *The Hungry Spirit* 26 Aug 1940; *St. Paul's of London* 14 October 1940; *Souvenir for Suzanne* 26 Mar 1941; *Garibaldi Remembers* 6 May 1941; *Family Reunion* (Francis

Dickie) 9 September 1941; *The Eagle of Oregon* 18 November 1941; *Maestro* 28 Apr 1942.

DRAMA

Appointment With Yesterday (Francis Dickie) 1941.

CBC *OTTAWA WORKSHOP*

Back to the Kitchen, Woman! (Gowan) 16 Jan 1941.

THE BIRTH OF CANADIAN FREEDOM

When Freedom Was a Dream 14 Jan 1942; *Radical Jack* 11 Feb 1942; *Elgin the Figurehead* [1942].

HEROES OF CANADA

script on Frank Oliver [1942].

MONTREAL DRAMA

The Strong and the Free 30 Sept 1942.

TALES FROM FAR AND NEAR (CBS Columbia School of the Air) 1943.

We Couldn't Leave Dinah (Mary Treadgold); *North After Seals* (Thames Williamson).

THESE ARE MY NEIGHBORS (CJCA, CFRN) 1943.

The Story of Steve Barclay; The Case of the Unofficial Parents; Ann Grierson and the Bogeyman.

LANDS OF THE FREE (NBC Inter-American University of the Air) 1943.

Canada Comes of Age; The Clipper Ship; The Road to Alaska; Silver and Quicksilver; They Came Bearing Gifts; Canada the Refuge.

MONTREAL PLAYHOUSE

Love Story, 9 Aug 1943.

CBC NATIONAL SCHOOL BROADCASTS

Explorers of the Dawn (Mazo de la Roche) 1945; *Edmonton – Gateway to the North* [1945-1946]; *I Was There . . . With the Cariboo Miners* 1950; *Young Bush Pilot* 1950; *Klondyke Gold* 1950; *British Columbia is Born* 1952.

PANORAMA

A Valentine to a Western Lady 14 Feb 1946.

RADIO REPERTORY

The Courting of Marie Jenvrin (Gwen Pharis Ringwood) 4 Apr 1946.

VANCOUVER THEATRE

Bump on a Log (Ted Belt) 17 Oct 1946.

THIS IS OUR STORY (CBC CJCA) 1946-1947.

Sister in the Gray Gown; The Harbor of the Air; Home Town . . . 1946; Breeches from Bond Street.

ON STAGE (CBC International Network)

Steamboat Bill and the Pirate 31 Oct 1949.

IN SEARCH OF CITIZENS

The Gateway 29 Nov 1949.

CURTAIN TIME

Breeches from Bond Street 5 Apr 1950.

IN SEARCH OF OURSELVES

Search for Martin Carlisle 25 Apr 1950.

CBC STAGE

The Last Caveman 7 May 1950.

SUMMER FALLOW

World on her Doorstep 1950; *John E. Lundberg – Advocate of the People* 1950; *Home Town . . . 1954* 1954; *This Land for my Sons* 1959.

CROSS SECTION

What About Oil? 1951.

PRAIRIE PLAYHOUSE

Maestro in Spite of Himself 27 Aug 1953; *The Blue Heron* 25 Jun 1959; *This Land for my Sons* [1959].

WESTERN GATEWAYS

This Land for my Sons 1953.

ALBERTA SCHOOLS BROADCASTS

Shaped Like a Question Mark 1953; *Want to go Hunting?* 1954.

SATURDAY PLAYHOUSE

The Unique Spirit 14 Aug 1954.

I WAS THERE

I was a Clerk in the Hudson's Bay Co. 1954.

WORKING TOGETHER

Glorious Journey 1954.

AS CHILDREN SEE US

This I Know 21 March 1955.

HALIFAX THEATRE

Burning Their Bridges Behind Them (Elsie Park Gowan and D.Wilson) 17 Jan 1956.

CBC PLAYHOUSE

The Man in the News 1967.

Individual Radio Plays (not all may have been broadcast)

The Latchstring: A Radio Play for Goodwill Day, written for the children of the Friendship Club, nd.

The Governor Works Fast, CBC 1940.

Printing, Messenger of Life, Edmonton local station 1940.

Greater Magic (Francis Dickie), submitted to Canadian historical play contest 1940.

The Men in the News, Winnipeg 12 March 1941, in *Confederation in Prose and Poetry for Canadians*, J.W. Chalmers ed. Toronto: Dent 1951.

The Lake of Gold, submitted to CBS School of the Air of the Americas 1942.

The Princess who Dreamed Too Much 1943, 1946, 1952.

How Big is Edmonton? CJCA, CFRN Edmonton 1943.

The Shop in Toad Lane – For the Centenary of Co-operative

Movement 1843-1943 1943-1944.

Marching with the Legion (Anthony Walsh and Elsie Park Gowan), not broadcast.

The Tale of the Lion (Francis Dickie) 1944.

One Who Looks at the Stars, CJCA Edmonton and CBC Western Network 1946, in *The Alberta Golden Jubilee Anthology* William George Hardy ed. Toronto: McClelland and Stewart 1955.

Lift up the Towers, CJCA and CBC Trans-Canada network 26 Apr 1947.

A Story for November, CJCA 1947.

The Branch of Rosemary, CBC 1953.

This is our Heritage, CJCA Drama Club on CBC Trans-Canada network 1955.

Journey with Louisa, based on a true story about Alderman Julia Kinisky, CJCA 1963-1971.

TELEVISION PLAYS

Stage Coach Bride, adaptation of *Breeches from Bond Street* (Gowan) 1956.

Here and There – Feeding the City, for the opening of Northern Alberta Jubilee Auditorium May 1957.

Here and There – Spirit in Stone, for the opening of Northern Alberta Jubilee Auditorium May 1957.

SHORT STORIES

"Don't Marry A Nudist" (Elsie Park Young) *Saturday Night* 19 Aug 1933.

"The Red Hat," manuscript, nd post 1946.

"The Freedom of Mrs. Radway," first broadcast over Trans Canada Matinee on "Bernie Braden Tells a Story" CBC, circa 1957. First published in *Strathcona Harvest* (Strathcona Writing Group) Edmonton 1978.

SPEECHES

"Woman in the Twentieth Century" [1935].

"The Girl Who Is Out Of Step," autobiographical script for CBC radio series *Growing Up* 1948.

"A Life Of My Own," autobiographical script for CBC Trans Canada Matinee 1947.

"Women and the Arts," speech to Coste House, Allied Arts Council, Calgary 1959.

"Are Women People?" or "Woman's Role in the World We Live In" [post 1954].

"On Being An Alberta Playwright," to the Friends of the Library 1979.

"The History of Edmonton," to the Historical Society of Alberta, Edmonton branch 1979.

"Are We Dramatic?," to the Historical Society of Alberta, Edmonton branch 1985.

ARTICLES

"Passport to Friendship" by Canadienne (on nudism) nd.

"Blitz Over Yew Tree" by Canadienne (on nudism) nd.

"About Radio Plays" [1945-1946].

"There's Drama in Them There Hills being an account of the Summer Drama Course at Banff," *Curtain Call*, Vol 7 No 14 Oct 1935.

"Powerful Social Force at Banff Drama School," Edmonton *People's Weekly* 14 Aug 1937.

"The Edmonton Little Theatre Past and Present," *Curtain Call*, Vol 12 No 6 Mar 1941.

"Lebensraum For Two," *Saturday Night* 13 Feb 1943.

"I Visit Everyman Theatre," *Stage Door* Vol 5 Jan 1947.

"Wanted – A Playwright's Workshop," *Stage Door* Vol 6 Dec 1947.

"Technique – Playwriting in Western Canada," *Western Theatre* Vol 1 Winter-Spring 1950.

"A Playwright Looks At the One-Act Play," *Alberta English Teacher* June 1963.

"History Into Theatre," *Canadian Author and Bookman* Vol 51 No 1 Fall 1975.

PAMPHLET

Editor of *Remembering Elizabeth*, Edmonton: Committee for Elizabeth Haynes Theatre Event 1974.

SECONDARY SOURCES

Olson, Steve, "The function of Radio Drama: An Alberta Perspective." MA University of Alberta Fall, 1991.

Wagner, Anton, "Elsie Park Gowan: Distinctively Canadian," *Theatre History in Canada* Vol 8 No 1 Spring 1987 68-82.

Whiting, Glynnis, "Elsie Park Gowan," *Edmonton Bullet* 2 Dec 1983.

Elsie Park Gowan Scrapbooks, University of Alberta Archives.

---

* This bibliography is an expansion of Anton Wagner's Preliminary Checklist, *Theatre History in Canada/Histoire du Théâtre au Canada* (Vol. 8 No. 1, Spring 1987, 79-81). Holdings are in the University of Alberta Archives.

** CBC, 30 min, unless otherwise indicated